WOMEN'S RIGHTS AND INTERNATIONAL LAWS

WOMEN'S RIGHTS AND INTERNATIONAL LAWS

D S Pradhan

MD PUBLICATIONS PVT LTD
NEW DELHI
www.mdppl.com

Published by :

MD Publications Pvt Ltd
"MD House", 11, Darya Ganj,
New Delhi - 110 002
Phone : +91-11-45355555
E-mail : contact@mdppl.com
Website: www.mdppl.com

ISBN: 978-81-7533-312-3

Published and Printed by Mr. Pranav Gupta on behalf of **MD Publications Pvt Ltd** at Mohit Enterprises, Delhi.

PREFACE

Women's rights and human rights are indivisible. All governments are obliged to uphold the basic human rights of each individual on an equal basis. States must recognize the unique context in which women experience human rights and take all necessary steps to protect women from discrimination and abuse in both the private and public spheres.

The term women's rights refer to freedoms and entitlements of women and girls of all ages. These rights may or may not be institutionalized, ignored or suppressed by law, local custom, and behavior in a particular society. These liberties are grouped together and differentiated from broader notions of human rights because they often differ from the freedoms inherently possessed by or recognized for men and boys and because activists for this issue claim an inherent historical and traditional bias against the exercise of rights by women and girls.

Women are in double jeopardy. Discriminated against as women, they are also as likely as men, if not more so, to become victims of human rights violations. Today, what unites women internationally-transcending class, race, culture, religion, nationality and ethnic origin-is their vulnerability to the denial and violation of their fundamental human rights, and their dedicated efforts to claim those rights. Women's rights are human rights. This notion is at once fundamental and revolutionary. In theory, women have never been overtly excluded from the concept of human rights.

I am very grateful to Mr. Pranav Gupta, Director of MD Publications Pvt Ltd, New Delhi, for his kind cooperation and support for this book.

D S Pradhan

Contents

1

Introduction

The term women's rights refer to freedoms and entitlements of women and girls of all ages. These rights may or may not be institutionalized, ignored or suppressed by law, local custom, and behaviour in a particular society. These liberties are grouped together and differentiated from broader notions of human rights because they often differ from the freedoms inherently possessed by or recognized for men and boys and because activists for this issue claim an inherent historical and traditional bias against the exercise of rights by women and girls.

Issues commonly associated with notions of women's rights include, though are not limited to, the right: to bodily integrity and autonomy; to vote (universal suffrage); to hold public office; to work; to fair wages or equal pay; to own property; to education; to serve in the military or be conscripted; to enter into legal contracts; and to have marital, parental and religious rights. Women and their supporters have campaigned and in some places continue to campaign for the same rights as modern men. Until the mid-nineteenth century, writers assumed that a patriarchal order was a natural order that had existed as John Stuart Mill wrote, since "the very earliest twilight of human society". This was not seriously challenged until the eighteenth century when Jesuit missionaries found matrilineality in native North American peoples.

In the middle Ages, an early effort to improve the status of women in Islam occurred during the early reforms under

Islam, when women were given greater rights in marriage, divorce and inheritance. Women were not accorded with such legal status in other cultures, including the West, until centuries later. The Oxford Dictionary of Islam states that the general improvement of the status of Arab women included prohibition of female infanticide and recognizing women's full personhood. "The dowry, previously regarded as a bride-price paid to the father, became a nuptial gift retained by the wife as part of her personal property." Under Islamic law, marriage was no longer viewed as a "status" but rather as a "contract", in which the woman's consent was imperative. "Women were given inheritance rights in a patriarchal society that had previously restricted inheritance to male relatives." Annemarie Schimmel states that "compared to the pre-Islamic position of women, Islamic legislation meant an enormous progress; the woman has the right, at least according to the letter of the law, to administer the wealth she has brought into the family or has earned by her own work."

According to Professor William Montgomery Watt, when seen in such historical context, Muhammad "can be seen as a figure who testified on behalf of women's rights." Some have claimed that women generally had more legal rights under Islamic law than they did under Western legal systems until more recent times. English Common Law transferred property held by a wife at the time of a marriage to her husband, which contrasted with the Sura: "Unto men (of the family) belongs a share of that which Parents and near kindred leave, and unto women a share of that which parents and near kindred leave, whether it be a little or much - a determinate share", albeit maintaining that husbands were solely responsible for the maintenance and leadership of his wife and family. "French married women, unlike their Muslim sisters, suffered from restrictions on their legal capacity which were removed only in 1965."

In the 16th century, the Reformation in Europe allowed more women to add their voices, including the English writers Jane Anger, Aemilia Lanyer, and the prophetess Anna Trapnell. However, it has been claimed that the Dissolution and resulting closure of convents had deprived many such women of one path to education. Giving voice in the secular context became more difficult when deprived of the rationale and protection of divine inspiration. Queen Elizabeth I demonstrated leadership amongst women, even if she was unsupportive of their causes, and subsequently became a role model for the education of women.

THE VINDICATION OF THE RIGHTS OF WOMAN

The Age of Enlightenment was characterized by secular intellectual reasoning, and a flowering of philosophical writing. The most important feminist writer of the time was Mary Wollstonecraft, often described as the first feminist philosopher. In A Vindication of the Rights of Woman (1792) Wollstonecraft argued that it was the education and upbringing of women that created limited expectations. Despite some inconsistencies reflective of problems that had no easy answers, this book remains a foundation stone of feminist thought.

In other parts of Europe, Hedvig Charlotta Nordenflycht was writing in Sweden, and what is thought to be the first scientific society for women was founded in Middelburg, in the south of Holland in 1785. This was the Natuurkundig Genootschap der Dames which met regularly until 1881, finally dissolving in 1887. However Deborah Crocker and Sethanne Howard point out those women have been scientists for 4,000 years. Journals for women which focused on science became popular during this period as well.

SUFFRAGE, THE RIGHT TO VOTE

The ideas that were planted in the late 1700s took root during the 1800s. Women began to agitate for the right to vote and participate in government and law making. The ideals of Women's suffrage developed alongside that of universal suffrage, and women's movements took lessons from those in other countries. Today women's suffrage is considered a right (under the Convention on the Elimination of All Forms of Discrimination Against Women), although a few countries, mainly in the Middle East, continue to deny voting rights to women.

United States

American women advocated women's right to vote from the 1820s onward. One colonial forerunner, Lydia Chapin Taft was granted the right to vote in 1756 by the town of Uxbridge, Massachusetts colony. In the United States, this was first achieved in the relatively sparsely-populated territories of Wyoming (1869) and briefly in Utah (1870), although Utah women were disenfranchised by the U.S. Congress in 1887. The push to grant women's suffrage in Utah was at least partially fueled by outsiders' belief that, given the right to vote, Utah women would dispose of polygamy. After Utah women exercised their suffrage rights in favor of polygamy the U.S. Congress disenfranchised Utah women. Other territories and states granted women the right to vote in the late 19th and early 20th centuries, but national women's suffrage did not come until the Nineteenth Amendment to the United States Constitution was ratified in 1920.

United Kingdom

For many years the ability to vote was restricted to wealthy property owners within British jurisdictions. This arrangement implicitly excluded women as property law and marriage law gave males ownership rights at marriage or inheritance until the 19th century. Although male suffrage broadened during the century, women were explicitly prohibited from voting nationally and locally in the 1830s by a Reform Act and the Municipal Corporations Act.

Throughout the 19th century women reformers developed their own dialogue through many various groups until, by 1903, they had formed into two distinct organisations; the democratic National Union of Women's Suffrage Societies, and the militant Women's Social and Political Union. Leaders in the struggle were the peaceful Millicent Fawcett and radical Emmeline Pankhurst with her daughter Christabel. Their fight also proved slow and frustrating. In 1918 the British Parliament finally passed a bill allowing women over the age of 30 to vote. In 1928 the age limit was lowered to 21.

Other examples

Women first won the right to vote in New Zealand in 1893, in Australia in 1902, and in Finland in 1906, preceding the United States and Britain in affirming full voting rights. However, in some of these countries only women in the ruling population were able to vote at first. For example, Aboriginal women in Australia were not allowed to vote until they became citizens in 1967.Many other nations have proved much slower to change. For example, in Switzerland women gained the right to vote only in February 1, 1959, after a referendum on women's suffrage.

MODERN MOVEMENT

In the subsequent decades women's rights again became an important issue in the English speaking world. By the 1960s the movement was called "feminism" or "women's liberation." Reformers wanted the same pay as men, equal rights in law, and the freedom to plan their families or not have children at all. Their efforts were met with mixed results. In the UK a public groundswell of opinion in favour of legal equality had gained pace, partly through the extensive employment of women in men's traditional roles during both world wars. By the 1960s the legislative process was being readied, tracing through MP Willie Hamilton's select committee report, his Equal Pay For Equal Work Bill, the creation of a Sex Discrimination Board, Lady Sear's draft sex anti-discrimination bill, a government Green Paper of 1973, until 1975 when the first British Sex Discrimination Act, an Equal Pay Act, and an Equal Opportunities Commission came into force.

With encouragement from the UK government, the other countries of the EEC soon followed suit with an agreement to ensure that discrimination laws would be phased out across the European Community. In the USA, the US National

Organization for Women (NOW) was created in 1966 with the purpose of bringing about equality for all women. NOW was one important group that fought for the Equal Rights Amendment (ERA). This amendment stated that "equality of rights under the law shall not be denied or abridged by the United States or any state on account of sex."

But there was disagreement on how the proposed amendment would be understood. Supporters believed it would guarantee women equal treatment. But critics feared it might deny women the right be financially supported by their husbands. The amendment died in 1982 because not enough states had ratified it. ERAs have been included in subsequent Congresses, but have still failed to be ratified. In the last three decades of the 20th century, Western women knew a new freedom through birth control, which enabled women to plan their adult lives, often making way for both career and family.

The movement had been started in the 1910s by US pioneering social reformer Margaret Sanger and in the UK and internationally by Marie Stopes. Over the course of the 20th century women took on a greater role in society. For example, many women served in government. In the U.S. government some served as U.S. Senators and others as members of the U.S. Cabinet. Many women took advantage of opportunities to become educated. In the United States at the beginning of the 20th century less than 20% of all college degrees were earned by women. By the end of the century this figure had risen to about 50%.

Opportunities also expanded in the workplace. Fields such as medicine, law, and science opened to include more women. At the beginning of the 20th century about 5% of the doctors in the United States were women. As of 2006, over 38% of all doctors in the United States were women, and today, women make almost 50% of the medical student population. While the numbers of women in these fields increased, many women still continued to hold clerical, factory, retail, or service jobs. For example, they worked as office assistants, on assembly lines, or as cooks.

UNITED NATIONS AND WOMENS' RIGHTS

In 1946 the United Nations established a Commission on the Status of Women. Originally as the Section on the Status of Women, Human Rights Division, Department of Social Affairs, and now part of the Economic and Social Council (ECOSOC). Since 1975 the UN has held a series of world conferences on women's issues, starting with the World Conference of the International Women's Year in Mexico City. These conferences created an international forum for women's rights, but also illustrated divisions between women of different cultures and the difficulties of attempting to apply principles universally Emerging from the 1985 Nairobi conference was a realization that feminism is not monolithic but "constitutes the political expression of the concerns and interests of women from different regions, classes, nationalities, and ethnic backgrounds.

There is and must be a diversity of feminisms, responsive to the different needs and concerns of women, and defined by them for themselves. This diversity builds on a common opposition to gender oppression and hierarchy which, however, is only the first step in articulating and acting upon a political agenda." At the Fourth World Conference on Women in Beijing, The Platform for Action was signed. This included a commitment to achieve "gender equality and the empowerment of women".

THE ELIMINATION OF ALL FORMS OF DISCRIMINATION AGAINST WOMEN

The Universal Declaration of Human Rights, adopted in 1948, enshrines "the equal rights of men and women", and addressed both the equality and equity issues. In 1979 the United Nations General Assembly adopted the Convention on the Elimination of All Forms of Discrimination against Women (CEDAW). Described as an international bill of rights for women, it came into force on 3 September 1981. The United States is the only developed nation that has not ratified the CEDAW.

The Convention defines discrimination against women in the following terms:

Any distinction, exclusion or restriction made on the basis of sex which has the effect or purpose of impairing or nullifying the recognition, enjoyment or exercise by women, irrespective of their marital status, on a basis of equality of men and women, of human rights and fundamental freedoms in the political, economic, social, cultural, civil or any other field.

It also establishes an agenda of action for putting an end to sex-based discrimination: States ratifying the Convention are required to enshrine gender equality into their domestic legislation, repeal all discriminatory provisions in their laws, and enact new provisions to guard against discrimination against women. They must also establish tribunals and public institutions to guarantee women effective protection against discrimination, and take steps to eliminate all forms of discrimination practiced against women by individuals, organizations, and enterprises. The CEDAW has been controversial for statements seen by some as promoting radical feminism. Particularly referenced is a 2000 report which said that in Belarus, "the Committee is concerned by the continuing prevalence of sex-role stereotypes and by the reintroduction of such symbols as a Mothers' Day and a Mothers' Award, which it sees as encouraging women's traditional roles."

MAPUTO PROTOCOL

The Protocol to the African Charter on Human and Peoples' Rights on the Rights of Women in Africa, better known as the Maputo Protocol, was adopted by the African Union on 11 July 2003 at its second summit in Maputo, Mozambique. On 25 November 2005, having been ratified by the required 15 member nations of the African Union, the protocol entered into force. The protocol guarantees comprehensive rights to women including the right to take part in the political process, to social and political equality with men, and to control of their reproductive health, and an end to female genital mutilation.

REPRODUCTIVE RIGHTS

Reproductive rights are rights relating to sexual reproduction and reproductive health. "Reproductive rights" are not recognised in international human rights law and is used as an umbrella term that may include some or all of the following rights: the right to legal or safe abortion, the right to control one's reproductive functions, the right to access quality reproductive healthcare, and the right to education and access in order to make reproductive choices free from coercion, discrimination, and violence. Reproductive rights may also be understood to include education about contraception and sexually transmitted infections, and freedom from coerced sterilization and contraception, protection from gender-based practices such as female genital cutting, or FGC, and male genital mutilation, or MGM.

Reproductive rights are understood as rights of both men and women, but are most frequently advanced as women's rights. The United Nations Population Fund (UNPF) and the World Health Organization (WHO) advocate for reproductive rights with a primary emphasis on women's rights. The ideas of these rights were first discussed as a subset of human rights at the United Nation's 1968 International Conference on Human Rights. The sixteenth article of the Proclamation of Teheran recognises reproductive rights as a subset of human rights and states, "Parents have a basic human right to determine freely and responsibly the number and the spacing of their children."

ABORTION

Women's access to safe and legal abortions is restricted in law or in practice in most countries in the world. Even where abortion is permitted by law, women may only have limited access to safe abortion services. Only a small number of countries prohibit abortion in all cases. In most countries and jurisdictions, abortion is allowed to save the pregnant woman's life, or where the pregnancy is the result of rape or incest.

Human Rights Watch considers abortion within the context of human rights, arguing:

"Abortion is a highly emotional subject and one that excites deeply held opinions. However, equitable access to safe abortion services is first and foremost a human right. Where abortion is safe and legal, no one is forced to have one. Where abortion is illegal and unsafe, women are forced to carry unwanted pregnancies to term or suffer serious health consequences and even death. Approximately 13% of maternal deaths worldwide are attributable to unsafe abortion–between 68,000 and 78,000 deaths annually."

They furthermore argue that "...international human rights legal instruments and authoritative interpretations of those instruments compel the conclusion that women have a right to decide independently in all matters related to reproduction, including the issue of abortion." Human Rights Watch argues that "the denial of a pregnant woman's right to make an independent decision regarding abortion violates or poses a threat to a wide range of human rights."

Basing its analysis on the authoritative interpretations of international human rights instruments by UN expert bodies Human Rights Watch states that where women's access to safe and legal abortion services are restricted, the following human rights may be at risk: the right to life, the right to health (or health care), right to freedom from discrimination, right to security of person, the right to liberty, the right to privacy, the right to information, the right to be free from cruel, inhuman, or degrading treatment, the right to decide the number and spacing of children (reproductive rights), the right to freedom of thought, and the right to freedom of religion.

Other groups however, such as the Catholic Church, regard abortion not as a right but as a 'moral evil'.

RAPE AND SEXUAL VIOLENCE

Rape, sometimes called sexual assault, is an assault by a person involving sexual intercourse with or sexual penetration of another person without that person's consent. Rape is generally considered a serious sex crime as well as a civil assault when part of widespread and systematic practices of rape and sexual slavery are now recognised as crime against humanity and war crime. Rape is also now recognised as an element of the crime of genocide when committed with the intent to destroy, in whole or in part, a targeted group.

Rape as an element of the crime of genocide

In 1998, the International Criminal Tribunal for Rwanda established by the United Nations made landmark decisions that rape is a crime of genocide under international law. The trial of Jean-Paul Akayesu, the mayor of Taba Commune in Rwanda, established precedents that rape is a element of the crime of genocide.

The Trial Chamber held that "sexual assault formed an integral part of the process of destroying the Tutsi ethnic group and that the rape was systematic and had been perpetrated against Tutsi women only, manifesting the specific intent required for those acts to constitute genocide."

Judge Navanethem Pillay said in a statement after the verdict: "From time immemorial, rape has been regarded as spoils of war. Now it will be considered a war crime. We want to send out a strong message that rape is no longer a trophy of war." An estimated 500,000 women were raped during the 1994 Rwandan Genocide.

The Akayesu judgement includes the first interpretation and application by an international court of the 1948 Convention on the Prevention and Punishment of the Crime of Genocide. The Trial Chamber held that rape, which it defined as "a physical invasion of a sexual nature committed on a person under circumstances which are coercive", and sexual assault constitute acts of genocide insofar as they were committed with the intent to destroy, in whole or in part, a targeted group, as such.

It found that sexual assault formed an integral part of the process of destroying the Tutsi ethnic group and that the rape was systematic and had been perpetrated against Tutsi women only, manifesting the specific intent required for those acts to constitute genocide.

RAPE AND SEXUAL ENSLAVEMENT AS CRIME AGAINST HUMANITY

The Rome Statute, which defines the jurisdiction of the International Criminal Court, recognises rape, sexual slavery, enforced prostitution, forced pregnancy, enforced sterilization, "or any other form of sexual violence of comparable gravity" as crime against humanity if the action is part of a widespread or systematic practice. Rape was first recognised as crime against humanity when the International Criminal Tribunal for the former Yugoslavia issued arrest warrants based on the Geneva Conventions and Violations of the Laws or Customs of War.

Specifically, it was recognised that Muslim women in Foca (southeastern Bosnia and Herzegovina) were subjected to systematic and widespread gang rape, torture and enslavement by Bosnian Serb soldiers, policemen and members of paramilitary groups after the takeover of the city in April 1992. The indictment was of major legal significance and was the first time that sexual assaults were investigated for the purpose of prosecution under the rubric of torture and enslavement as a crime against humanity. The indictment was confirmed by a 2001 verdict of the International Criminal Tribunal for the former Yugoslavia that rape and sexual enslavement are crimes again humanity. This ruling challenged the widespread acceptance of rape and sexual enslavement of women as intrinsic part of war.

2

Legal Rights of Women

The Legal rights of women refer to the social and human rights of women. One of the first women's rights declarations was the Declaration of Sentiments. From women's involvement within the abolition movements, women of the early 1800s became aware of the male dominance in society (patriarchy). From then on women struggled for equality, and were largely rewarded. The dependent position of women in early law is proved by the evidence of most ancient systems.

WOMEN IN INDIA

There is no doubt that we are in the midst of a great revolution in the history of women. The evidence is everywhere; the voice of women is increasingly heard in Parliament, courts and in the streets. While women in the West had to fight for over a century to get some of their basic rights, like the right to vote, the Constitution of India gave women equal rights with men from the beginning. Unfortunately, women in this country are mostly unaware of their rights because of illiteracy and the oppressive tradition. Names like Kalpana Chawla: The Indian born, who fought her way up into NASA and was the first women in space, and Indira Gandhi: The Iron Woman of India was the Prime Minister of the Nation, Beauty Queens like Aishwarya Rai and Susmita Sen, and Mother Teresa are not representative of the condition of Indian women.

CONSTITUTIONAL RIGHTS

The Constitution of India guarantees equality of sexes and in fact grants special favours to women. These can be found in three articles of the Constitution. Article 14 says that the government shall not deny to any person equality before law or the equal protection of the laws. Article 15 declares that government shall not discriminate against any citizen on the ground of sex. Article 15 (3) makes a special provision enabling the State to make affirmative discriminations in favour of women. Moreover, the government can pass special laws in favour of women. Article 16 guarantees that no citizen shall be discriminated against in matters of public employment on the grounds of sex. Article 42 directs the State to make provision for ensuring just and humane conditions of work and maternity relief.

Above all, the Constitution imposes a fundamental duty on every citizen through Articles 15 (A) (e) to renounce the practices derogatory to the dignity of women. All these are fundamental rights. Therefore, a woman can go to the court if one is subjected to any discrimination. When we talk about constitutional rights of women in India, we mainly pertain to those areas where discrimination is done against women and special laws formulated to fight those bigotries.

The most important issues stand as those pertaining to marriage, children, abortion, crimes against women, and inheritance. Before modern Hindu laws were passed, child marriages were the norms, inter-caste marriages were banned, the girl became a part of the husband's family, and polygamy was common. In the 19th century, the British rulers passed several laws to protect customs and traditions while abolishing detestable practices like Sati. Some such revolutionary laws were Hindu Widows Remarriage Act 1865 and the Brahmo Samaj Marriage Act 1872, the forerunner of the present Special Marriage Act. In the beginning, the Act sets four essential conditions for a valid Hindu marriage. They are:

1. Monogamy
2. Sound mind

3. Marriageable age
4. The parties should not be too closely related

Polygamy was permitted among Hindus before the Act was passed in 1955. However, after the act was passed, any man marrying again while his wife is living will be punished with fine and imprisonment up to seven years. Formerly, child marriages were common. The Child Marriage Act of 1929 was not very effective as such marriages were continued to be performed. Now, however, the bridegroom must be 21 years old and the bride 18 years. However, there is a separate Muslim Code of Conduct, which allows polygamy of up to four wives as per Islamic laws. A marriage may be invalid without the boy or the girl realizing it at the time of the wedding.

A civil marriage would be void if four essential conditions are not complied with. These conditions are listed in the Special Marriage Act (Section 4), as enumerated below:

- If it is bigamy.
- If either party was suffering from mental disorder.
- If the boy has not completed 21 years and the girl 18 years
- The boy and the girl are too closely related, or in legal language, are "within degrees of prohibited relationship" unless custom governing at least one party permits the marriage between them. Prohibited relationships are listed in he Special Marriage Act.
- A fifth reason for invalidating a marriage is impotence of either party.

There are some grounds available to the wife only, both in Hindu and civil marriages. One such ground available exclusively to the wife is her husband's commission of rape, sodomy or bestiality. Under the Hindu Adoptions and Maintenance Act 1956, a Hindu wife is entitled to be maintained by her husband. Section 125 of the Criminal Procedure Code also deals with maintenance of wife and children. If there is a decree of maintenance against the husband and the couple has been living apart for over one year, it would be a ground for the wife to seek dissolution of marriage. Here again the Muslim Personal Law has a different set of conditions for the annulment of an Islamic marriage.

The Dowry Prohibition Act of 1961 says that any person who gives, takes, or abets the giving or taking of dowry shall be punished with imprisonment, which may extend to six months or with fine up to Rs. 5,000 or with both. Dowry that started off as a practice to give away presents to the departing daughter, usually some resources to begin her new married life, slowly assumed extraordinary proportions and turned into a social evil. Brides were expected to bring the "gifts" regardless of their personal willingness. The bride's family could no longer have an individual say; lists were prepared and sent to the girl's house before the final agreement between the two families. The condition being that the boy would marry the girl only if the demands were met. Such a custom is being practiced not only in India but also in other countries like Bangladesh and Nepal.

The reason behind this custom is the poor economical condition of the people along with a lack of education; unawareness of legal rights among women and a general bias against the women. Crimes like rape, kidnapping, eve teasing and indecent exposure can be grouped as crimes against women. Rape is the worst crime against women after murder and the maximum punishment under the Indian Penal Code (IPC) is life imprisonment. An abortion or miscarriage due to natural causes is not an offence. Therefore, the law does not deal with it. However, violent and forceful abortion is a crime. Sections 312 and 316 of the Indian Penal Code deal with abortion as crime. Section 313 deals with abortion without the consent of the woman. The punishment could even be life imprisonment. The Hindu Succession Act gives male and female heirs almost equal right to inheritance. Section 14 says that any property possessed by a female Hindu shall be held by her as full owner and not as a limited owner.

WOMEN'S CONTRIBUTION TO THE ECONOMY

Although most women in India work and contribute to the economy in one form or another, much of their work is not documented or accounted for in official statistics. Women plough fields and harvest crops while working on farms, women weave and make handicrafts while working in household industries, women sell food and gather wood while working in the informal sector. Additionally, women are traditionally responsible for the daily household chores (e.g., cooking, fetching water, and looking after children). Since Indian culture hinders women's access to jobs in stores, factories and the public sector, the informal sector is particularly important for women.

There are estimates that over 90 percent of workingwomen are involved in the informal sector. The informal sector includes jobs such as domestic servant, small trader, artisan, or field labourer on a family farm. Most of these jobs are unskilled and low paying and do not provide benefits to the worker. More importantly, however, cultural practices vary from region to region. Though it is a broad generalization, North India tends to be more patriarchal and feudal than South India. Women in northern India have more restrictions placed on their behaviour, thereby restricting their access to work. Southern India tends to be more egalitarian, women have relatively more freedom, and women have a more prominent presence in society.

Cultural restrictions however are changing, and women are freer to participate in the formal economy, though the shortage of jobs throughout the country contributes to low female employment. But in the recent years, conditions of working women in India have improved considerably. More and more women find themselves in positions of respect and prestige; more and more workplaces are now populated with women who work on equal terms as men. Working is no longer an adjustment, a mere necessity; but a means to self worth and growth. Women have now not only found their place in work places but are also part to the governance.

In recent years there have been explicit moves to increase women's political participation. Women have been given representation in the Panchayati Raj system as a sign of political empowerment. There are many elected women representatives at the village council level. At the central and state levels too women are progressively making a difference. Today we have women Chief Ministers in five large states of India. The Women's reservation policy bill is slated to further strengthen political participation.

WOMEN'S RIGHTS AND WRONGS

The All India Muslim Personal Law Board proclaims that triple talaq is a social evil, but it is equally assertive that this social evil should not be removed by legislative reform. There is no question of banning the practice. Maulana Sayed Rabey Al-Hasani Naqvi, the Board president, says: "our laws are based on divine inspiration and triple talaq comes from the same inspiration, that is, Shariat. We have no powers to amend or abolish it. So the triple talaq is irrevocable." It is difficult to understand how what is divine can at the same time be evil.

The Hindu religion has also been replete with many social evils that Hindu women had to face. The practice of sati which forced Hindu woman to sit on the funeral pyre of her husband was abolished by the Sati Regulation Act, 1829, itself the result of a social reform movement launched by Raja Rammohun Roy. The reform was taken to its logical conclusion with the Widows Remarriage Act of 1856. Among Hindus, polygamy too was rampant. Yet it was abolished first in Bombay State by the Bombay Prevention of Hindu Bigamous Marriages Act, 1946. Later, the Hindu Marriage Act, 1955, put an end to polygamy throughout the country.

Marriage among Hindus had been held to be sacrosanct, something that could not be dissolved – yet the Hindu Marriage Act, 1955, provides for dissolution of marriage both by husband and wife on the grounds stated in the Hindu Marriage Act. The Indian Divorce Act has also been recently amended to do away with inequality between women and men in matters of divorce among Christians. Untouchability, yet another social evil, was outlawed by Article 17 of our Constitution. Social and legal reforms must move together to ensure that all social evils are banished.

It is often said that personal laws are outside the purview of challenge under Article 13 of the Constitution of India. But this has no constitutional or legal basis. The fact is that what is inhuman is both unconstitutional and illegal. A very interesting answer to the argument of the Muslim Personal Law Board lies in the fact that in several Muslim countries triple talaq has been banned or restricted. There are several countries where there is a uniform law of divorce, for all citizens irrespective of their religion. The power to legislate on marriage and divorce is specifically conferred in entry 5, List III, Schedule VII of our Constitution.

WOMEN'S HUMAN RIGHT

Millions of women throughout the world live in conditions of abject deprivation and attacks against their fundamental human rights for no other reason than that they are women. Considering this position, human rights for women, as for all individuals, are protected in international law. The international community has tried to play a decisive role in protecting human rights of women. And in furtherance to this objective, vigilant and concerted actions have been taken and which includes documenting human rights violations, publicizing these as widely as possible and campaigning to press government authorities seeking an end to the abuses and confronting governments which fail to protect fundamental human rights with full force of international condemnation.

INTERNATIONAL INSTRUMENTS AND WOMEN

International instruments relating to women fall into three distinct categories. The protective conventions, which came earliest, seek to shield women in their employment conditions, such as by prohibiting night work, employment in mines, and certain types of plantation labour. The second category of convention is corrective in nature, intended to ameliorate a distinct social problem or restriction. This type of convention covers matters such as loss of nationality at time of marriage, restrictions on prostitution, sale of women for forced labour, slavery and similar practices, child labour, and other personal abuses. The third category, which is the most recent, is intended to prevent discrimination on the basis of sex in a wide variety of fields, with normative sex-neutral provisions as the underlying rationale.

GENERAL DUTIES OF THE STATE UNDER INTERNATIONAL LAW

Generally, international conventions impose three types of duties on the state. First, the state has a duty to respect rights. Second, the state has a duty to protect rights - that is, to prevent the violation of rights by private persons and organizations who are not themselves bound by international treaties. A state's failure to organize the governmental apparatus and, in general, all the structures through which public power is exercised, so that they are capable of juridical ensuring the free and full enjoyment of human rights constitutes a breach of this duty. Third, the state has a duty to fulfill rights. Upon ratifying international treaties, states must take appropriate legislative, administrative, judicial, budgetary, economic and other measures to achieve individual's full realization of their human rights. In addition, the duty to fulfill rights requires states to alleviate persistent obstacles to the exercise of these rights.

VARIOUS INTERNATIONAL INSTRUMENTS RELATING TO WOMEN

Universal Declaration of Human Rights, 1948

Nearly all international human rights instruments adopted by the United Nations bodies since 1948 elaborate principles set out in the Universal Declaration of Human Rights. The drafters of the Universal Declaration of Human Rights considered women as part of humanity and granted them all rights as were granted to men.

Convention on the Political Rights of Women, 1952

The Convention on the Political Rights of Women provides for equal political rights for women. Under this Convention, states are obligated to ensure that women have the right to vote in elections, to be elected to publicly elected bodies, and to hold public office on equal terms with men.

Women are entitled to be free from discrimination in the exercise of these rights.

Though the Convention does not specifically mention affirmative action for women to increase their participation in political as well as public life, it does recognize the discriminatory practices that hinder women's participation and obligates the state party to equalize the status of men and women in the enjoyment and exercise of political rights.

International Covenant on Civil and Political Rights, 1966

The ICCPR, which was ratified in 1966, is a treaty of paramount importance to the international community which sets forth numerous provisions to ensure the enjoyment of civil and political freedom for all people. The Civil Covenant assures women's civil rights, as well as access to the political process.

International Covenant on Economic, Social and Cultural Rights, 1966

The Economic Covenant, in contrast, recognizes positive rights, such as the rights to food, shelter, health care, and education. The Economic Covenant is linked to distributive justice for the most vulnerable, who are everywhere disproportionately female. The Economic Covenant emphasizes the importance of non-discrimination on the basis of sex by reiterating it in two articles (Articles 2 and 3), and it supports the concept of affirmative action.

Declaration on the Elimination of All Forms of Discrimination against Women, 1967

In 1967, the United Nations promulgated the Declaration on the Elimination of all Forms of Discrimination Against Women. This Declaration recognized the particular nature of discrimination against women as worthy of a separate legal response.

The declaration called for member states to submit reports on the status of women in their own countries. The Indian government released its report, Toward Equality, in 1971. The report illuminated the poor conditions of women in India with regard to economic freedom, education, family and legal rights and helped the more educated and politicized Indians to see that something needed to be done to achieve full equality in Indian society.

Declaration on the Protection of Women and Children in Emergency and Armed Conflict, 1974

The General Assembly had taken on a true hybrid approach, citing both IHL and human rights law. Through this Declaration, the Assembly demanded states abide by the Geneva Conventions and other instruments of international law relative to respect for human rights in armed conflicts. It specifically noted the relevance in armed conflict of the UDHR, the International Covenant on Civil and Political Rights (ICCPR), the International Covenant on Economic, Social and Cultural Rights (ICESCR), and the Declaration of the Rights of the Child.

Although this document fails to address specifically the issue of wartime rape, the preamble does acknowledge that women are too often the victims of inhuman acts during periods of armed conflict and are in need of special protection. The Declaration also establishes mistreatment of women during war as a criminal offence. While the document adds validity to the need for recognizing women's issues in conflict situations, it is only a nonbinding declaration and, thus, plays a limited role in ending foreseeable, gender-specific war crimes.

Convention on the Elimination of all Forms of Discrimination against Women, 1979

Since the first years of the 1970s, the international community was convinced of the need to gather, in one single compulsory instrument, the great bulk of norms enunciated in the resolutions, declarations, and recommendations of the international organizations and the provisions of Conventions and Covenants already adopted. This included the principles contained in the Declaration on the Elimination of All Forms of Discrimination Against Women, approved by the UN General Assembly in 1967 (Declaration of 1967).

This Convention has been rightly called the "Charter of the Human Rights of Women." In sixteen articles legally related to one another, several principles that had been set forth at the international level in the Declaration of 1967 are confirmed. Also, it emphasizes those established in the Covenants of Human Rights, or in some other specific conventions, such as the 1952 Convention on the Political Rights of Women.

It is important to point out that the Convention, once opened to the signature and ratification of states, was one of three multilateral instruments to achieve in the least time the greatest number of ratifications or accessions, thereby surpassing the International Covenants on Human Rights of 1966. Thus, since 1980, the year in which it was opened to signature, thru October, 2000, 166 states have ratified or acceded to it.

The Convention is structured in six parts. Part I is devoted to general principles and commitments. Part II refers to the civil and political rights of women. Part III corresponds to the social areas, with special attention to rural women. Part IV is devoted to equality before the law and within the family. Part V contains the follow-up and surveillance provisions for the implementation of the Convention and also establishes the Committee on the Elimination of Discrimination Against Women (CEDAW). Finally, Part VI refers to issues of procedure, entering into force, solution of controversies, and presentation of reservations.

The Convention obliges governments to prohibit discrimination against women on the one hand, and ensure their equality on the other, equality being one of the Convention's goals. There is not, at present, any procedure for complaints under this Convention, though it is under active consideration. The Convention prohibits any distinction, exclusion or restriction based on sex, or marital status, which is either intended to, or has the effect of, impairing women's fundamental rights and freedoms, in any field. This covers unintentional (or indirect) discrimination, as well as deliberate acts that disadvantage women, and it affects the protection of rights in private (or family) life as well as public life.

Declaration on the Elimination of Violence against Women, 1993

The United Nation's 1993 Declaration on the Elimination of Violence against Women defines gender-based violence broadly to include any gender-based act that causes physical, sexual, or psychological harm. The final Declaration on the Elimination of Violence against Women, which was adopted by the United Nations General Assembly in 1993 making it applicable to all United Nations member states, condemned both public and private physical, sexual, or psychological harm or suffering to women, specifically naming violence within families and female genital mutilation as human rights violations. This Declaration noted that these rights were already protected among several international conventions, including the Universal Declaration of Human Rights and the International Covenant on Civil and Political Rights.

The efforts done till now though have bettered the position of women, however, we have not reached the stage of fully protecting the human rights of women. There are still many instances occurring around the world that are absolutely violative of women's human right. For example, combatants and their sympathizers in conflicts, such as those in Sierra Leone, Kosovo, the Democratic Republic of Congo, Afghanistan, and Rwanda, have raped women as a weapon of war with near complete impunity. Men in Pakistan, South Africa, Peru, Russia, and Uzbekistan beat women in the home at astounding rates, while these governments alternatively refuse to intervene to protect women and punish their batterers or do so haphazardly and in ways that make women feel culpable for the violence.

As a direct result of inequalities found in their countries of origin, women from Ukraine, Moldova, Nigeria, the Dominican Republic, Burma, and Thailand are bought and sold, trafficked to work in forced prostitution, with insufficient government attention to protect their rights and punish the traffickers. In Guatemala, South Africa, and Mexico, women's ability to enter and remain in the work force is obstructed by private employers who use women's reproductive status to exclude them from work and by discriminatory employment laws or discriminatory enforcement of the law. In the U.S., students discriminate against and attack girls in school who are lesbian, bi-sexual, or transgendered, or do not conform to male standards of female behaviour.

Women in Morocco, Jordan, Kuwait, and Saudi Arabia face government-sponsored discrimination that renders them unequal before the law - including discriminatory family codes that take away women's legal authority and place it in the hands of male family members - and restricts women's participation in public life. Hence it is necessary that the campaign to protect women's human rights is waged on more specific fronts and specific issues in addition to protecting general human rights. The efforts be made successful and the concept of women's human right remains prosaic and revolutionary.

They should be used to lobby for legislative and policy changes at local, national and international levels, equally and used as important tool for grassroots organizing. As the women's human rights not only teach women about the range of rights that their governments must honour; it also functions as a kind of gestalt by which to organize analyses of their experiences and plan action for change. The human rights framework creates a space in which the possibility for a different account of women's lives can be developed. What is so useful about this framework is that it provides women with principles by which to develop alternative visions of their lives without suggesting the substance of those visions.

The fundamental principles of human rights that accord to each and every person the entitlement to human dignity give women a vocabulary for describing both violations and impediments to the exercise of their human rights. The large body of international covenants, agreements and commitments about human rights gives women political leverage and a tenable point of reference. And finally, the idea of women's human rights enables women to define and articulate the specificity of the experiences in their lives at the same time that it provides a vocabulary for women to share the experiences of other women around the world and work collaboratively for change.

Woman is in no way inferior to her counterpart, man. A major civilization transformation has taken place throughout the 20th century: the evolving empowerment of women together with the recognition of women's rights as human rights. 8th of March is universally acknowledged as International Women's Day which means that the woman of today has come of age and wants to lead a dignified life of equality with man. The slogan raised today by the women of the world is: "Equality, Dignity and Self-Respect is what we want". This slogan is indicative of the new awareness among women the world over. Modern women have raised their voices against the male dominated and feudalistic society.

Level of consciousness, emergence of successive generations of women at the forefront of knowledge, and growing numbers of women with enough education to investigate the conditions, aspirations and perspectives among the poor - all this was an impulsion to react to the need for change in societal patterns. Other factors also contributed to this process: the growth of women studies in many universities throughout the world supplemented by burgeoning networks of the cross fertilization of ideas, approaches, tactics and strategies. Added to these was the active role played by women in the struggle for democracy against oppressive regimes in Latin America, Africa and Asia. The role of women as a separate issue of more than merely token significance entered international debate at the first UN Conference on Population and Development, held in Bucharest (Romania) in 1974.

The United Nations Conferences on women and other development and socio-economic issues, held since 1975, have helped to heighten the visibility of the role, the plight and the potential of women on the international scene. To quote United Nations Development Program (UNDP's) Human Development Report "human development is impossible without gender equality".

Woman is in no way inferior to her counterpart, man. From time immemorial, woman represents history in all its grace and distress in terms of time and space, social ups and down, political subjugation and freedom. In religion, social intercourse, education, literature, art and culture, her status was never in doubt. As a significant measure towards initiating women's empowerment, equal-pay legislation should be adopted and expanded in all countries so as to incorporate the principle of equal pay for work of equal value.

This would allow for a re-evaluation of women's professional and 'pink-collar' occupations, with increases in both pay and status. Affirmative-action measures might include the provision of day-care centres, flexible working hours, women's quotas in retirement, promotion, and retraining; and outlawing and prosecuting sexual harassment in the work place. Labour laws need also to be expanded to provide better conditions, benefits and job security for domestic and agricultural workers, part-time, temporary, and miscellaneous workers in the home, and employees in export-processing zones. More research should be conducted on the contribution of women's unpaid work to family and national economies - including work in subsistence agriculture, livestock husbandry, domestic work, child-care, and care for the elderly, the disabled, and this time.

This analysis should incorporate time-use data, and should be used in the design of future policy. All new development initiatives and economic and social planning should be subject to a 'gender audit' to assess their effects on women's quality of life as well as on the inequalities persisting between men and women. The majority of the world's women are poor citizens of the poor countries; they are 'deprived' and 'backward'. About 40% of females worldwide are children under the age of 15. The World Health Report 1995 highlighted the grim prospects facing a baby girl born in one of the least developed countries, where one-sixth of all births occur annually. Equity demands that the conditions of such deprived infants and children be improved without delay.

There is a need to formulate a comprehensive global action plan for girls and adolescent females. It will redress many of the prevalent injustices suffered by women. The greatest need of the hour is to change the social attitude to women. Women's empowerment means a lot, but the ultimate goal of the equalization of man and woman would materialize only when her complimentary role is recognized by the society.

FUNDAMENTAL FOR WOMEN'S RIGHTS

The relationship of women with the state in Pakistan appears to depend on three interrelated sets of relationships: (i) the relation between the state and the individual citizen; (ii) the relation between the state and the ethnic or religious group to which a citizen belongs; and (iii) the relation between women and the ethnic or religious group with which they identify. The extent to which a woman is allowed or denied her fundamental rights granted by the state is mediated by her ethnic or religious group and its relationship with the state. In a liberal bourgeois democracy these relationships are further complicated by the need to accommodate ethnic and religious parties in coalition arrangements. Elections increasingly deliver ethnically split verdicts in which no single party gets a simple majority and the party with the largest number of seats is forced to rely on others to form its government.

In return for support the smaller parties extract their pound of flesh in the form of ministries, lucrative positions and compromise on certain ideological standpoints. This not only creates large cabinets it also requires backtracking by political parties on clearly enunciated principles. In political bargains the greatest backtracking is invariably witnessed on the issues of women's rights and equality. The clearest evidence of such political manoeuvring is the manner in which the PPP inducted two ministers, Israrullah Zehri as minister for postal services and Hazar Khan Bijarani as minister for education. Israrullah Zehri is on record defending the brutal murder of five women who it is alleged were buried alive in Balochistan. Hazar Khan Bijarani is said to have presided over a jirga that ordered that five girls aged two to five be handed over to a rival clan to settle a dispute.

The overriding need to accommodate people from the smaller provinces and minority ethnic groups to ensure their support for the government has negated the fundamental rights to life and security for women. Such political compromise for expediency ignores the manifesto of the party which states: "The Pakistan People's Party has an unflinching commitment to the cause of gender equality ever since it was founded in 1967" and "The party will take institutional initiatives to prevent crimes against women in the name of tribalism, such as honour killings and forced marriages". Despite repeated protests by various sections of society this travesty of justice has not been reversed.

Other parties with stated commitments to women's rights and equality have also exhibited misogynist biases against women by failing to show a modicum of respect for their female colleagues. The remarks about two women being equal to one man by Ishaq Dar of the PML-N, and the subsequent refusal by party members to allow Sherry Rehman to record her protest is an incident reflective of the deeply prejudiced attitudes of our lawmakers.

The bewildering insensitivity was further demonstrated by Chaudhry Nisar Ali's nomination of Hanif Abbasi as head of the National Assembly's Standing Committee on Women's Affairs despite the presence of a number of worthy women candidates in the parliament. The heartening fact is that the PML-N women parliamentarians themselves protested. The PML-N's manifesto also promises to "promote participation of women in national development and their social, political and economic empowerment". One wonders how women's political empowerment would be possible when even their most basic rights to represent themselves are not acknowledged.

As if all this were not enough there are rumours circulating that the Ministry of Women Development would be given to the JUI-F. Apart from this party's known aversion to women's equality and freedom, it is vital to remember that its members had stated that the implementation of the Protection of Women Bill 2006 was like challenging God. One of the demands of the JUI-F for supporting Asif Zardari's presidential bid was the revocation of parts of the Women Protection Act. Maulana Fazlur Rahman and his associates were seen roaring with laughter over an anti-women song at the maulana's brother's kalima reception. The song was about marrying four times as one wife was not sufficient.

Patriarchal and misogynist attitudes are deeply ingrained in our social, economic, political and ideological structures. It is too much to hope that those entrusted with making the country's laws would reflect a morality higher than the rest of the nations. However, one can expect the lawmakers to have read the constitution and know that killing citizens, men or women, is murder and that murder is a crime. The country's law does not allow so-called honour to be invoked as a justification for vile murder. It is also reasonable to expect that lawmakers would not pass statements contrary to the law to justify crimes.

Since one cannot depend on individuals to rise above their ethnic or religious prejudices, one has to rely on systems. The assumption underlying liberal democracy was that over time it would eliminate the pre-modern identities of caste, clan, tribe and sect and create the modern identity of the citizen whose relation to the state would be a direct one and not mediated through local, cultural and customary structures. It was also assumed that broad-based political parties, premised on shared economic issues, would replace narrow sub-nationalist, ethnic, sectarian and fundamentalist outfits.

Instead, politics itself became ethnicised, and sub-national, sectarian and tribal sentiments were articulated in the political arena. The state capitulated to such sentiments in the process itself becoming tribal and sectarian. Multiple legal systems distorted democracy and laws came to be premised on religion and tribal customs. The Qisas and Diyat law is a major example of a tribal law becoming entrenched in the state's legal structure. The tribal state allows parliamentarians like Ajmal Khattak, Salim Mazari, Israrullah Zehri and Hazar Bijarani to legitimise the murder and trafficking of women as cultural tradition.

The sectarian state allows violence against women to be condoned through laws made in the name of religion. Political compulsions force parties like the PPP to establish the Sharia in parts of Pakistan like Malakand. With the collusion between the Sharia, tribal and customary law, and Anglo-Saxon legal principles, women's rights and equality are sacrificed at the altar of political expediency. If democracy has reinforced rather than weakened tribal, sectarian, fundamentalist and ethnic articulations, it is because Pakistan's social and economic structures were not transformed significantly to meet the needs of a viable democracy.

The most fundamental requirement for democracy is secularism so that the legal system of the country can ensure equality and justice to all citizens irrespective of religion, sex or ethnic belonging. A single legal system based on democratic and secular principles would eliminate parallel ones and establish a direct relation between women citizens and the state. Their relation to the state would then not be mediated by the immediate reference group but by their status as equal citizens.

WOMEN EQUALITY AND THE U.S. CONSTITUTION

At a time when women are astronauts and truck drivers, it is hard to believe that the U.S. Constitution does not guarantee women the same rights as men. For most women, equality is a bread-and-butter issue. Women are still paid less on the job and charged more for everything from dry cleaning to insurance. The value of a woman's unpaid work in the home is often not taken into account in determining divorce settlements and pension benefits. When women turn to the courts to right these wrongs, they are at a distinct disadvantage because of what has and hasn't happened to the Constitution.

In 1776 Abigail Adams urged her husband, John, that he and other framers of our founding documents should, "Remember the ladies." John, who went on to become our second president responded, "Depend upon it. We know better than to repeal our masculine systems," and women were left out of the Constitution. Nearly a hundred years later, Congress adopted amendments to the Constitution to end slavery and provide justice to former slaves. The 14th Amendment, passed in 1868, guaranteed all "persons" the right to "equal protection under the law." However, the second section of the amendment used the words "male citizens," in describing who would be counted in determining how many representatives each state gets in Congress.

This was the first time the Constitution said point blank that women were excluded. Similarly, the 15th Amendment in 1870 extended voting rights to all men – but not to any women. It wasn't all doom and gloom for women in the 19th and early 20th centuries, though. Two women active in world anti-slavery efforts, Lucretia Mott and Elizabeth Cady Stanton, were leaders at the first-ever "Women's Rights Convention" in Seneca Falls, N. Y., in 1848. Their "Declaration of Sentiments" included this play on the Declaration of Independence, "We hold these truths to be self-evident: that all men and women are created equal."

These women and others went on to form what became known as the suffrage movement. We now consider the suffragists the "first wave" of the U.S. feminist movement. During their long campaign to win women the right to vote, they used strategies including marches, pickets, arrests and hunger strikes. They triumphed in 1920 when the states ratified the 19th Amendment to the Constitution, which corrected the long-time injustice the 15th Amendment had put into writing. Suffragist leader Alice Paul authored the Equal Rights Amendment (ERA) to remedy women's exclusion from the 14th Amendment. Introduced in 1923, the ERA was buried in Congress for nearly 50 years. In the late 1960s, the "second wave" of feminist activists took up Alice Paul's cause.

After getting the ERA voted out of Congress, we held marches, organized boycotts, lobbied and worked on election campaigns to try to get it passed by the necessary three-fourths of the states. When an arbitrary time limit expired in 1982, the ERA was just three states short of the 38 required for ratification. The history of Supreme Court rulings on women's rights makes clear why a constitutional guarantee of women's equality is needed. During the first 200 years of our country's history, the Supreme Court justices never saw a discriminatory law against women they didn't like. Illinois wanted to keep women from practicing law? The court in 1873 cited "the law of the Creator" as good enough reason to protect these delicate creatures – grown women – from being sullied by the corruption of legal and business practices.

Time and again, women were really being protected from making too much money. Oregon wanted to limit the number of hours women could work? The court in 1908 ruled that women must "rest upon and look to (men) for protection" and also – in a contradictory view of men – that the law was needed "to protect (women) from the greed as well as the passion of man." Michigan wanted to allow women to work as waitresses but keep them out of higher-paid bartender jobs? The court in 1948 did not see this as a violation of the Constitution's guarantee of "equal protection." In modern times, Supreme Court rulings on women's rights have zigged and zagged, backward and forward. In a 1961 case, the justices upheld Florida's virtual exclusion of women from juries because "women are the center of home and family life." The defendant had bludgeoned her husband to death and wanted jurors who might understand how she could be driven to such a deed.

Finally, in 1971, pioneering feminist attorney Ruth Bader Ginsburg made the first breakthrough in the court's "anything goes" attitude toward sex discrimination. She convinced the court to throw out an Idaho law that automatically gave preference to a man over an equally qualified woman when appointing the person responsible for disposing of the property of someone who has died. Ginsburg went on to become the second woman appointed to serve on the Supreme Court. In 1973, the Court struck down a U.S. Air Force policy that automatically gave a married man family housing and medical allowances, while a married woman had to prove she was the "head of household," i.e., that she provided all of her own expenses plus at least half of her families in order to qualify for the family benefits.

But in 1977 the justices were back to an old-fashioned view, a more narrow reading of women's equality. A bright eighth-grade girl, named Susan, who'd won science awards wanted to attend Philadelphia's all-boys Central High. It was an academically superior public school; even the school board admitted Girls High had inferior science facilities. But the Supreme Court upheld Central High's exclusion of Susan solely because she was a girl. More recently, in a 1987 decision that is the only Supreme Court case dealing with affirmative action for women, the justices upheld a county's voluntary plan. The justices allowed the promotion to stand, and the women became the first ever promoted to one of the country's 238 skilled craft jobs.

A qualified woman was promoted over a man who had a slightly higher score based on interviews with a team of three men. One of them had called the woman a "rabble rousing skirt" and another had refused to issue her the required coveralls for a previous job. A case that was before the court in its 1996-1997 term drove home the inequities that still exist at the dawn of the 21st century. A jury had convicted a judge of violating the civil rights of five women by raping, sexually assaulting and harassing the women. An appeals court overruled the jury. Even though courts have ruled repeatedly that it is a violation a person's civil rights to be beaten by a police officer, the appeals court could not see anything in the Constitution that would put this judge on notice that it is just as wrong to rape a woman.

Without a constitutional guarantee of women's equality, even favorable rulings and good laws on women's rights can be ignored, revoked or overruled. Feminist activists have not given up on a women's equality amendment. We know that to get women into the Constitution we will have to elect a lot more people who support that idea. We look to the young women and men who are addressing issues of equality and justice in high schools across the country. We are confident that this "third wave" will soon be ready to accept the baton.

WOMEN'S MARCH TO EQUALITY

A human being is born free. In other words every individual has the right to a life of freedom. Women are neither ethereal damsels nor dolls nor bundles of passions and nerves. They are as much human beings as men are and they are filled with the same urge for freedom. But in the name of social customs and traditions the woman of this country is bound by the chains of slavery forged by men and her freedom is being negated. The widow has to observe very hard rules in respect of her food, dress and habits. The peasant labour women do not get wages equal to those of men. The common women become victims to the cruelty of their husbands. They are even haunted by punishment here on earth and elsewhere in imaginary hell after their death for breach of duty towards their male counterparts.

The old institutions like caste, patriarchal family, religious mores and dominant social value systems still reign supreme with considerable vigour. All these institutions and ideologies are surcharged with the spirit of male dominance. The dowry system, the bride burning, the exploitation of the sex symbol images of women in advertising are the proofs of gross injustice against women. Manu, the ancient law giver of Indian society ordained that, a woman is not entitled to freedom and independence and that she shall be protected by her father in childhood, by her husband in her youth and by her male children in old age. Hence the concept that women are inferior to men was universally accepted by people in the ancient period and the doors to self development were closed to them. But at the time of British rule, Mahatma Gandhi, knowing the potential of women, advocated the cause of womens' emancipation and influenced them to participate in the freedom struggle of India.

Pandit Jawaharlal Nehru also supported womens' cause and declared that "In order to awaken the people it is the women who have to be awakened, when women are on the move, the village moves, the household moves and the country moves." After the independence, the crowning achievement of modern Indian History is the recognition and granting of equal status to women through the constitution of free sovereign India. The constitution has proclaimed the equality of man and woman in all domains of life. As declared in the constitution, "The state shall not discriminate against any citizen, on ground only of religion, race, caste, sex, place or any of them." Further in the 16th article it is mentioned that, "there shall be equality of opportunity for all citizens in matters relating to employment or appointment to any office under the state."

In pursuance of the constitutional provisions, the Govt. has enacted a series of legislations relating to inheritance, adoption, marriage, divorce and maintenance to ensure that women should be treated in equality and also to safeguard their rights. The constitution again has elaborated, in Directive Principles of State Policy which relates to a variety of issues like equal pay for equal work, human conditions of work for women, maternity relief etc. Action has been taken like the passing of the Equal Remuneration Act, which gives right for equal pay for equal work. It is now high time to change our social outlook towards women. Their understanding, cooperation and effective participation are essential for bringing about the desirable social changes. To quote Smt. Indira Gandhi, "If women are neglected, humanity is deprived of half of its energy and creativity."

Therefore for the development of community and nation, for reducing the male dominance and in order to minimise the discrimination against women, they should be brought into the mainstream of socioeconomic field of the country. To combat against male dominance and injustice, first of all, women have to become aware of their social positions. Unless they realise that they are in bonds, they cannot aspire for freedom. They should have to get rid of mental slavery and should cultivate a scientific outlook coupled with a spirit of modernism and develop thought, based on rationalism. When once, they begin to question age old beliefs and time worn ideas then solutions will automatically appear on their mental horizon. In order that, women receive emancipation and equality of status with their male counterpart, it is imperative to impart vocational education to them.

In the words of Pandit Jawaharlal Nehru, our first Prime Minister and architect of nation "Freedom depends on economic conditions even more than political and if the woman is not economically free and self earning, she will have to depend on her husband or someone else and dependants are never free."

Swami Vivekananda, the famous India monk had declared that education is the only panacea for the upliftment of the nation. But we are having an outmoded system of education. This educational system was evolved by the British with a calculated objective of producing men and women suitable for white collar jobs in their administrative hierarchy. But now our thinking is that, our education should be programmed to train men and women not only who seek employment but also those who would create employment. Therefore the education should also develop such skill and attitude for potential employment. Women should be given proper vocational education and general education, consistent with the need of the society.

By proper employment, the women will be able to enhance their family income, their standard of living and can thereby able to raise their social positions and respectability. Though the Government has adopted some progressive legislation, the women have to take a lead in fighting for their rights and for this as the first step; they should have knowledge of their existing legal rights. The different women organisations and the privileged women should strive for developing awareness in the minds of their poor and illiterate sisters through mass media, such as folk dance, cinema, etc. about women's all round contribution to the family welfare so that men treat women with respect, understanding and equality.

A CASE STUDY

Equality for Hindu women

In the case of C. Masilamani Mudaliar vs. Idol of Shri Swaminathathaswam! (ALR-1996-SC-1697) the Supreme Court was required to determine the scope of right of Hindu Female to dispose of property acquired or possessed under a will executed prior to the Commencement of the Hindu Succession Act. 1956. The Court said that Section 14 of The Hindu Succession Act should be construed harmoniously consistent with the Constitutional goal of removing gender-based discrimination and effectuating economic empowerment of Hindu Females.

Applying this principle of interpretation the Apex Court held that right derived by widow (who had bequeathed the property to the appellant) under the will of her husband (even though before the enactment of the Hindu Succession Act. 1956) should be considered to have developed into a right of absolute ownership by virtue of operation of Section 14 of the Hindu Succession Act.

The Supreme Court said that - "it is seen that after the Constitution came into force the right to equality and dignity of person enshrined in the Preamble of the Constitution. Fundamental Rights and Directive Principles which are a trinity intended to remove discrimination or disability on grounds only of social status of gender removed the pre-existing impediments that stood in the way of female or weaker segments of the society."

What follows is significant. The Supreme Court said further -"the personal laws conferring inferior status on women is anathema to equality.Personal laws are derived not from the Constitution, but from the religious scriptures. The laws thus derived must be consistent with the Constitution lest they became void under Article 13 if they violate fundamental rights. Right-to equality is a fundamental right.'

This view is consistent with international documents on women's rights. In this connection, it will be useful to refer to a canon of interpretation approved by the Supreme Court in a J980 case of Jolly George Varghese Vs. Bank of Cochin that - with regard to interpretation it is a principle generally recognized in national legal systems, that in the event of doubt, the national rule is to be interpreted in accordance with the State's international obligations."

As regards the scope of Women's right, the Supreme Court in the present case of C. Masilamani Mudaliar, therefore, rightly derived, support from the UN Declaration updated 4- I2- J986 on "The Development of.the Right to Developments", in which the India played a crusader's role for its adoption and ratified the same. Relying upon Article 6(I), 6(2), and 6(3) of the said declaration, the Supreme Court said that - "effective measures should be undertaken to ensure that women have an active role in the development process. Appropriate economic and social reforms should be carried out with a view to eradicate all social injustice."

The Supreme Court also derived similar support from Vienna Declaration on the elimination of all forms of Discrimination against Women, which was ratified by the UNO on 18-12-1979.' The Government of India has ratified the same on J9-6-1993. The Supreme Court concluded that - "the right to equality, removing handicaps and discrimination against a Hindu Female by reason of operation of existing law should be in conformity with the right to equality enshrined in the Constitution and the personal law against needs to be in conformity with the Constitutional goal.'

In the case of Madhu Kishwar vs. State of Bihar the Supreme Court directed the State of Bihar to comprehensively, examine the question of gender discrimination prevalent in the form of certain tribal customs among the tribes (who are exempted from Hindu Succession Act. 1956 vide Section 2(2) of the said Act) JO. Applying this dictum of the Supreme Court should we not examine some provisions of the Hindu Law (codified as well as uncodified law) from the viewpoint of equal rights for women? If we find any provision loaded with discrimination against women, endeavor should be made to remove discrimination either by process of interpretation or if necessary by suitable legislative amendments. In that context, we notice that -

i. In the matter of adoption under the Hindu Adoption and Maintenance Act. 1956, a Hindu male whether married or unmarried divorced or widowed can adopt a child. A married male, however can adopt one with the consent of his wife so far as good. But a married lady cannot adopt a child even with the consent of her husband.

ii. In uncodified Hindu Law (Mitakshara school), females and not Co-partners - which is a bastion of males only. A daughter therefore cannot tile a suit for partition of properties held by her father. It is a different matter, however, if her brothers file a suit. In that event, she would be entitled to her legitimate share.

iii. Discrimination is writ large against women even in the matter of intestate succession to the property of Hindu females. Section 15 provides that the property of a female Hindu dying intestate shall firstly devolve upon her children and then upon the heirs of the husband. In the absence of her children, the manner of devolution depends upon the fact whether her property had been inherited from her father or from her husband. If the property left behind her is the property inherited from her father, the heirs of her father will inherit the property. If the property left behind her is the property inherited from her husband, different rules will apply, viz., that the heirs of her husband will inherit the property. Thus, ultimately her husband's dominating role ensures even after her dying intestate. One can be sanguine that our courts and legislators will notice such anti-female bias in our codified and uncodified Law of Succession and take remedial measures.

3

Gender Equality
Women, Communal Violence, and Rights Rhetoric

Recent television footage and reports from Gujarat have shown Hindu families, including women participating in violence and attacks on Muslims. Communal violence has spread beyond the traditional geographical confines of the walled city to middle-class localities, especially in cities like Ahmedabad. 'Spontaneous' acts of rioting and arson that involve lumpen elements have always been suspected as the cause of many riots in India. Though targeted violence was occasionally a factor at times in some earlier urban outbreaks, large scale mobilisation for targeted violence came into its own as part of the Ram Janmabhoomi movement. While scholars like Tanika Sarkar have provided a lot of insight into the increasing participation of women in Hindu fundamentalist bodies and movements, specific attention to the nature, prevalence and severity of women's participation in violence is something that requires more attention.

Much of the literature on this subject relates women's violence to the mobilisation and wooing of women by Sangh Parivar organisations. At the height of the Ram Janmabhoomi movement, and during the destruction of the Babri Masjid, women participated in large numbers in destructive and violent activity, especially in Mumbai and several cities in

Gujarat. But the kind of violence we are observing now, where entire families, women and children included, participate in arson, looting, and murder, points to a new situation - active and aggressive participation in violence during riots has become a 'normal' social activity, suitable for the participation of all family members. How else can one explain or understand women in their nineties coming out on to the terraces of their houses, egging their men on, and even throwing stones at neighbours belonging to a different community?

Newspapers have reported seeing Hindu women with weapons going around as part of mobs committing arson and attacking Muslims. There have also been reports that closed circuit cameras have captured images of women participating in the looting of shops. Activists on fact-finding missions have also reported observing women participating in violence, and Muslim women have complained of being "betrayed" by their (female) neighbours. Citing the active participation of women in the violence against members of the Muslim community, the Head of the All India Muslim Women's Conference termed it as a division of women along religious lines. In a society where social and family norms do not even permit women to show their faces outside of their homes, what changes have led to women participating in violent activities along with men? Has the legitimacy given to violence among groups provided legitimacy to changes in women's behaviour as well? Has the strategy of the Sangh Parivar in bringing women into their fold also led to their greater participation in violence?

Women often bear the brunt of violence at the hands of their husbands and other kin without protection. Have their 'collective mentalities' been transformed by the Sangh Parivar led outbreaks of communal violence? Did it so 'empower' them that they could have broken through the norms that usually require them to accept without effective protest, the violence inflicted upon them? Did it impel them to engage in acts of violence and rioting when sanctioned by these same oppressors? Is it possible to explain a significant portion of violence by a woman on members of another community as just the pent-up emotions of victims of violence being released?

Did the fact that she wasn't likely to be harmed for expressing it, rather applauded for doing so contribute in some way?

Some writers claim that when Hindu women assume militant roles they do so "without violating the norms of Hindu womanhood." The implication in some of these analyses is that, while women may be part of militant outfits, provide informed consent to violence by male members of their community, and even participate in public protests, they stop short of actually indulging in violence, since that would go against the norms of womanhood, Hindu or otherwise. The sight of women actively participating in such acts as looting, arson and stone throwing leads one to question the current applicability of these interpretations.

Two discrete but interrelated streams of discourse and action seem to be at the heart of this social-political transformation in the last two decades. The first is the reactionary mobilisation of upper castes to oppose the increasing empowerment of the Dalit-Bahujans, reflected especially in the anti-reservation movements in the second half of the 1980s and the early 1990s. The first large scale violence that took place in Ahmadabad outside of the walled city and involved active middle class participation was during the anti-reservation riots in 1985, which later turned communal.

During the nationwide anti-reservation violence against the Mandal Commission report, large scale violence was mostly treated benignly by the state machinery. For the first time many middle class young people, especially women, were involved in the violence. For many, it was the first time that they had come out on the streets and participated in public protests. The transformation of anti-reservation riots into attacks on members of other communities has been observed in many areas throughout the country. It is not an accident that the rise of the BJP in coastal Andhra has occurred in those areas notorious for atrocities on Dalits.

The political linkages between the movement for the mandir and the anti-Mandal agitation are well known. Scholars have also established the ways in which the 'Manuvadi' forces have been working to incorporate some of the cadres from the Ambedkarite movement into their own ranks as supporters of hindutva. However we also need to understand the particular ways in which the anti-Mandal agitation marked a watershed in Indian politics. Especially to be noted is the rhetoric the agitation's leaders used to justify the rights they claimed as a supposed meritocracy. This claim dramatically shifted aspects of reservation policy away from their previous ostensible focus on remediating bias against marginalised groups. Sections of the media, intellectuals, and politicians aided Manuvadi leaders colluded in distorting the logic behind reservations by focussing on nothing but income differences, rather than on the strong effects of social inequality and discrimination.

Their proposed substitute for the previous reservation policy, which was justified as a means of achieving substantive equality, developed via a new rhetoric, a version of equality that highlighted 'merit' and 'equality of opportunities' as superior to reservations which are a recompense for historically based bias and discrimination. More importantly, the movement actively encouraged direct violent action against other vulnerable groups. At the same time, they attacked the weak attempts by law enforcement agencies to prevent their attacks and to provide protection to their victims. They consistently regarded members of these vulnerable groups as legitimate scapegoats, eligible targets for their attacks. Through their political and social influence among those supposed to enforce the law, they confidently anticipated they would never be held to account in any way for their acts of oppressive violence.

This immunity from reproach by the law or retaliation by the victimized vulnerable groups, emboldened a new form of middleclass violence. The debased logic used to justify the attacks was assertively propagated by some middle class intellectuals who deliberately overlooked the vulgar nature of the justifications for the anti-reservation movement, and ignored its mindless violence, as well as the defiance of the law and breach of moral norms prevalent among the middle classes. These intellectuals betrayed their vocation in support of direct, illegal, violence for what they believed were their group interests. They helped provide shape and legitimation to an ideology based on a singular and unexamined concept of 'merit.' They considerably shifted the national discourse away from the goal of reducing societal inequality. They made a major contribution to changing the terms of discourse as far as policies regarding equality, social mobility, and the rights of marginalised groups were concerned.

The savarna men and women who came out into the streets as part of the anti-reservation movement had little knowledge about the social structure of India, the history of its struggles to mitigate discrimination by constitutional methods, and its many other attempts to reduce social and political repression. In such a situation, Manuvadi propaganda focused on a crude and obfuscating notion of 'merit', created and sanctified by some liberal intellectuals who addressed meetings and wrote popular articles in newspapers and magazines. This resulted in an ideological atmosphere in which traditional caste and other group based notions of hierarchy and superiority got reinforced, well reflected in the extremely derogatory statements made against Dalit-Bahujans.

For example, demonstrators often taunted them by associating them with occupations Manuvadis considered shameful. They displayed their hatred and contempt of those who have been the victims of discrimination by displaying vulgar caricatures of members of these groups engaged in some traditional urban occupations such as polishing shoes and sweeping the roads. Most young men and women who demonstrated at that time were extremely proud of their participation in their displays of hatred and contempt, and their riskless violence against weaker groups. One often heard their boastful accounts of brutal acts recounted with glee and pride. It is interesting that this was the first time that many of them had participated in any form of public protests. Interestingly, many had received parental sanction for them to participate.

Many fathers were not only tolerant of their children staying out late to take part in 'strategy' meetings, but also approved of their throwing stones at unprotected vulnerable people and burning up buses and other public property. It is this sanctioning of brutality that may help explain women's violence during such demonstrations. Perhaps women are only willing to take part when and if their family legitimates their participation in violence. These women will gain approval from members of their family for expressing/redirecting previously forbidden impulses to violence they were not allowed to express toward those who brutalised them. This is one time when they find that male heads of the family cannot or will not impose restrictions against their expressing violence or participating in what are described as reprisals.

Just as fear of further and more severe violence against them as well as other forms of reprisal within the family keeps many women in check and ensures their conformity to dominant norms and ensures that they do not reply in kind, the very absence of such fears during riots gives them the sanction to do things which they otherwise would not do. Perhaps, when women engage in such violence, it is just a form of catharsis or release for these women. Perhaps it also provides them with some feeling of empowerment. What is also important is that they get a sense of being included in a major public act of family and community members, an arena where they rarely participate. This possible partial explanation for women's participation points to a need to pay more scholarly attention to the new ways of belonging and inclusion developed for individuals by the hindutva movements.

As Arvind Rajagopal has pointed out, more emphasis has been given to the disruptive effects of participation rather than to the possible role they play in generating a greater sense of inclusion. The puzzle of increased participation in the hindutva movements of groups such as Dalits, OBCs, and women who have all had to bear the brunt of Brahminical, patriarchal violence may in part be explained by this kind of analysis. The lack of adequate support structures for women is frequently given as the reason women are afraid to confront violence within the family. What we need to understand is how the same women become active collaborators in violence committed during riots. One explanation may be related to the way in which the majority of people in this country - male and female - view domestic violence.

Despite the long history of legal action to protect women's rights, and constant attempts by women's organisations to get laws passed and courts to intervene on issues related to violence against women, a majority of women do not perceive domestic violence as a crime that is defined by law. This is partly an outcome of the way in which political parties have related to such issues. Even left of centre parties have 'ghettoised' the women's wing of their parties, refusing to mainstream their issues, leaving them to be taken up solely by their women's wing (AIDWA, Mahila Dakshata Samiti, etc.). Many women's organisations affiliated to political parties have simply not had their party's political support to launch struggles to change public awareness as well as make the laws against domestic violence more stringent and enforceable, though there has been no dearth of attempts to do so. Thus, struggles relating to women's issues have often been reduced to ineffectual forms of 'social' struggles, in the form of failed public awareness campaigns, as well as the sporadic, momentary and inconclusive attention given to individual atrocities against women.

It is interesting to note that a government official in Gujarat during the recent riots stated that rape cases must be taken up by NGOs, because the government's duty is only to look into 'law and order' cases, implying thereby the non-criminal nature of rape. Also, as is well known, women leaders in the hindutva movement have themselves spoken about the 'normality' of male domestic violence, and the consequent need for women to 'adjust' to violent domestic life. Wife beating, for instance, they have said, is caused by the wife who 'irritates' her husband. These beatings are likened to the acts of parents admonishing their children. Sarkar (1999) mentions one respondent who blames rapes of women on those women who protest against their victimisation; they are viewed as forfeiting their "older modes of honour and motherhood" by participating in struggles for equality and rights. The implication is that women should retreat from such forms of politics into passive forms of domesticity to avoid rape.

When women who struggle for such rights meet male oppression and violence, this repression is considered justifiable. Both female and male leaders of Hindu fundamentalist organisations argue that 'adjustment' and obedience of girls and wives to parents and husbands will avert male domestic violence. Domestic violence is thereby removed from the public sphere of illegal behaviour, and at the same time justified by attributing its occurrence to women's own 'deviant' behaviour. In their view, women should endure male violence in order to further strengthen the norms of the culture and keep the family together. The combined effect of a) family and group legitimacy that enable attacks on members of other communities; and b) the failure to label domestic violence as criminal and illegitimate, have created a situation where women often find it much easier to collaborate with their own oppressors in inflicting violence upon others than to combat oppression within the family.

Social codes relating to violence, the circumstances under which it may be legitimately inflicted on others, and the extent of enforcement of legal and other sanctions against violence, are important factors in understanding why some people engage in acts of violence more than others. Again, while the knowledge that such illegitimate acts will not be punished is a significant factor in explaining why people are violent and in understanding socialisation practices, it is also true that levels of exposure to violence, and political mobilisation against violent oppression - all determined by one's location in social space - are important in explaining why some people engage in violence against others. Deciding to participate in violence against others for most individuals, but especially for women, is not a simple act; it requires a coherent explanation.

This is especially true of the participation of women in communal violence, which has become far more notable in recent years, and is a dangerous and disturbing development. It is precisely at this juncture that intellectuals need to be more cautious and careful about how they explain this new development. Public space in India is already vitiated by ideologies that justify and legitimise violence, partly through the rhetoric of communal resentments and presumptions of justified exercise of special rights, and partly through recourse to some distorted versions of the traditional liberal idea of social contract. This is evident also in the rejection of the jurisdiction of courts in certain spheres of social life. Another important point is the constant newspeak regarding past and possibly future attacks on 'Hindus' by members of the minority community.

This propaganda is used to recruit men and women for training in physical 'self-defence' activities. In recent times, through rumours, propaganda pamphlets, public agitation and other such channels, fear has been created among Hindu women by providing mostly fictional accounts of attacks by male members of other communities on Hindu women. The fear is now being specifically focused on violation of women's own bodies. This strategy is meant to bring about a radical change in the attitude of women toward willingness to sanction and even engage in violence against minorities. Those who promote such violence can then presumably claim to have a greater degree of legitimacy for its use against members of other groups. Some intellectuals in this country seem to be similarly influenced by a distorted idea of social contract theory that results in their either ignoring or supporting organised violence against the state and other communities. This is justified by appealing to a special normative order they believe exists within the confines of their own group.

What they forget is that in the context of a hierarchical, stratified society, where even basic rights are yet to be realised for some groups, justification of certain anti-state movements in the name of a putative group-defined normative order may reinforce a discriminatory and unequal social order. Violence by women as part of such a movement, and their complicity in male violence on members of other communities, reinforces their own oppression by patriarchal structures. Some women may temporarily be given an exalted status for their participation in such movements, whether it is an anti-minority pogrom, or the movement which brought down the Babri Masjid structure. Just as fundamentalist leaders justify participation in violence in the name of a distorted normative order which justifies violence and delegitimises constitutional bodies and norms, so also some neo-liberal advocates shift the rights discourse by justifying violence either through popular groups or through the state that acts in the name of a specific unconstitutional normative order.

Such violence usually targets the weak and the marginalised, the Dalits, Tribals, and others among the poor, including pavement dwellers, street hawkers, and slum dwellers. These groups are not allowed to use their identities, their rights are abrogated whenever they clash with mainstream 'development' policies, and their very existence is deemed illegitimate. There is very little public outcry against their forcible illegal displacement. There is also an extreme lack of concern regarding their rights and welfare. The overall shift in the way in which rights are discussed, the condoning of violent actions targeted at the marginalised, and the refusal to recognise certain forms of social and political mobilisation among the underprivileged, all have contributed to an overall rise in the legitimisation of violent repressive actions by the powerful - be they men, upper castes, the state, or particular communities.

Some liberals are yet to learn that certain claims to group identities also are valid claims to human rights. Therefore, they differentiate among the many identities asserted by these communities for different purposes. Their lack of sensitivity considerably enhances the possibilities of movements by the oppressed getting co-opted by fascist and fundamentalist movements, as we are observing now. A colleague never tires of reminding me of Gandhi's approach to public issues - it is not just enough to be right, but one must be right for the right reason, for the right cause.

GENDER EQUALITY

Gender equality (also known as gender equity, gender egalitarianism, or sexual equality) is the goal of the equality of the genders or the sexes, stemming from a belief in the injustice of myriad forms of gender inequality. World bodies have defined gender equality as related to human rights, especially women's rights, and economic development. UNICEF defines gender equality as "levelling the playing field for girls and women by ensuring that all children have equal opportunity to develop their talents." The United Nations Population Fund declared gender equality "first and foremost, a human right." "Gender equity" is one of the goals of the United Nations Millennium Project, to end world poverty by 2015; the project claims, "Every single Goal is directly related to women's rights and societies where women are not afforded equal rights as men can never achieve development in a sustainable manner."

Thus, promoting gender equality is seen as an encouragement to greater economic prosperity. For example, nations of the Arab world that deny equality of opportunity to women were warned in a 2008 United Nations-sponsored report that this disempowerment is a critical factor crippling these nations' return to the first rank of global leaders in commerce, learning and culture.

WOMEN IN HINDUISM

The role of women in Hinduism is often disputed, and positions range from quite fair to intolerant. Hinduism is based on numerous texts, some of which date back to 2000 BCE or earlier. They are varied in authority, authenticity, content and theme, with the most authoritative being the Vedas. The position of women in Hinduism is widely dependent on the specific text and the context. Positive references are made to the ideal woman in texts such as the Ramayana and the Mahabharata, while some texts such as the Manu Smriti advocate a restriction of women's rights. In modern times the Hindu wife has traditionally been regarded as someone who must at all costs remain chaste or pure.

This is in contrast with the very different traditions that have prevailed at earlier times in 'Hindu' kingdoms, which included highly respected professional courtesans (such as Amrapali of Vesali) sacred *devadasis*, mathematicians and female magicians (the basavis, the Tantric kulikas). Some European scholars observed in the nineteenth century Hindu women were "naturally chaste" and "more virtuous" than other women, although what exactly they meant by that is open to dispute. In any case, as male foreigners they would have been denied access to the secret and sacred spaces those women often inhabited. In ancient India, women occupied a very important position, in fact a superior position to, men. It is a culture whose only words for strength and power are feminine -"Shakti" means "power" and "strength."

All male power comes from the feminine. Literary evidence suggests that kings and towns were destroyed because a single woman was wronged by the state. For example, Valmiki's Ramayana teaches us that Ravana and his entire clan were wiped out because he abducted Sita. Veda Vyasa's *Mahabharatha* teaches us that all the Kauravas were killed because they humiliated Draupadi in public. Elango Adigal's Sillapathigaram teaches us Madurai, the capital of the Pandyas was burnt because Pandyan Nedunchezhiyan mistakenly killed her husband on theft charges. In Vedic times women and men were equal as far as education and religion was concerned. Women participated in the public sacrifices alongside men. One text mentions a female rishi Visvara.

Some Vedic hymns, are attributed to women such as Apala, the daughter of Atri, Ghosa, the daughter of Kaksivant or Indrani, the wife of Indra. Apparently in early Vedic times women also received the sacred thread and could study the Vedas. The Haritasmrti mentions a class of women called brahmavadinis who remained unmarried and spent their lives in study and ritual. Panini's distinction between arcarya (a lady teacher) and acaryani (a teacher's wife), and upadhyaya (a woman preceptor) and upadhyayani (a preceptor's wife) indicates that women at that time could not only be students but also teachers of sacred lore. He mentions the names of several noteworthy women scholars of the past such as Kathi, Kalapi, and Bahvici. The Upanishads refer to several women philosophers, who disputed with their male colleagues such as Vacaknavi, who challenged Yajnavalkya. The Rig Veda also refers to women engaged in warfare.

One queen Bispala is mentioned, and even as late a witness as Megasthenes (fifth century B.C. E.) mentions heavily armed women guards protecting Chandragupta's palace. Louis Jaccoliot, the celebrated French author of the Bible in India: Hindu Origin of Hebrew and Christian Revelation said: "India of the Vedas entertained a respect for women amounting to worship; a fact which we seem little to suspect in Europe when we accuse the extreme East of having denied the dignity of woman, and of having only made her an instrument of pleasure and of passive obedience." He also said: "What here is a civilization, which you cannot deny to be older than your own, which places the woman on a level with the man and gives her an equal place in the family and in society."

Recent incidents of sati and rash of "dowry murders" have made headlines not only in India, but all around the world, and have focused attention to women's issues in India. In the wake of the discussion it emerged that Indian women's problems are not only problems of Hindu women or problems caused by traditional Hinduism. Media paints India as a dangerous place. But if statistics can be trusted, a study by Hindus against the Abuse of Women presented at the Second International Conference on Bride Burning and Dowry Deaths in India puts USA in the lead of familial femicide. It says USA murders of women committed by "intimate relations" are 15 per year per million populations.

Too often the underbelly of the West is not reported in their media whereas; the English media in India makes a living out of pouring hate and bile on India and her culture. (Refer to Killings of new, expectant mothers mount in USA - Many pregnant women like them have been slain in Maryland and Mississippi, in California and Kansas, in Ohio and Illinois. A year-long examination by The Washington Post of death-record data in states across the country documents the killings of 1,367 pregnant women and new mothers since 1990. This is only part of the national toll).

The rate in Pakistan is 6.44 per million. India's is 6.25 per million. The study says excessive need for control and greed may be the underlying causes, not cultural or religious factors. India recently passed a law making husbands and in-laws guilty until proven otherwise if a bride dies within the first year of marriage and since then, the rate of women killed by intimate relations dropped by more than 50%. Tiny Switzerland is home to a mere 7.2 million people. It is extremely rich, modern, industrialised and democratic with excellent health care and a 100 per cent literacy rate. So why has this proud nation with its fiercely democratic traditions failed to curb violence against women? This is why the statistics for wife beating are about the same in the developed and the developing world. It is fallacious to think that there is a link between democracy, prosperity, education levels and domestic violence," counters Elizabeth Rod-Grangé, a Swiss sociologist and activist with Solidarité Femme, a women's rights group that runs shelters for battered women in Geneva.

According to the report, one in every three women suffers violence in her lifetime. The statistics in Europe are as appalling as anywhere else. In France, six women die each month at the hands of men who profess to love them. In Britain, one woman is killed by a partner every three days, one woman in four experiences domestic violence and attacks on partners account for a quarter of all violent crime. Despite media campaigns and shocking statistics, domestic violence continues to be one of Europe's most under-reported crimes. Watch the movie - The Magdalene Sisters (2002) treatment of "wayward women" run by the Catholic Church in Ireland in 1964. According to the Amnesty report, one in every three women suffers violence in her lifetime.

The statistics in Europe are as appalling as anywhere else. In France, six women die each month at the hands of men who profess to love them. In Spain, some 100 women are killed each year by abusive spouses or boyfriends with over 30,000 complaints of severe physical violence, while in Switzerland, one of the wealthiest countries in Europe where "direct democracy" rules supreme, the number of women who suffer physical and psychological abuse tops 20 per cent. In France, the subject became front-page news after the film actress, Marie Trintrignant, was beaten to death by her lover, singer Bertrand Cantat. In Europe - Women earn less than men in all 27 European Union countries, according to a recent European Commission report. In 2005, the "pay gap" was 15% across the European Union. Refer to Western Women - Liberated or Exploited in a materialistic society? - The system demands that their bodies are exploited for advertising purposes. Refer to Anorexia and Eating Disorders.

Dowry practice plagues Christian community in India - The practice of dowry, normally prevalent among the Hindus, is now making its presence in the Christian community as well. In fact, despite a high literacy rate, Kerala continues to be one of the epicenters of dowry practice in the country. While the Church is aware of this practice, its leaders say there is little they can do about it. Far from being a solemn ceremony, marriages have now become an occasion to flaunt wealth and social status. And in a consumer state like Kerala it seems just everyone wants to shell out as much as he can on marriages. Hindu religion has been occasionally criticized as encouraging inequality between men and women, towards the detriment of Hindu women. This inaccurate presumption again arises when people combine social and religious issues.

GENDER OF GOD

There is a wide variety of viewpoints within the different schools and sects of Hinduism concerning the exact nature and gender (where applicable) of the Supreme person or being; there are even sects that are sceptical about the existence of such a being. Shaktism, for example, focuses worship on the goddess Devi as the supreme embodiment of power, or Shakti (feminine strength; a female form of God). Vaishnavism and Shaivism both worship Lakshmi with Vishnu and Parvati with Shiva respectively as beings on an equal level of magnitude (the male and female aspects of God). In some instances such as with Gaudiya Vaishnavism, specific emphasis is placed on the worship of God's female aspect (Radharani) even above that of her paramour Krishna. Thus it could be said that Hinduism considers God to have both male and female aspects, as the original source of both.

Male deities (such as Shiva and Indra) are believed, in some traditions, to themselves offer worship to the Goddess, Durga:

Elsewhere Shiva and Vishnu are also described as possessing feminine qualities represented through their Ardhanarishvara and Mohini forms respectively. There have also been male devotees who have claimed to be incarnations of goddesses, such as Narayani Peedam and Bangaru Adigalar of Melmaruvathur, Tamil Nadu who claim to be forms or avataras of the goddess Narayani.

Hindu feminists such as Phoolan Devi have also used the goddess Durga as their icon. Traditions which follow the advaita philosophy consider that ultimately the Supreme Being is formless without any particular gender, or is transcendental to such considerations.

PROPERTY RIGHTS

Arthashastra and Manusamhita are sources about the woman's right to property or 'Stridhan', (literally meaning, property of wife). It is of two types: maintenance (in money or land given by the husband), and anything else like ornaments given to her by her family, husband, in-laws and the friends of her husband. Manu further subdivides this into six types - the property given by parents at marriage, given by the parental family when she is going to her husband's house, given by her husband out of affection (not maintenance which he is bound to give), and property given separately by brother, mother and father. Pre-nuptial contracts are also mentioned where the groom would agree to give a set amount of bride price to both parents and the bride. Such property belonged to the wife alone and was not to be touched by the groom or her parents except in emergencies (in sickness, in famine, threaten by robbers, or for performing holy deeds). At the same time, the Manu Smriti contradicts itself by declaring that a wife has no property and the wealth earned is for the husband.

Daughters and sons equally inherited their mother's property; but some scriptures insist that a mother's property belongs solely to the daughters, in order of preference: unmarried daughters, married but poor daughters, married and rich daughters. When a father died, unmarried daughters had to be given a share in their father's property, equal to one-fourth from every brother's share [since it is assumed that the married daughter had been given her share at marriage]. If the family has no sons, the (appointed) daughter is the sole inheritor of the property.

Study of scriptures

Several women sages and seers are mentioned in the Upanishads, the philosophical part of the Vedas, notable among them being Gargi and Maitreyi. The Sanskrit word for female teachers as Acharyâ (as opposed to Acharya for teacher and Acharyini for teacher's wife) reveal that women were also given a place as Gurus. The Harita Dharmasutra (of the Maitrayaniya school of Yayurveda) declares that there are two kinds of women: Sadhyavadhu who marry, and the Brahmavaadini who are inclined to religion, they can wear the sacred thread, perform rituals like the agnihotra and read the Vedas. Bhavabhuti's Uttararamacharita 2.3 says that Atreyi went to Southern India where she studied the Vedas and Indian philosophy. Shankara debated with the female philosopher Ubhaya Bharati, and Madhava's Shankaradigvijaya (9.63) mentions that she was well versed in the Vedas. Tirukkoneri Dasyai (15th century) wrote a commentary on Nammalvar's Tiruvaayamoli, with reference to Vedic texts like the Taittiriya Yajurveda.

The Bhagavata Purana states that the Mahabharata was written specifically for women and also men who were not in the priestly Brahmin caste:

"Out of compassion, the great sage thought it wise that this would enable men to achieve the ultimate goal of life. Thus he compiled the great historical narration called the Mahabharata for women, laborers and friends of the twice-born." In several schools for Vedic priests, many graduates are women.

WIDOWHOOD AND REMARRIAGE

In traditional families, widows were, and in some cases are, required to wear white sarees, and give up their ornaments, including the bindi, which signified auspiciousness; their presence at religious rites was considered inauspicious, and they were supposed to devote their lives to an austere pursuit of religion. These restrictions were traditionally strongest in the highest castes, in which the head was frequently shaved as well, and which had the severest restrictions on remarriage. These restrictions are now strictly observed only by a small minority of widows, though some degree of ritual inauspiciousness remains.

In NAsmR 12.45-48, there are three types of punarbhu, or remarried widow: The virgin widow, the woman who abandons her husband to take up with another man and then returns to her husband, and the woman who has no brothers-in-law who can give her offspring. Although this list is not exhaustive, it makes it clear that a punarbhu was not just any widow; she may not have been a widow at all (the second case). In the other two cases, she is a childless widow, which is an important distinction that should not be ignored. It is important to mention that although many texts do seem to admit to the existence of the remarriage of widows and sometimes allow it, it is not considered an ideal situation.

A punarbhu would not be given the same rights as a woman who was married only once. I think you must also mention that the son of a punarbhu, a punarbhava, is often listed as one who is unfit to invite to a sacrifice, as is the husband of a remarried woman. The punarbhava also did not inherit as would a 'natural son'. As of 2007, 3 per cent of the population of India consists of widows. Most of the widows are left to survive on charity; many are reduced to begging on the streets. Some surveys show that steeped in their religious beliefs and fearful of violating social customs they were brought up to believe in, many widows themselves do not want to remarry.

WOMEN'S PROPERTY RIGHTS MOVEMENT

Nepal is still running under strong feudalistic social values and norms. There were no clear provisions regarding Nepalese women and property rights until 1975. Following the UN Declaration of 1975, which was International Women's Year, the Nepali government began to celebrate International Women's Day on the 8th of March. That same year, the Civil Code was amended and a clause on women's inheritance and property rights included. The clause states that if a woman remains unmarried up to 35 years of age, she would have a right to inherit property. However, the amendment limits itself as it continues "if she gets marriage after having property that should be returned back to the brothers by deducting the marriage cost."

With the restoration of multiparty democracy in 1990, the new constitution guaranteed that no one should be discriminated against on the basis of sex. Furthermore, in 1991, the government ratified the UN Convention on the Elimination of all forms of Discrimination Against Women (CEDAW-1979). The nation's Women's Movement demanded that all inequalities in Nepali law be eliminated and focused attention on the equal right of women to inherit property. All political parties have included this demand in their respective election manifestos. The opposition party in parliament, the Communist Party of Nepal-Unified Marxist-Leninist, has raised this issue repeatedly but the government has neither considered it seriously, nor taken any initiation to amend discriminatory laws.

In 1993, a case was finally filed in the Supreme Court with a demand to amend the Civil Code to give women equal rights over property. After two years, in 1995, the Supreme Court issued a directive to the government to introduce a Bill in parliament that would guarantee a woman's rights to inherit property. Following the Supreme Court directive, the Ministry of Women and Social Welfare drafted a Bill, popularly known as the "Women's Property Rights Bill" in order to amend the existing Civil Code. It was tabled for discussion in the 11th session of Parliament. It took almost six years more to be passed through parliament, despite a number of other Bills being adopted in this time parliament. During this period, different political parties and parliamentary committees have made a number of changes to the original Bill.

On July 17, 2001, a parliamentary committee unanimously declared that women should have equal rights to inherit property. However, the ruling Nepali Congress party expressed some disagreement and proposed that inherited property "should be returned back to respective brother/s if she gets marriage". The ruling party passed the Bill with a majority vote in the Lower House of Parliament in October 2001. But, the Upper House - National Assembly, which is dominated by the opposition party, failed the Bill and it was sent back to the Lower House for reconsideration. In due process, the Bill came back to the Lower House. Here, the ruling party was pressing for the Bill to be adopted while the main opposition party, supported by almost all women organizations, was pressing hard to guarantee inherited property rights for women equivalent to that of their brother's.

In this situation, there was a risk that the Bill would not be passed again and it might take several more years to go through another round of discussion. At this point, the opposition party made the tricky decision to vote for a Bill with its reservation on the provision, which do not recognize the equal right of sons or daughters to inherited property after marriage.

Major Achievements through 11th Amendment in Civil Code-2020 (1963)

After all these turning points, the bill was finally passed in parliament on March 14, 2002. It was sent to the King for his seal of approval and came into effect from September 27, 2002. The major achievements of this amendment are as follows:

- Women's Right to Property

Today, women in Nepal can enjoy their right to inherit property from birth. But when they marry any property will be returned to the parent's family. The new law establishes a wife's equal right to her husband's property immediately after marriage, rather than after she reaches 35 years of age or has been married for 15 years as before. A widow's right to claim her share of property from the joint family after the death of her husband, and to use this property even if she gets re-married, is now also established in law.

- Women's Right to Divorce

The Bill gives women the right to seek divorce from her husband if he harasses her physically or psychologically; if he establishes sexual relationships with other women; if he is incapable of producing children; or if he is affected by an STD, including HIV/AIDS. Previously, the law allowed a wife to claim only food stuff from her husband for the five years following their divorce. Today, a woman can also claim property.

- Increase Penalty for Polygamy

Polygamy is still rampant in Nepal, though it was declared illegal in 1975. Previously, those who violate the law in this regard face a punishment of 1 to 3 months in prison or a fine of 1000 to 2000 Rupees, or both. The new amendment increases these punishments; a man can now face 1 to 3 years in prison or a fine of 5000 - 25,000 Rupees, or both.

- Women's Right to Abortion

Previously, abortion was illegal unless a doctor advised that a mother's life was endangered unless a fetus was aborted. Charged with this crime, more than five dozen women are imprisoned across Nepal. The new law legalizes abortion with some conditions. In normal cases a woman can make her own decision to go through with an abortion, though only within the first 12 weeks of pregnancy. However, if the child's delivery endangers the mother's life, or if a women becomes pregnant through rape or incestuous sexual relations then abortions can take place within 18 weeks of pregnancy. Nepal is the first South Asian country to legalize abortion in this way.

- Stern Action against persons involved in Rape

Rape is one of the major issues that have been raised by the women's movement in Nepal. In this regard, the amendments to the civil code make the law stronger and increase the punishment for rapists. According to the new provisions, a rapist can be imprisoned for 10-15 years, if their victim is below 10 years of age; 7-10 years of imprisonment, if their victim is between 10 and 16 years of age; and 5 - 7 years of imprisonment, if the victim's age is above 16 years.

In each category, an additional five years of prison can be given if the victim is a pregnant or disabled woman.

Lacunas still remain

It is a big achievement that women have been granted more legal rights with this amendment. But, there remain issues to be addressed. One major issue is to establish equal rights of property inheritance regardless of a women's marital status. The struggle to achieve rights based on gender is ongoing. If gender equality has not been achieved even when important goals are met then the struggle should continue.

Challenges ahead

There is a bigger challenge ahead of the women's movement. Until and unless women and men in wider society are aware of these new legal instruments, they cannot bring any remarkable change to the real lives of Nepalese women. In this regard, it is the role and responsibility of the women's movement to make women and men aware of their legal rights. At the same time, social and bureaucratic structures including those in civil society and government must institutionalize these changes. Only in this way will feudal and traditional attitudes towards women's rights change.

To ensure the impact of these legal rights, authority should be delegated in a practical way and the implementing apparatus should be correctly managed. The women's movement can lead the campaign to make people aware and to check that the law is implemented properly. We can prove that legal instruments are important tools and play a crucial role in creating gender equality in society.

WOMEN'S MOVEMENT SCENARIO

Nepal is one of the least developed countries in the world. Our socio-economic life and hence the national life is largely dependent on agriculture. 42 percent of the national income is being contributed by agriculture and almost 81 percent of the population is employed in this sector. However, agriculture itself is in a very miserable condition. It has become away of life to majority of the population, but its fruitfulness is decreasing every year. In the Nepalese context, the women struggle started against British imperialism. Patriotic struggle against British imperialism dates back to the battle of 1814 at Nalapani. Women marched shoulder to shoulder with men in the civil right movement of 1948. Women took active part in the democratic revolution of 1951 which overthrew the 104 year autocracy of the Rana family. Its goal was to overthrow the 104 years of Rana autocracy from Nepal.

The first women organization the "Nepal Women Association" was established in 1948, it worked to inculcate political awareness among women. After the fall of the Rana regime and dawn of democracy in 1951, political parties became active. Women's organization began to be affiliated with various political parties. During the thirty year rule (1960-1990) of the party-less Panchayat system, all political parties and independent women 5 organizations were banned. However, the left democratic forces continued their struggle against the suppressive political system. The communist organized peasants and workers to fight against the exploitative regime. Women came out in large number during the struggle for democracy. The All Nepal Women Association (ANWA) functioning under the party, was very active in organizing revolutionary women.

It is during this period of struggle that ANWA established itself as a revolutionary wing of the party. Many members of ANWA were tortured by the rulers. The persistence in the struggle attracted women to join the movement. The movement was successfully expanded throughout the country. Also there were some sectoral women movements in existence against the feudal exploitation of landlord and Rana regime. But they were limited in coverage and could not take larger shape to include women from all over the nation. In order to understand the shaping of the movement, it is necessary to mention how the women's political and organized form of movement was connected with the political parties. The first underground mass meeting of All Nepal Women Association was held in 1980. The gathering discussed and analyzed situation of the country, set goals and strategies of women struggle to achieve the women's rights and liberation. It formulated the long term and short term national policy and programme for the women struggle.

The period of eighties is the most active and important period for Nepalese women movement. The oppression from the then rulers was intolerable. Many women activists were jailed and tortured, more than 70 women activists were full-time underground and semi-underground activists. They developed thousands of activists who were over-ground, and they continued their underground activities. It played a crucial role in creating political awareness and played significant role in organizing women of different class, profession and strata. During its underground political training, the All Nepal Women Association equipped its cadre with true ideals in the struggles for political rights, social justice and economic equality. It also made best use of the 8th March International Women's Day (started since 1972, 8th march), and national festival such as Tij (exclusive women festival) and Tihar (festival of light) celebrated each year for five days culminating the worshipping of brothers by sisters on the last day.

On this day women folk gather at their parental houses, hence an opportunity to make best use of gathering. ANWA organized its first National Conference in 1989 in underground way, second National Conference in 1992 and the third National Conference in 1995 with the theme "Social Security and Employment, Equal Rights in all Sectors". All members of ANWA and other women organizations cultivated a dream-a dream of new progressive and democratic Nepal where women participation in all walks of national life is ensured. In spite of all these struggles, sacrifices and enthusiasm, women have been marginalized in politics as in any other sectors. The paternalistic structures of the family, society and the male-dominated political organizations gave little space to women. There exist a big gap between saying and doing, preaching and practicing about women's participation and leadership in Nepal.

Constitutionally, 5 percent seats of the total candidacy in the parliamentary election are reserved for women, in each political party. Recently the government has decided to provide 15 percent reservation in each VDC and Municipality. Altogether there are 4000 VDCs and 58 Municipalities and in each VDC there are 9 Wards (Unit). Each ward of the VDC will have 5 members including chairperson elected. Among four members one seat is reserved for women. There is a provision of Advisory Committee in VDC and municipality and participation of women is provisioned. Thus, at the local level altogether more than 120,000 women will be mobilized representing all parties. It is a welcome step forward to include women in politics at the local levels.

The position of women in civil service is also very bleak. While the 1990 High Level Administration Reform Commission gave suggestions to improve the situation, only 5 percent of the civil servants at officer level were women in 1992. National and international efforts have been made to bring multilateral and bilateral agencies for aid and assistance for women's cause. In spite of all these efforts, gender gap is still very wide. Inequalities are rampant in all fronts—cultural, social, economic, and political and in education. Women have no separate identity of her. They are identified in relation to her father, husband, son and grandson.

The Patriarchal system is the root cause of social injustice in Nepal. Sons are preferred over daughters. Sons are considered economic insurance in old age. They carry the family name, perform death rituals and rites. Girls are considered as other's property to be given away in marriage. They are unwanted, neglected and overworked. They are seen as auxiliary contributors to the household. Thus, the women are caught in the corrupt circle of the family system of exploitation and deprivation. The socialization pattern of Nepalese society is very discriminative. From the childhood, boys are groomed towards productive work and decision making and girls are confined to an "inside world" conditioned to be home makers, dutiful wives, loving mothers and service providers. A woman is subjected to the protection of man and has no mobility. Women are controlled by men and are considered as a property of men. Hence they do not have their own property. Even religion, education and rituals are denied to women. A women's life is not for her self.

Health status of Nepalese women is deplorable. Nepal is one of the three countries in the world where the life expectancy of women is lower than that of men. In Nepal 20 percent of pregnancies are said to be in the "high risk" category. Violence on girl-child and child prostitution is alarmingly increasing.

Trafficking of girls into India are increasing and of those trafficked 20 percent are minors under 16 years of age. The overall health condition is alarmingly poor in Nepal. The average life expectancy is 55.9 for males and 53.5 for females. Only 10 percent of the pregnant women get maternal service. The maternal mortality rate is 850 per 100,000 live births. Average child bearing age among 40 percent of women is 15 to 19 years. The fertility rate is as high as 5.7. Women have been the focus of population policies and the main target for family planning and fertility control.

The girl malnutrition rate is double than that of boy under 5 years. 78 percent of rural women suffer by anaemia in the delivery period. 85 percent of women depend upon the traditional birth attendants instead of health post and hospital services. Even in the urban areas, the maternal mortality rate is 8.5 per 1000 but in rural and geographically distanced rural area the MMR is 15.4 per 1000.

ECONOMIC STATUS OF WOMEN

Nepal is an underdeveloped agricultural country with a per capita GDP of US $ 202 (1994). Almost half of its population is below the poverty line. It ranks second among the poorest countries of the world. Studies have shown that women's contribution in the economy is large and significant with 57 percent of agricultural activities being carried out by women. They contribute about half of household income and work 11 hours a day. Despite women's substantial contributions both as cultivators and managers in the production process, all their labour is unnoticed, undervalued and unaccounted in the economy.

Women as the workers

Women constitute a little over one-half of the Nepalese population. 95 percent of employed women are confined to agricultural work compared to 75 percent for men. Besides agriculture, women are again mostly confined to traditional jobs such as sewing and knitting. They are rarely engaged in professional and technical jobs. Very few are in community services, commerce, manufacturing etc. Jobs are low-paid, requiring relatively simple skills. In the service sector, women are mostly engaged in teaching, health and financial institutions. Women lag far behind in the legal field and media service. Only 6 percent are found at officer level positions in the civil services. Women in Nepal generally work for longer hours compared to men, and rural women devote much longer hours than urban women. His Majesty's Government of Nepal has fixed the minimum wage and salaries in the industrial and organized sectors without any gender discrimination but in practice such discrimination are noticed. Discrimination in organized sectors is more prominent.

Effective and in built participation of women in the development process, both as a producer and consumer of development output, has been accepted as a necessary condition for balanced, equitable and sustainable growth. But Nepalese women are yet to obtain such participation. In terms of labour force participation, women are behind men, are predominantly confined to agriculture, account for the majority of unpaid family workers, number predominantly among the unemployed and are heavily concentrated in low-paid jobs, The constraints against women's employment in industry can be summarized as follows:

- Women are poorly qualified or not suitably trained.
- Protective legislation has acted as a deterrent to women's employment.
- Women are prepared to work for lower wage.
- Both women and men look upon women's income as supplementary.
- There is no solidarity and no unions among women.
- They lack entrepreneurial knowledge.

Women are facing problems created by government new economic policy of privatization and liberalization. The policy of privatization and liberalization is yet to show its full impact in Nepalese economy. Even then we expect to encounter the following problems in the field of women workers and employment in the days to come.

1. The employer may prefer men to women or unmarried to married one.
2. Difference in salary of men and women may persist.
3. Government may not be responsible for capacity building program for women.
4. The dignity of women workers might erode as they will be treated as commodity by their employers.
5. Prostitution, sex tourism and sexual harassment will grow together with success of privatization and liberalization.
6. Women will have to be restricted to low skilled and low paid jobs.

The new policy will reduce the opportunities for formal education and vocational training for upgrading the skills, with a result that women do not qualify for promotions, job up gradation and higher wage. For a long time, education was a privilege for a few in Nepal. The first government school for girls opened in 1948 a year after the Civil Rights Movement.

It was only in 1951 that education was gradually prompted throughout the country. The literacy rate in the country is 40 percent. Literacy rate among women is only 25 percent. In the schools the dropout and irregularity of girls are higher compared to that of boys.

Progress in the promotion of girl's education has been made as a result of international women's year and the international women's decade. Several measures have been taken to augment girl's education. Female teachers were appointed in each school. Nevertheless, education is yet to be effective in empowering women in Nepal. Education in Nepal is not yet linked with the lives of the people. Equality and empowerment of women is simply a lip-service.

Government Policy and Women's Advancement

There have been some changes in the interests and attitudes of the policy planners after the change in the political system. However, the changes are not satisfactory and are still sectoral. A new ministry looking after women issues has been created. The ministry is to coordinate and further the policies and programs related to the women.

Women constitute half of the population in Nepal. Unless they participate fully in the nation building task, economic development of the country will not be possible. Taking this reality into account sectoral strategy and working policy were outlined in the eighth plan (1992-97), the first plan of fully democratic. The strategies to be followed as outlined in the plan are:

- Encouraging women's participation in traditional as well as non traditional sectors.
- Extending access to be formal and non-formal education to women.
- Adopting affirmative action in training program.
- Increasing women's access to health facilities especially FP/MCH facilities.
- Increasing women's access to credit, technical knowledge, entrepreneurship development programs, marketing facilities and employment opportunities.

- Extending to rural areas those kinds of technological changes which reduce the time spend in gathering an fetching fuel fodder, water and household work.
- Revising laws discriminatory to women.

Though the government of Nepal started a policy on Women in Development (WID) since sixth five year plan (1980-85) which aimed to promote the status of women by recognizing them as development agents. The plans stressed on technical and non technical fields of training for women. The Women Training Centre was formed under the Ministry of Local Development (MOLD) for skill development of rural women. Of course there have been some changes in the interests and attitudes among politicians and policy makers. However the change is not overall satisfactory and still is sectoral. Women should be recognized as partner and not as subordinate to men. No doubt, the newly formed Ministry of Women and Social Welfare should take up a leading role in asserting this concept.

Girls trafficking and prostitution as major Social Problems of Women in Nepal

In Nepal girls trafficking and prostitution problem are becoming similar to that of problems in Thailand, the Philippines, Sri Lanka and Taiwan. Over 200,000 Nepali girls/ women are reported to be indulged into prostitution in India. It is said that between 5000 to 7000 young girls are trafficked to India annually; of which one-third are trafficked forcefully. According to the Indian Health Organization (IHO) 100,000 Nepali girls/women are working as prostitutes in Calcutta, Mumbai and New Delhi alone. IHO estimates that of the 15,000 prostitutes working in the state of Uttar Pradesh, 12,000 are Nepali girls and women.

The Girls, sold against their will, are subjected to severe mental and physical torture. Most of the girls and women engaged in prostitution are usually from broken families while others come from poor families. Many innocent teenage girls are abducted or lured from their homes in the countryside and are forced into the job. They are either lured or deceived on fake promises and sold to the brothel houses in Indian cities by the middlemen. As such the Nepali girls/women are found serving as prostitutes in almost every city and towns of India and the practice is, unfortunately increasing. Intra-regional and Inter-regional trafficking has also increased rapidly as more and more people migrate to the cities. There are more than 5000 girls/women from surrounding countryside working as prostitutes in Kathmandu and it is said that there are more than 200 brothels in Kathmandu city alone.

Similarly, major market centers work as transit centers for ultimate trafficking into India. The East-west Highway is a fertile ground for prostitution which is being called commonly as highway prostitution. Some reports and investigations have revealed that large number of girls/women have been trafficked via carpet and garment factories. Many who fall victim are those destitute and helpless women who are neglected, abused and abandoned by their husbands and relatives. Many women belonging to lower castes are also made to be the victims. No doubt the trafficking of girls/women to the urban areas of Nepal and to the brothels of foreign countries tells us a story of fraud exploitation, domination as well as despair frustration and poverty.

We need to look beyond the facade of economic problems and try to come with the possible reasons within a larger cultural, historical and socio-political framework. While the subjects of sex remain taboo in Nepalese society, prostitution has gained a big momentum. It is no longer limited to the traditional red light areas of Salyan, Pyuthan and Dang districts where the women of the "Badi" community adopt prostitution as profession. They adopt prostitution as a social practice. Under the "Deuki" system the girls are surrendered to temples by people by the way of religious gift or "Bhakal". The Deukies are not expected to marry and thus, they adopt prostitution as a means of livelihood when they grow up.

The Deuki system has been operating under the guise of religious and cultural beliefs. The cultural practice of Deuki system and Badi community have given way to socially recognized prostitution in Nepal. In Nepal as banning of prostitution remains a matter of dispute, there can be no question on the urgent need to address the issue that force girls and women into the flesh trade. The immediate risk groups like the poor and ignorant girls in the countryside, girls children working in the carpet and garment factories and the children on the streets should be made the immediate target for protection activities. All the government and non government organizations and the conscious citizens need to act actively to abolish the practice of flesh trade.

Everybody should realize the gravity of the problem which is posing a big threat to a very fabric of Nepalese society. Everyone should work to contribute for his prevention and control of prostitution and girls trafficking. Well coordinated efforts need to be made in creating the congenial environment to discourage the sexual exploitation of women. There should be an effective implementation of laws relating to trafficking of girls. Income and employment generating programs such as knitting, sewing, weaving, bamboo work, sericulture etc. are necessary so that economic status of women in the countryside, the fertile ground for the traffickers is bettered.

The profession of flesh trade can not be checked with the legal measures alone. Alternative means for survival are necessary. Both income generating activities as well as programs generating awareness are equally important in this respect. Despite all the existing laws, the enforcement and the threat of AIDS, girls/women trafficking and prostitution still remain a growing problem in Nepal. Nevertheless, it is a matter of great satisfaction that since the last few years some of the NGO and INGOs have started taking keen interests on the issue of women trafficking and practice of forced prostitution in Nepal. Similarly, the international and United Nations agencies have also started creating awareness against girls trafficking and immoral prostitution practices.

In the western and far western part of Nepal there is residue of slavery system called Karnaiya. The bonded labourers do not receive their full labour cost. They have to work free of charge for 15-18 hours/day. The system is spread in 5 districts of Kailali, Kanchanpur, Banke, Dang and Bardiya. In all these districts there is approximately 50 thousands Kamaiya. Generally women from Kamaiya family are required to work free for the landlord. Women under Kamaiya system are more exploited even than the Kamaiyas themselves. Physical and sexual abuses are common among Kamaiya women.

GLOBAL CONTEXT OF AND ITS EFFECT TO WOMEN

In the present context globalization has inflicted its worse effect all over the world. Globalization is generally used to designate an aggregate of policy measures which seek to expand market relations on world level and to enlarge the scope for the free movement of capital internationally. Some of the key components of globalizations are trade liberalization i.e. breakdown of tariff barriers, privatization of formerly public sector companies and the reduction of state intervention and the promotion of export oriented production for instance pf cash crops agriculture. In the countries of the south, such policies are generally imposed by WB, IMF, in the name of structural adjustment. while the ideology of globalization states that such polities serve to promote human welfare an increasingly large body of literature migration from rural areas and to a shift from secure to insecure forms of employment and production.

Under structural adjustment programmes, government world wide have been compelled to sell of public sector companies to the private sector, and such transfers to the private sector have frequently been accompanied but massive dismissals and the flexibilization of labour relations under structural adjustment and liberalization, workers loose various forms of minimal security previously provided by the state or state owned companies. The declarations and programs of action adopted at the four global women's conferences held since 1975 have added important dimensions on the empowerment of women. The second global conference in

Copenhagen in 1980 and the third one in Nairobi in 1985 contributed to the adoption of the advancement of women by the year 2000. Now the UN is working on the fourth phase of progress of women. All the four conferences have the message that no progress is possible without a full and equal participation of men and women. Although in many countries women remain most deprived, discriminated and powerless in most societies.

With this global context we should raise some pertinent points regarding Nepalese women's movement which will give the picture of Nepalese women, their social, cultural, economic and political status that are the threshold for the 21st century. From the mid 1980s women's movement in Nepal can be characterized in three distinct features. Firstly, women's movement was all activism. The role of academia was insignificant. But now there has been forging links between these two in a variety of ways in different fora, conferences, conventions, and demonstrations. A strong belief among many groups has emerged that the struggle against gender inequalities can not be waged in isolation from struggle in many other fronts. Thirdly, the women's movement is not secluded within the country and is increasingly interconnected with the international women's movement. The four international conferences on women have been successful in bringing women's all over the world in common platform of action.

4

International Law on Women's Right

International law is the term commonly used for referring to the system of implicit and explicit agreements that bind together nation-states in adherence to recognized values and standards. It differs from other legal systems in that it primarily concerns states rather than private citizens. However, the term "international law" can refer to three distinct legal disciplines:

- Public international law, which involves for instance the United Nations and other international organizations, maritime law, international criminal law and the Geneva conventions.
- Private international law, or conflict of laws, which addresses the questions of (1) in which legal jurisdiction may a case be heard; and (2) the law concerning which jurisdiction(s) apply to the issues in the case.
- Supranational law or the law of supranational organizations, which concerns at present regional agreements where the special distinguishing quality is that laws of nation states are held inapplicable when conflicting with a supranational legal system.

The two traditional branches of the field are:

- Jus gentium – law of nations
- Jus inter gentes – agreements among nations

Sources of international law are the materials and processes out of which the rules and principles regulating the international community developed. They have been influenced by a range of political and legal theories. During the 20th century, it was recognised by legal positivists that a sovereign state could limit its authority to act by consenting to an agreement according to the principle pacta sunt servanda. This consensual view of international law was reflected in the 1920 Statute of the Permanent Court of International Justice, and preserved in Article of the 1946 Statute of the International Court of Justice.

PUBLIC INTERNATIONAL LAW

Public international law (or international public law) concerns the relationships between the entities or legal persons which are considered the subjects of international law, including sovereign nations, international organizations (including especially intergovernmental organizations such as the United Nations), and in some cases, movements of national liberation (wars of national liberation) and armed insurrectional movements. Norms of international law have their source in either i) custom, or customary international law (consistent state practice accompanied by opinio juris), ii) globally accepted standards of behaviour (peremptory norms known as jus cogens or ius cogens), or iii) codifications contained in conventional agreements, generally termed treaties.

Article 13 of the United Nations Charter obligates the UN General Assembly to initiate studies and make recommendations which encourage the progressive development of international law and its codification. Evidence of consensus or state practice can sometimes be derived from intergovernmental resolutions or academic and expert legal opinions (sometimes collectively termed soft law). International law has existed since the Middle Ages, but much of its modern corpus began developing from the mid-19th century. In the 20th century, the two World Wars and the formation of the League of Nations (and other international organizations such as the International Labour Organization) all contributed to accelerate this process and established much of the foundations of modern public international law.

After the failure of the Treaty of Versailles and World War II, the League of Nations was replaced by the United Nations, founded under the UN Charter. The UN has also been the locus for the development of new advisory (non-binding) standards, such as the Universal Declaration of Human Rights. Other international norms and laws have been established through international agreements, including the Geneva Conventions on the conduct of war or armed conflict, as well as by agreements implemented by other international organizations such as the ILO, the World Health Organization, the World Intellectual Property Organization, the International Telecommunication Union, UNESCO, the World Trade Organization, and the International Monetary Fund. The development and consolidation of such conventions and agreements has proven to be of great importance in the realm of international relations.

CONFLICT OF SUPER LAW

Conflict of laws, often called "private international law" in civil law jurisdictions, is less international than public international law. It is distinguished from public international law because it governs conflicts between private persons, rather than states (or other international bodies with standing). It concerns the questions of which jurisdiction should be permitted to hear a legal dispute between private parties, and which jurisdiction's law should be applied, therefore raising issues of international law. Today corporations are increasingly capable of shifting capital and labour supply chains across borders, as well as trading with overseas corporations. This increases the number of disputes of an inter-state nature outside a unified legal framework and raises issues of the enforceability of standard practices. Increasing numbers of businesses use commercial arbitration under the New York Convention 1958.

CONFLICT OF LAWS

Conflict of laws (or private international law) is that branch of international law and international interstate law that regulates all lawsuits involving a "foreign" law element where different judgments will result depending on which jurisdiction's laws are applied as the lex causae. In civil law systems, private international law is a branch of the internal legal system dealing with the determination of which state law is applicable to situations crossing over the borders of one particular state and involving a "foreign element" (élément d'extranéité), (collisions of law, conflict of laws). Lato sensu (at large) it also includes international civil procedure and international commercial arbitration (collisions of jurisdiction, conflict of jurisdictions), as well as citizenship law (which strictly speaking is part of public law).

In common law systems, conflict of laws, firstly, is concerned with determining whether the proposed forum has jurisdiction to adjudicate and is the appropriate venue for dealing with the dispute, and, secondly, with determining which of the competing state's laws are to be applied to resolve the dispute. It also deals with the enforcement of foreign judgments. There are two major streams of legal thought on the nature of conflict of laws. One group of researchers regards Conflict of Laws as a part of international law, claiming that its norms are uniform, universal and obligatory for all states. This stream of legal thought in Conflict of Laws is called "universalism". Other researchers maintain the view that each State creates its own unique norms of Conflict of Laws pursuing its own policy. This theory is called "particularism" in Conflict of Laws.

Private international law is divided on two major areas:

- Private international law "sensu stricto" (narrow sense) comprising conflict of laws rules which determine the law of which country (state) is applicable to specific relations.
- Private international law "sensu lato" (broader sense) which comprises private international law "sensu stricto"

(conflict of laws rules) and material legal norms which have direct extraterritorial character and are imperatively applied (material norms of law crossing the borders of State) - usually regulations on real property, consumer law, currency control regulations, insurance and banking regulations.

Its three different names– conflict of laws, private international law, and international private law– are generally interchangeable, although none of them is wholly accurate or properly descriptive. The term conflict of laws is primarily used in jurisdictions of the Anglo-American legal tradition, such as in the United States, England, Canada, and Australia. Private international law (droit international privé) is used in France, as well as in Italy, Greece, and the Spanish and Portuguese speaking countries. International private law (internationales Privatrecht) is used in Germany and other German-speaking countries.

Within the federal systems where legal conflicts among federal states require resolution, as in the United States, the term conflict of laws is preferred simply because such cases do not involve an international issue. Hence, conflict of laws is a general term to refer to disparities among laws, regardless of whether the relevant legal systems are international or inter-state. The term, however, can be misleading when it refers to resolution of conflicts between competing systems rather than "conflict" itself. The term conflict of laws is usually used by common law countries, while for civil law countries the term private international law is more appropriate. The term private international law was coined by American lawyer and judge Joseph Story, but was abandoned subsequently by common law scholars and embraced by civil law lawyers.

The first instances of conflict of laws in the Western legal tradition can be traced to Greek law. Ancient Greeks dealt straightforwardly with multistate problems, and did not create choice-of-law rules. Leading solutions varied between the creation of courts for international cases, or application of local law, on the grounds that it was equally available to citizens of all states. More significant developments can be traced to Roman law. Roman civil law (jus civile) being inapplicable to non-citizens, special tribunals had jurisdiction to deal with multistate cases. The officers of these specialized tribunals were known as the praetor peregrini.

The Praetor peregrini did not select a jurisdiction whose rules of law should apply. Instead, they "applied" the "jus gentium." The jus gentium was a flexible and loosely-defined body of law based on international norms. Thus the praetor peregrini essentially created new substantive law for each case.Today, this is called a "substantive" solution to the choice-of-law issue. An early private international law was established in classical Islamic law and jurisprudence as a result of the vast Muslim conquests and maritime explorations during the early Middle Ages giving rise to various conflicts of laws. A will, for example, was "not enforced even if its provisions accorded with Islamic law if it violated the law of the testator."

Islamic jurists also developed elaborate rules for private international law regarding issues such as contracts and property, family relations and child custody, legal procédure and jurisdiction, religious conversion, and the return of aliens to an enemy country from the Muslim world. The religious laws and courts of other religions, including Christianity, Judaism and Hinduism, were also usually accommodated in classical Islamic law, as exemplified in Islamic Spain, Islamic India, and the Ottoman Empire. The modern conflict of laws is generally considered to have begun in Northern Italy during the late Middle Ages and in particular at trading cities such as Genoa, Pisa and Venice.

The need to adjudicate issues involving commercial transactions between traders belonging to different cities led to the development of the theory of statuta, whereby certain city laws would be considered as statuta personalia "following" the person whereby it may act, and other city laws would be considered as statuta realia, resulting in application of the law of the city where e.g. the res would be located (cf. lex rei sitae). Maritime law was also a great driver of international legal rules; providing for the enforcement of contracts, the protection of shipwrecked sailors and property, and the maintaining of harbours. The modern field of conflicts emerged in the United States during the 19th century with the publishing of Joseph Story's treatise on the Conflict of Laws in 1834. Story's work had a great influence on the subsequent development of the field in England such as those written by A.V. Dicey. Much of the English law then became the basis for conflict of laws for most commonwealth countries.

The stages in a conflict case:

1. The court must first decide whether it has jurisdiction and, if so, whether it is the appropriate venue given the problem of forum shopping.
2. The next step is the characterisation of the cause of action into its component legal categories which may sometimes involve an incidental question (also note the distinction between procedural and substantive laws).
3. Each legal category has one or more choice of law rules to determine which of the competing laws should be applied to each issue. A key element in this may be the rules on renvoi.
4. Once the applicable law is decided, that law must be proved before the forum court and applied to reach a judgment.
5. The successful party must then enforce the judgment which will first involve the task of securing cross-border recognition of the judgment.

In those states with an underdeveloped set of Conflict rules, decisions on jurisdiction tend to be made on an ad hoc basis, with such choice of law rules as have been developed embedded into each subject area of private law and tending to favour the application of the lex fori or local law. In states with a more mature system, the set of Conflict rules stands apart from the local private civil law and adopts a more international point of view both in its terminology and concepts. For example, in the European Union, all major jurisdictional matters are regulated under the Brussels Regime, e.g. the rule of lis alibi pendens from Brussels 1 Regulation applies in the Member States and its interpretation is controlled by the European Court of Justice rather than by local courts.

That and other elements of the Conflict rules are produced supranationally and implemented by treaty or convention. Because these rules are directly connected with aspects of sovereignty and the extraterritorial application of laws in the courts of the signatory states, they take on a flavour of public rather than private law because each state is compromising the usual expectations of their own citizens that they will have access to their local courts, and that local laws will apply in those local courts. Such aspects of public policy have direct constitutional significance whether applied in the European context or in federated nations such as the United States, Canada, and Australia where the courts have to contend not only with jurisdiction and law conflicts between the constituent states or territories, but also as between state and federal courts, and as between constituent states and relevant laws from other states outside the federation.

Choice of law rules

Courts faced with a choice of law issue have a two-stage process:

1. The court will apply the law of the forum (lex fori) to all procedural matters (including, self-evidently, the choice of law rules); and
2. It counts the factors that connect or link the legal issues to the laws of potentially relevant states and applies the laws that have the greatest connection, e.g. the law of nationality (lex patriae) or domicile (lex domicilii) will define legal status and capacity, the law of the state in which land is situated (lex situs) will be applied to determine all questions of title, the law of the place where a transaction physically takes place or of the occurrence that gave rise to the litigation (lex loci actus) will often be the controlling law selected when the matter is substantive, but the proper law has become a more common choice.

For example, suppose that Alexandre who has a French nationality and residence in Germany, corresponds with Bob who has American nationality, domicile in Arizona, and residence in Austria, over the internet. They agree to the joint purchase of land in Switzerland, currently owned by Heidi who is a Swiss national, but they never physically meet, executing initial contract documents by using fax machines, followed by a postal exchange of hard copies. Alexandre pays his share of the deposit but, before the transaction is completed, Bob admits that although he has capacity to buy land under his lex domicilii and the law of his residence, he is too young to own land under Swiss law.

The rules to determine which courts would have jurisdiction and which laws would be applied to each aspect of the case are defined in each state's laws so, in theory, no matter which court in which country actually accepts the case, the outcome will be the same (albeit that the measure of damages might differ from country to country which is why forum shopping is such a problem). In reality, however, moves to harmonise the conflictual system have not reached the point where standardisation of outcome can be guaranteed.

CONFLICT OF LAW RULES IN MATRIMONIAL CASES

In divorce cases, when a court is attempting to distribute marital property, if the divorcing couple is local and the property is local, then the court applies its domestic law lex fori. The case becomes much more complicated if foreign elements are thrown into the mix, such as when the place of marriage is different from the territory where divorce was filed; when the parties' nationalities and residences do not match; when there is property in a foreign jurisdiction; or when the parties have changed residence several times during the marriage. Each time a spouse invokes the application of foreign law, the process of divorce slows down, as the parties are directed to brief the issue of conflict of laws and provide translations of the foreign laws.

Different jurisdictions follow different sets of rules. Before embarking on a conflict of law analysis, the court must determine whether a property agreement governs the relationship between the parties. The property agreement must satisfy all formalities required in the country where enforcement is sought. Whereas commercial agreements or prenuptial agreements generally do not require legal formalities to be observed, when married couples enter a property agreement, stringent requirements are imposed, including notarization, witnesses, and special acknowledgment forms. In some countries, these must be filed (or docketed) with a domestic court, and the terms must be "so ordered" by a judge. This is done in order to ensure that no undue influence or oppression has been exerted by one spouse against the other.

Upon presenting a property agreement between spouses to a court of divorce, that court will generally assure itself of the following factors: signatures, legal formalities, intent, later intent, free will, lack of oppression, reasonableness and fairness, consideration, performance, reliance, later repudiation in writing or by conduct, and whichever other concepts of contractual bargaining apply in the context.

In the absence of a valid and enforceable agreement, here's how the conflict of law rules work:

- Movable v. Real Estate - In general, applicable matrimonial law depends on the nature of the property. Lex situs is applied to immovable property (i.e., real estate), and the law of matrimonial domicile applies to movable property, provided there has been no subsequent change in the spouses' domicile.
- Full Mutability Doctrine - property relations between spouses are governed by their latest domicile, whether acquired before or after the marriage. This is also the norm in England, except for a few cases where severe injustice results from a harsh application. In those cases, the court also examines whether newly acquired property can be traced back to property owned before the change.

- Immutability Doctrine - the original personal law of the parties at the time of marriage continues to govern all property including subsequently acquired property, regardless of a later change in domicile or nationality. This is the Continental approach in France, Germany and Belgium. Also in Israel: "property relations between spouses shall be governed by the law of their domicile at the time of the solemnisation of the marriage, provided that they may by agreement determine and vary such relations in accordance with the law of their domicile at the time of making the agreement". Note that the Israeli application of the Immutability Doctrine does not distinguish between personal and real property. Both are subject to the law of domicile at marriage.
- Partial Mutability or Mutability of New Acquisition - this is the American approach to conflicts of law in matrimonial property division cases. All movable property acquired during the marriage is subject to the parties' domicile law at the time of acquisition, and not that of the original or intermediate domicile. What was acquired before the marriage is governed by the law of the parties' domicile at the time of marriage. Thus, if rights vested in a property when and where it was purchased, it would not be adversely affected by a later change of domicile.
- Lex Fori - In many cases, courts simply avoid this complicated and expensive analysis by applying their local law to the parties' entire property, even if there is a foreign element. This is based on the assumption that laws around the world are basically similar in their treatment of marriage as a co-partnership. Since the partnership can be placed in the forum, the forum's law applies to all its aspects.

Note that Lex Fori also applies to all procedural relief (as opposed to substantive relief). Thus, issues such as the ability to grant pre-trial relief, procedure and form, as well as statutes of limitations are classified as "procedure" and are always subject to domestic law where the divorce case is pending.

PRE-DISPUTE PROVISIONS

Many contracts and other forms of legally binding agreement include a jurisdiction or arbitration clause specifying the parties' choice of venue for any litigation (called a forum selection clause). Then, choice of law clauses may specify which laws the court or tribunal should apply to each aspect of the dispute. This matches the substantive policy of freedom of contract. Judges have accepted that the principle of party autonomy allows the parties to select the law most appropriate to their transaction. Obviously, this judicial acceptance of subjective intent excludes the traditional reliance on objective connecting factors, but it does work well in practice.

THE STATUS OF FOREIGN LAW

Generally, when the court is to apply a foreign law, it must be proved by foreign law experts. It cannot merely be pleaded, as the court has no expertise in the laws of foreign countries nor in how they might be applied in a foreign court. Such foreign law may be considered no more than evidence, rather than law because of the issue of sovereignty. If the local court is actually giving extraterritorial effect to a foreign law, it is less than sovereign and so acting in a way that is potentially unconstitutional. The theoretical responses to this issue are:

- (a) that each court has an inherent jurisdiction to apply the laws of another country where it is necessary to achieving a just outcome; or
- (b) that the local court creates a right in its own laws to match that available under the foreign law. This explanation is sustainable because, even in states which apply a system of binding legal precedents, any precedent emerging from a conflicts case can only apply to future conflicts cases. There will be no ratio decidendi that binds future litigants in entirely local cases.
- (c) that the national court, when applying a foreign law, does not give an extraterritorial effect but recognizes, through its own "conflict of laws rule", that the situation at hand falls under the scope of application of the foreign

rule. In order to understand this argument one must first define the notion of extraterritorial application of a rule. This notion is susceptible to two distinct meanings:

On the one hand, this notion is used to describe the situation where a local court applies a rule other than the Lex fori (local law). On the other hand, it could mean that the rule is being applied to a factual situation that occurred beyond the territory of its state of origin. As an example of this situation, one can think of an American court applying British tort statutes and case law to a car accident that took place in London where both the driver and the victim are British citizens but the lawsuit was brought in before the American courts because the driver's insurer is American. One can then argue that since the factual situation is within the British territory, where an American judge applies the English Law, he does not give an extraterritorial application to the foreign rule. In fact, one can also argue that the American judge, had he applied American Law, would be doing so in an extraterritorial fashion.

Once the lex causae has been selected, it will be respected except when it appears to contravene an overriding mandatory rule of the lex fori. Each judge is the guardian of his own principles of ordre public (public order) and the parties cannot, by their own act, oust the fundamental principles of the local municipal law which generally underpin areas such as labour law, insurance, competition regulation, agency rules, embargoes, import-export regulations, and securities exchange regulations. Furthermore, the lex fori will prevail in cases where an application of the lex causae would otherwise result in a fundamentally immoral outcome, or give extraterritorial effect to confiscatory or other territorially limited laws.

In some countries, there is occasional evidence of parochialism when courts have determined that if the foreign law cannot be proved to a "satisfactory standard", then local law may be applied. In the United Kingdom, in the absence of evidence being led, the foreign law is presumed to be the same as the lex fori. Similarly, judges might assume in default of express evidence to the contrary that the place where the cause of action arose would provide certain basic protections, e.g. that the foreign court would provide a remedy to someone who was injured due to the negligence of another. Finally, some American courts have held that local law will be applied if the injury occurred in an "uncivilized place that has no law or legal system."

If the case has been submitted to arbitration rather than a national court, say because of a forum selection clause, an arbitrator may decide not to apply local mandatory policies in the face of a choice of law by the parties if this would defeat their commercial objectives. However, the arbitral award may be challenged in the country where it was made or where enforcement is sought by one of the parties on the ground that the relevant ordre public should have been applied. If the lex loci arbitri has been ignored, but there was no real and substantial connection between the place of arbitration and the agreement made by the parties, a court in which enforcement is sought may well accept the tribunal's decision. But if the appeal is to the courts in the state where the arbitration was held, the judge cannot ignore the mandatory provisions of the lex fori.

HARMONIZATION

To apply one national legal system as against another may never be an entirely satisfactory approach. The parties' interests may always be better protected by applying a law conceived with international realities in mind. The Hague Conference on Private International Law is a treaty organisation that oversees conventions designed to develop a uniform system. The deliberations of the conference have recently been the subject of controversy over the extent of cross-border jurisdiction on electronic commerce and defamation issues.

There is a general recognition that there is a need for an international law of contracts: for example, many nations have ratified the Vienna Convention on the International Sale of Goods, the Rome Convention on the Law Applicable to

Contractual Obligations offers less specialised uniformity, and there is support for the UNIDROIT Principles of International Commercial Contracts, a private restatement, all of which represent continuing efforts to produce international standards as the internet and other technologies encourage ever more interstate commerce. But other branches of the law are less well served and the dominant trend remains the role of the forum law rather than a supranational system for Conflict purposes.

Even the EU, which has institutions capable of creating uniform rules with direct effect, has failed to produce a universal system for the common market. Nevertheless, the Treaty of Amsterdam does confer authority on the Community's institutions to legislate by Council Regulation in this area with supranational effect. Article 177 would give the Court of Justice jurisdiction to interpret and apply their principles so, if the political will arises, uniformity may gradually emerge in letter. Whether the domestic courts of the Member States would be consistent in applying those letters is speculative.

SUPRANATIONAL LAW

Supranational law is a form of international law, based on the limitation of the rights of sovereign nations between one another. It contrasts to public international law, which involves the United Nations, the Geneva conventions, or the law of the sea, because in supranational law, nations explicitly submit their right to make decisions on the international playing field to a set of common institutions.

Supranational theory

Supranationalism can be contrasted to intergovernmentalism as a form of decision making, and is worthy of study. Speaking in relation to Europe, Joseph H. H. Weiler, in his seminal work "The Dual Character of Supranationalism" states that there are two main concerns to European supranationalism. These are:

- Normative Supranationalism: The Relationships and hierarchy which exist between Community policies and legal measures on one hand and the competing policies and legal measures of the Member states on the other. (The Executive Dimension)

- Decisional Supranationalism: The institutional framework and decision making by which such measures are initiated, debated, formulated, promulgated and finally executed. (The Legislative-Judicial Dimension)

In many ways the split sees the separation of powers confined to merely two branches.

EUROPEAN UNION LAW

The Law of the European Union is the unique legal system which operates alongside the laws of Member States of the European Union (EU). EU law has direct effect within the legal systems of its Member States, and overrides national law in many areas, especially in areas covered by the Single Market. The EU is not a federal government; as established by the European Court of Justice, the Community constitutes "a new legal order" in international law. It is sometimes classified as supranational law. Currently there are around 500 million EU citizens in 27 Member States subject to EU law, making it one of the most encompassing modern legal systems in the world.

Like the EU itself, EU law can be divided into three pillars. The first of these, the European Community pillar, comprises the majority of law produced by the EU and is where the European Court of Justice has the most power. The EU can also enact legislation under the second and third pillars - relating to criminal law and foreign policy respectively - although the powers of the Court of Justice are much reduced and direct effect does not apply. EU laws are more detailed when compared with member states' laws. Similarly with federal states, the legal system is used to ensure political results from the member states, because of the decentralized nature of the political system. Decisions are taken at the EU level but, implementation is overwhelmingly done by member states. By contrast, decision making and implementation inside member states is usually done by the same actors.

The development of law of the European Community has been largely moulded by the European Court of Justice (ECJ). In the landmark case of Van Gend en Loos in 1963, the ECJ ruled that the European Community, through the will of Member States expressed in the Treaty of Rome, "constitutes a new legal order of international law for the benefit of which the states have limited their sovereign rights albeit within limited fields." The distinction between European Community (EC) law and European Union law is that based on the Treaty structure of the European Union. The European Community constitutes one of the 'three pillars' of the European Union and concerns the social and economic foundations of the single market.

The second and the third pillars were created by the Treaty on European Union (the Maastricht Treaty) and involve Common Security and Defence Policy and Internal Security. Decision-making under the second and third pillars is not subject to majority voting at present. The Maastricht Treaty created the Justice and Home Affairs pillar as the third pillar. Subsequently, the Treaty of Amsterdam transferred the areas of illegal immigration, visas, asylum, and judicial co-operation to the European Community (the first pillar). Now Police and Judicial Co-operation in Criminal Matters is the third pillar. Justice and Home Affairs now refers both to the fields that have been transferred to the EC and the third pillar.

Several principles such as subsidiarity, proportionality, the principle of conferral, and the precautionary principle have become prominent in the development of European Union law. Scholars such as Catherine Barnard argue that the Four Freedoms form the substantive law of the EU: free movement of goods, services, capital, and labour within the internal market of the EU.

CRIMINAL LAW

In 2006, a toxic waste spill off the coast of Côte d'Ivoire, from a European ship, prompted the Commission to look into legislation against toxic waste. Environment Commissioner Stavros Dimas stated that "Such highly toxic waste should never have left the European Union". With countries such as Spain not even having a crime against shipping toxic waste Franco Frattini, the Justice, Freedom and Security Commissioner, proposed with Dimas to create criminal sentences for "ecological crimes".

His right to do this was contested in 2005 at the Court of Justice resulting in a victory for the Commission. That ruling set a precedent that the Commission, on a supranational basis, may legislate in criminal law - something never done before to outlined in treaties. So far though, the only other use has been the intellectual property rights directive. Motions were tabled in the European Parliament against that legislation on the basis that criminal law should not be an EU competence, but was rejected at vote. However in October 2007 the Court of Justice ruled the Commission could not propose what the criminal sanctions could be, only that there must be some.

INTERNATIONAL HUMANITARIAN LAW

International humanitarian law (IHL), often referred to as the laws of war, the laws and customs of war or the law of armed conflict, is the legal corpus "comprised of the Geneva Conventions and the Hague Conventions, as well as subsequent treaties, case law, and customary international law." It defines the conduct and responsibilities of belligerent nations, neutral nations and individuals engaged in warfare, in relation to each other and to protected persons, usually meaning civilians. The law is mandatory for nations bound by the appropriate treaties. There are also other customary unwritten rules of war, many of which were explored at the Nuremberg War Trials. By extension, they also define both the permissive rights of these powers as well as prohibitions on their conduct when dealing with irregular forces and non-signatories.

THE LAW OF GENEVA AND THE LAW OF THE HAGUE

Modern International Humanitarian Law is made up of two historical streams: the law of The Hague referred to in the past as the law of war proper and the law of Geneva or humanitarian law. The two streams take their names from a number of international conferences which drew up treaties relating to war and conflict, in particular The Hague Conventions of 1899 and 1907, and the Geneva Conventions, the first which was drawn up in 1863. Both are branches of jus in bello, international law regarding acceptable practices while engaged in war and armed conflict.

The Law of The Hague or the Laws of War proper, "determines the rights and duties of belligerents in the conduct of operations and limits the choice of means in doing harm." In particular, it concerns itself with the definition of combatants, establishes rules relating to the means and methods of warfare, and examines the issue of military objectives. Systematic attempts to limit the savagery of warfare only began to develop in the 19th century. Such concerns were able to build on the changing view of warfare by states influenced by the Age of Enlightenment. The purpose of warfare was to overcome the enemy state and this was obtainable by disabling the enemy combatants. Thus, "the distinction between combatants and civilians, the requirement that wounded and captured enemy combatants must be treated humanely, and that quarter must be given, some of the pillars of modern humanitarian law, all follow from this principle."

THE LAW OF GENEVA

The massacre of civilians in the midst of armed conflict has a long and dark history. Selected examples include: Moses, speaking for the god of the Israelites, ordering the killing of all the Midianite women and male children; the massacres of the Kalingas by Ashoka in India, the massacre of some 100,000 Hindus by the Muslim troops of Timur (Tamerlane) or the Crusader massacres of Jews and Muslims in the Siege of Jerusalem (1099), to name a few examples drawn from a long list in history. Fritz Munch sums up historical military practice before 1800: "The essential points seem to be these: In battle and in towns taken by force, combatants and non-combatants were killed and property was destroyed or looted In the 17th century, the Dutch jurist Hugo Grotius wrote "Wars, for the attainment of their objects, it cannot be denied, must employ force and terror as their most proper agents."

HUMANITARIAN NORMS IN HISTORY

However, even in the midst of the carnage of history, there were expressions of humanitarian norms to protect the victims of armed conflicts, i.e. the wounded, the sick and the shipwrecked which date back to ancient times. In the Old Testament, the King of Israel prevents the slaying of the captured following the prophet, Elisha's admonition, to spare enemy prisoners: In answer to a question from the King, he said, "You shall not slay them. Would you slay those whom you have taken captive with your sword and with your bow? Set bread and water before them, that they may eat and drink and go to their master."

In ancient India there are records, for example the Laws of Manu, describing the types of weapons that should not be used. "When he fights with his foes in battle, let him not strike with weapons concealed (in wood), nor with (such as are) barbed, poisoned, or the points of which are blazing with fire. There is also the command not to strike the enemy "who folds his hands in supplication....Nor one who sleeps, nor one who has lost his coat of mail, nor one who is naked, nor one who is disarmed, nor one who looks on without taking part in the fight..."

Islamic law indicates that "noncombatants who did not take part in fighting such as women, children, monks and hermits, the aged, blind, and insane" were not to be molested. The first Caliph, Abu Bakr, proclaimed "Do not mutilate. Do not kill little children or old men or women. Do not cut off the heads of palm trees or burn them. Do not cut down fruit trees. Do not slaughter livestock except for food." Islamic jurists have held that a prisoner should not be killed as he "cannot be held responsible for mere acts of belligerency." Islamic law did not spare all non-combatants. In the case of those who refused to convert to Islam or pay an alternative tax, "were allowed in principle to kill any one of them, combatants or noncombatants, provided they were not killed treacherously and with mutilation."

CODIFICATION OF HUMANITARIAN NORMS

However, it wasn't until second half of the 18th century that more systematic approach was initiated. In the United States, a German immigrant, Francis Lieber, drew up a code of conduct in 1863, the Lieber Code, for the Northern army which included the humane treatment of civilian populations in the areas of conflict. It also forbade the execution of POWs. At the same time, the involvement of a number of individuals such as Florence Nightingale during the Crimean War and Henry Dunant a Genevese businessman who had worked with wounded soldiers at the Battle of Solferino led to more systematic efforts to try and prevent the suffering of war victims. Dunant wrote a book, A Memory of Solferino, which described the horrors he had witnessed. His reports led to the founding of the International Committee of the Red Cross (ICRC) in 1863 and the convening of a conference in Geneva in 1864 which drew up the Geneva Convention for the Amelioration of the Condition of the Wounded in Armies in the Field.

The Law of Geneva, is directly inspired by the principle of humanity. It relates to those who are not participating in the conflict as well as military personnel hors de combat. It provides the legal basis for protection and humanitarian assistance carried out by impartial humanitarian organizations such as the ICRC. This focus can be found in the Geneva Conventions.

GENEVA CONVENTIONS

The Geneva Conventions are the result of a process that developed in a number of stages between 1864 and 1949 which focused on the protection of civilians and those who can no longer fight in an armed conflict. As a result of World War II, all four conventions were revised based on previous revisions and partly on some of the 1907 Hague Conventions and readopted by the international community in 1949. Later conferences have added provisions prohibiting certain methods of warfare and addressing issues of civil wars.

The Geneva Conventions are:

- First Geneva Convention "for the Amelioration of the Condition of the Wounded and Sick in Armed Forces in the Field" (first adopted in 1864, last revision in 1949)
- Second Geneva Convention "for the Amelioration of the Condition of Wounded, Sick and Shipwrecked Members of Armed Forces at Sea" (first adopted in 1949, successor of the 1907 Hague Convention X)
- Third Geneva Convention "relative to the Treatment of Prisoners of War" (first adopted in 1929, last revision in 1949)
- Fourth Geneva Convention "relative to the Protection of Civilian Persons in Time of War" (first adopted in 1949, based on parts of the 1907 Hague Convention IV)

In addition, there are three additional amendment protocols to the Geneva Convention:

- Protocol I (1977): Protocol Additional to the Geneva Conventions of 12 August 1949, and relating to the Protection of Victims of International Armed Conflicts. As of 12 January 2007 it had been ratified by 167 countries.
- Protocol II (1977): Protocol Additional to the Geneva Conventions of 12 August 1949, and relating to the Protection of Victims of Non-International Armed Conflicts. As of 12 January 2007 it had been ratified by 163 countries.
- Protocol III (2005): Protocol Additional to the Geneva Conventions of 12 August 1949, and relating to the Adoption of an Additional Distinctive Emblem. As of June 2007 it had been ratified by 17 countries and signed but not yet ratified by an additional 68 countries.

While the Geneva Conventions of 1949 can be seen as the result of a process which began in 1864, today, they have "achieved universal participation with 194 parties." This means that they apply to almost any international armed conflict.

CONVERGENCE BETWEEN IHL AND THE LAWS OF WAR

With the adoption of the 1977 Protocols to the Geneva Conventions, the two strains of law began to converge. Already before, articles focusing on humanity could be found in the Law of The Hague (i.e. the protection of certain prisoners of war and civilians in occupied territories) articles which were later incorporated into the Law of Geneva in 1929 and 1949). However the Protocols of 1977 relating to the protection of victims in both international and internal conflict not only incorporated aspects of both the Law of The Hague and the Law of Geneva, but also important human rights aspects.

Basic rules of IHL:

1. Persons hors de combat and those not taking part in hostilities shall be protected and treated humanely.
2. It is forbidden to kill or injure an enemy who surrenders or who is hors de combat.
3. The wounded and sick shall be cared for and protected by the party to the conflict which has them in its power. The emblem of the red cross or the red crescent must be respected as the sign of protection.
4. Captured combatants and civilians must be protected against acts of violence and reprisals. They shall have the right to correspond with their families and to receive relief.
5. No one shall be subjected to torture, corporal punishment or cruel or degrading treatment.
6. Parties to a conflict and members of their armed forces do not have an unlimited choice of methods and means of warfare.
7. Parties to a conflict shall at all times distinguish between the civilian population and combatants. Attacks shall be directed solely against military objectives.

Examples

Well-known examples of such rules include the prohibition on attacking doctors or ambulances displaying a

Red Cross. It is also prohibited to fire at a person or vehicle bearing a white flag, since that indicates an intent to surrender or a desire to communicate. In either case, the persons protected by the Red Cross or white flag is expected to maintain neutrality, and may not engage in warlike acts; in fact, engaging in war activities under a white flag or red cross is itself a violation of the laws of war.

These examples of the laws of war address declaration of war, (the UN charter (1945) Art 2, and some other Arts in the charter, curtails the right of member states to declare war; as does the older and toothless Kellogg-Briand Pact of 1928 for those nations who ratified it but used against Germany in the Nuremberg War Trials), acceptance of surrender and the treatment of prisoners of war; the avoidance of atrocities; the prohibition on deliberately attacking civilians; and the prohibition of certain inhumane weapons. It is a violation of the laws of war to engage in combat without meeting certain requirements, among them the wearing of a distinctive uniform or other easily identifiable badge and the carrying of weapons openly. Impersonating soldiers of the other side by wearing the enemy's uniform and fighting in that uniform, is forbidden, as is the taking of hostages.

INTERNATIONAL COMMITTEE OF THE RED CROSS

The International Committee of the Red Cross (ICRC) is a private humanitarian institution based in Geneva, Switzerland. The community of states has given the ICRC a unique role, based on international humanitarian law of the Geneva Conventions as well as customary international law, to protect the victims of international and internal armed conflicts. Such victims include war wounded, prisoners, refugees, civilians, and other non-combatants. The ICRC is part of the International Red Cross and Red Crescent Movement along with the International Federation and 186 National Societies. It is the oldest and most honoured organization within the Movement and one of the most widely recognized organizations in the world, having won three Nobel Peace Prizes in 1917, 1944, and 1963.

VIOLATIONS AND PUNISHMENT

During conflict, punishment for violating the laws of war may consist of a specific, deliberate and limited violation of the laws of war in reprisal. Soldiers who break specific provisions of the laws of war lose the protections and status afforded as prisoners of war but only after facing a "competent tribunal". At that point they become an unlawful combatant but they must still be "treated with humanity and, in case of trial, shall not be deprived of the rights of fair and regular trial", because they are still covered by GC IV Art 5.

Spies and "terrorists" are only protected by the laws of war if the power which holds them is in a state of armed conflict or war and until they are found to be an unlawful combatant. Depending on the circumstances, they may be subject to civilian law or military tribunal for their acts and in practice have been subjected to torture and/or execution. The laws of war neither approve nor condemn such acts, which fall outside their scope. Countries that have signed the UN Convention Against Torture have committed themselves not to use torture on anyone for any reason. After a conflict has ended, persons who have committed any breach of the laws of war, and especially atrocities, may be held individually accountable for war crimes through process of law.

CUSTOMARY INTERNATIONAL LAW

Customary international law are those aspects of international law that derive from custom. Coupled with general principles of law and treaties, custom is considered by the International Court of Justice, jurists, the United Nations, and its member states to be among the primary sources of international law. For example, laws of war were long a matter of customary law before they were codified in the Hague Conventions of 1899 and 1907, Geneva Conventions, and other treaties.

The vast majority of the world's governments accept in principle the existence of customary international law, although there are many differing opinions as to what rules are contained in it. The Statute of the International Court of Justice acknowledges the existence of customary international law in Article 38(1)(b), incorporated into the United Nations Charter by Article 92: "The Court, whose function is to decide in accordance with international law such disputes as are submitted to it, shall apply...international custom, as evidence of a general practice accepted as law."

Customary international law "... consists of rules of law derived from the consistent conduct of States acting out of the belief that the law required them to act that way." It follows that customary international law can be discerned by a "widespread repetition by States of similar international acts over time (State practice); Acts must occur out of sense of obligation (opinio juris); Acts must be taken by a significant number of States and not be rejected by a significant number of States." A marker of customary international law is consensus among states exhibited both by widespread conduct and a discernible sense of obligation.

A peremptory norm (also called jus cogens, Latin for "compelling law") is a fundamental principle of international law which is accepted by the international community of states as a norm from which no derogation is ever permitted. Examples include various international crimes; a state which carries out or permits slavery, genocide, war of aggression, or crimes against humanity is always violating customary international law. Other examples of customary international law include the principle of non-refoulement, immunity of visiting foreign heads of state, and the right to humanitarian intervention.

INTERNATIONAL HUMAN RIGHTS LAW

International human rights law is a system of laws, both domestic, regional and international, designed to promote human rights. Human rights law is made up of various international human rights instruments which are binding to its parties (nation-states that have ratified the treaty).

An important concept within human rights law is that of universal jurisdiction. This concept, which is not widely accepted, is that any nation is authorized to prosecute and punish violations of human rights wherever and whenever they may have occurred. Some customary peremptory norms of human rights are also recognised, and these are considered binding on all nations, even those that have not ratified the relevant treaty. In principle human rights law is enforced on a domestic level and nation states that ratify human rights treaties commit themselves to enact domestic human rights legislations.

In addition to international human rights law, human rights law has been created on a regional level. The three regional human rights instrument that form binding human rights law to party states are: African Charter on Human and Peoples' Rights, the American Convention on Human Rights (the Americas) and the European Convention on Human Rights. Human rights law is related to, but not the same as International Humanitarian Law and Refugee Law. War crimes, crimes against humanity and genocide have their own treaty law.

Universal Declaration of Human Rights

The Universal Declaration of Human Rights is a declaration that does not form binding international human rights law. Although some legal scholars cite the UDHR as evidence for customary international law and more broadly the UDH has become an authoritative human rights reference. The UDHR has provided the basis for subsequent international human rights instruments that form binding international human rights law.

The Two Covenants

The Universal Declaration of Human Rights (UDHR) was adopted as binding international treaty into two distinct and different covenants, the International Covenant on Civil and

Political Rights(ICCPR) and the International Covenant on Economic, Social and Cultural Rights (ICESCR). The two Covenants form treaty law, that is international human rights law, and ratifying parties (nation states) to the Covenant commit themselves to implement the contained rights in their domestic jurisdictions. Note that some states have signed but not ratified the Covenants. Both covenants came in force in 1976 when a sufficient number of countries had ratified the Covenants.

International Human Rights Treaties

Since the adoption of the two Covenants a number of other treaties (pieces of legislation) have been adopted at the international level.

They are generally known as human rights instruments. Some of the most significant include:

- Convention on the Elimination of All Forms of Racial Discrimination (CERD) (adopted 1966, entry into force: 1969)
- Convention on the Elimination of All Forms of Discrimination Against Women (CEDAW) (entry into force: 1981)
- United Nations Convention Against Torture (CAT) (adopted 1984, entry into force: 1984)
- Convention on the Rights of the Child (CRC) (adopted 1989, entry into force: 1989)
- International Convention on the Protection of the Rights of All Migrant Workers and Members of their Families (ICRMW) (adopted 1990)

Regional Human Rights Instruments

There are three key regional human rights instruments which have established human rights law on a regional basis. These are:

- The African Charter on Human and Peoples' Rights for Africa (1981, in force since 1986)

- The American Convention on Human Rights for the Americas (1969, in force since 1978)
- The European Convention on Human Rights for Europe (1950, in force since 1953)

Organization of American States and Council of Europe, like UN, háve also adopted (but, unlike UN, later) separate treaties (with weaker implementation mechanisms) containing catalogues of economic, social and cultural rights, as opposed to their aforementioned conventions dealing mostly with civil and political rights.

- European Social Charter for Europe (1961, in force since 1965, complaints mechanism created under 1995 Additional Protocol, in force since 1998)
- Protocol of San Salvador to the ACHR for the Americas (1988, in force since 1999)

ENFORCEMENT OF HUMAN RIGHTS LAW

There is currently no international court to administer international human rights law, however, quasi-judicial bodies exists under some UN treaties (e.g., Human Rights Committee under ICCPR). The International Criminal Court (ICC) has jurisdiction over the crime of genocide, war crimes and crimes against humanity. While the European Court of Human Rights, and the Inter-American Court of Human Rights enforce regional human rights law.

The United Nations Human Rights Bodies do have some quasi legal enforcement mechanisms. These include the Treaty Bodies attached to the current seven active treaties, and the Human Rights Council complaints procedures, known as the 1235 and 1503 mechanisms. The enforcement of international human rights law is the responsibility of the Nation State, and it is the primary responsibility of the State to make human rights a reality. In practice, many human rights are very difficult to legally enforce due to the absence of consensus on the application of certain rights, the lack of relevant national legislation or of bodies empowered to take legal action to enforce them.

In over 110 countries national human rights institutions (NHRIs) have been set up to protect, promote or monitor human rights with jurisdiction in a given country. Although not all NHRIs are compliant with the Paris Principles, the number and effect of these institutions is increasing. The Paris Principles were defined at the first International Workshop on National Institutions for the Promotion and Protection of Human Rights in Paris on 7-9 October 1991, and adopted by United Nations Human Rights Commission Resolution 1992/54 of 1992 and the General Assembly Resolution 48/134 of 1993. The Paris Principles list a number of responsibilities for national institutions.

UNIVERSAL JURISDICTION

Universal jurisdiction is a controversial principle in international law whereby states claim criminal jurisdiction over persons whose alleged crimes were committed outside the boundaries of the prosecuting state, regardless of nationality, country of residence, or any other relation with the prosecuting country. The state backs its claim on the grounds that the crime committed is considered a crime against all, which any state is authorized to punish. The concept of universal jurisdiction is therefore closely linked to the idea that certain international norms are erga omnes, or owed to the entire world community, as well as the concept of jus cogens.

In 1993 Belgium passed a *law of universal jurisdiction* to give its courts jurisdiction over crimes against humanity in other countries, and in 1998 Augusto Pinochet was arrested in London following an indictment by Spanish judge Baltasar Garzón under the universal jurisdiction principle. The principle is supported by Amnesty International and other human rights organisations as they believe certain crimes pose a threat to the international community as a whole and the community has a moral duty to act, but others, including Henry Kissinger argue that "widespread agreement that human rights violations and crimes against humanity must be prosecuted has hindered active consideration of the proper role of international courts. Universal jurisdiction risks creating universal tyranny – that of judges".

PRIVATE INTERNATIONAL LAW

Lawyers and their clients often face the prospect of litigation in foreign jurisdictions. This area of law is called 'Private International Law' or 'Conflict of Laws'. The Private International Law Section of the Australian Government Attorney-General's Department provides information and assistance to governments, practitioners and members of the public on procedures for transmitting documents for service, taking of evidence for foreign proceedings, the enforcement of foreign judgments and jurisdictional issues. The Department also works to promote international cooperation on civil legal procedures.

The Australian Government Attorney-General's Department may be able to provide information and assistance on a range of private international law matters, including the:

a. Service of Foreign Court Process in Australia
b. Service of Australian Court Process Abroad

The permitted methods for serving Australian court documents in a foreign country depend upon:

- The Court Rules of the relevant Australian jurisdiction which regulate service abroad, and
- Tthe domestic laws of the foreign country.

A list of relevant legislation can be accessed from the menu under 'Relevant State and Territory legislation'. The information sheets accessible from the main menu under 'A-Z Country list' provide information on the procedures that the foreign country will allow. The information sheets also provide information on enforcement of judgments.

c. The Taking of Evidence in Australia for use in Foreign Proceedings

The information sheets on the taking of evidence in Australia are currently being updated. Please contact the Australian Government Attorney-General's Department if you require assistance.

d. The Taking of Evidence in Foreign Jurisdictions for use in Australian Court Proceedings

The information sheets on the taking of evidence in foreign jurisdictions are currently being updated. Please contact the Australian Government Attorney-General's Department if you require assistance. Australia is a party to the Hague Convention on the Taking of Evidence Abroad in Civil or Commercial Matters. This Convention provides procedures for the taking of evidence between foreign countries which are parties to the Convention. Our public international law practice advises states, international organisations and multinational companies on both contentious and non-contentious issues.

This includes territorial and boundary disputes; international maritime law; air and water rights; treaty negotiations and accession to treaties; state responsibility; sovereign and diplomatic privilege and immunity; project-specific international agreements between host states; foreign corrupt practices; extra-territorial jurisdiction for worker safety liability; offshore oil and gas (and other resources); human rights (including their relevance in the context of corporate social responsibility and alien tort claims); economic sanctions; expropriations; international environmental law; bilateral investment treaties; and sovereign debt questions; state and diplomatic immunity; privileges and immunities of international organizations; treaty obligations; human rights; international environmental law; law of the sea; proceedings before specially constituted claims tribunals; proceedings before other international courts and tribunals including the International Court of Justice.

International law deals with the relationships between states, or between persons or entities in different states. It subdivides into "public international law" and "private international law" (also called conflict of laws). When used without an adjective, "international law" generally refers to "public international law." Thus, public international law defined as "is the system of law which regulates the activities of entities possessing international personality."

Public international law has assumed greater importance with the increasing globalisation of business. We work on international project finance and major infrastructure projects, energy projects, international financing and privatisations, and trade and customs disputes. Our particular strength lies in combining public international law knowledge with wide commercial experience. International law is extremely relevant to any corporation or organisation with a presence in multiple jurisdictions, and to anyone involved in trans-national trade, commerce and investment. In a shrinking world, global and regional cooperation increases the need for corporations to understand international law and the impact of international and extra-territorial regulation.

We advise corporations, sovereign States and international organisations on the complex and far-reaching effects of international law including economic sanctions; export control legislation; anti-money laundering, anti-corruption and anti-terrorism regulations; alien torts legislation; bilateral investment treaties and investment protection; international environmental law and regulation; international trade law, including the WTO regime and its provisions; risk assessments for international projects and investments.

HAGUE CONFERENCE ON PRIVATE INTERNATIONAL LAW

The Hague Conference on Private International Law (or HCCH, for Hague Conference/Conférence de la Haye) is the preeminent organisation in the area of private international law. Since its formation in 1893, the purpose of HCCH has been to "work for the progressive unification of the rules of private international law". It has pursued this goal by creating and assisting in the implementation of multilateral conventions promoting the harmonisation of conflict of laws principles in diverse subject matters within private international law. Sixty-five nations are currently members of the Hague Conference, including China, Russia, the United States, and all member states of the European Union.

Recent developments

The 20th Diplomatic Session of the Conference, held from 14 to 28 June 2005, saw two major developments. First, the statute of the Conference was amended (for the first time in over 50 years) to expand the possibility of membership to Regional Economic Integration Organisations such as the European Union. Second, the Conference concluded and opened for ratification the Hague Convention on Choice of Court Agreements, a project which had been in negotiation for nearly 15 years. States applying this instrument agree to recognize and enforce decisions reached by courts of another signatory State if the dispute was governed by a valid choice of court agreement concluded between the parties to the dispute.

THE HAGUE SECURITIES CONVENTION

In July 2006 Switzerland and the United States jointly signed the Hague Securities Convention, providing legal certainty to modern forms of holding and transferring securities. This marked an important step in the development of the new legal infrastructure needed to match modern systems for the holding, transfer, and pledge of securities. The vast quantity of securities are nowadays held, transferred, and pledged by electronic entries to accounts with clearing and settlement systems and other intermediaries, rather than directly in physical form or directly by issuers.

The global financial market, which for the OECD countries alone has a volume of more than $2 billion US a day, is in need of a legal regime that deals effectively with this new reality. There is broad agreement in the financial world that the traditional legal rules, based on physical transfers and direct holdings, are too diverse, out-dated, and inadequate. The result is legal uncertainty, increased risk, and higher costs for global clearing and settlement, with repercussions at all levels of the global financial market.

The Hague Securities Convention ensures that there is a clear and certain answer to questions such as which law governs the determination of the legal nature of the rights resulting from a credit of securities to a securities account, the steps required for a transfer or pledge of securities to such accounts to be enforceable among the parties and third parties, and the steps required to realise a pledge of securities credited to such accounts. The European Commission at the same time concluded that "adoption of the Convention would be in the best interest of the Community" and recommended that the Convention "be signed after or with at least two of its main trading partners, the USA included."

WOMEN'S HOUSING RIGHTS UNDER INTERNATIONAL HUMAN RIGHTS LAW

Human rights apply to everyone, everywhere, regardless of gender. The right to adequate housing is established in many international human rights instruments and yet it remains far from being realised for most of the world's poor. Women, due to ongoing gender disparity, have suffered disproportionately from violations of the right to adequate housing. It has indeed been very positive that recent years have seen even more major advancements in the protection of women's housing rights at national, regional and international levels. At the international level, the landscape for women's housing rights has expanded, ushering in a new era of progress for women's rights advocates and deepening our understandings of the indivisibility of all women's human rights.

All aspects of women's housing rights touch upon the themes of a woman's rights to non-discrimination and equality. Indeed, the very ideas of non-discrimination and equality are cornerstone human right principles which themselves have enjoyed rich development. International human rights law has repeatedly set forth the overarching right to non-discrimination, a principle which applies to all aspects of housing, land and property. Nevertheless, there is a stark gap between the law and the reality for women. Gender discrimination in relation to housing security continues to characterise the daily reality of women in all corners of the world.

In 1996, the international community acknowledged gender equality in housing rights during the second United

Nations Conference on Human Settlements (Habitat II). At the Habitat II conference States pledged, inter alia, to remedy gender discrimination related to housing; to provide "legal security of tenure and equal access to land to all people, including women and those living in poverty," and to "undertake legislative and administrative reforms to give women full and equal access to economic resources, including the right to inheritance and to ownership of land and other property," and to eliminate gender bias in access to housing.

5

Equality of Rights between Men and Women

The Committee has decided to update its general comment on article 3 of the Covenant and to replace General Comment No. 4 (thirteenth session, 1981), in the light of the experience it has gathered in its activities over the last 20 years. The present revision seeks to take account of the important impact of this article on the enjoyment by women of the human rights protected under the Covenant. Article 3 implies that all human beings should enjoy the rights provided for in the Covenant, on an equal basis and in their totality. The full effect of this provision is impaired whenever any person is denied the full and equal enjoyment of any right. Consequently, States should ensure to men and women equally the enjoyment of all rights provided for in the Covenant.

The obligation to ensure to all individuals the rights recognized in the Covenant, established in articles 2 and 3 of the Covenant, requires that States parties take all necessary steps to enable every person to enjoy those rights. These steps include the removal of obstacles to the equal enjoyment of such rights, the education of the population and of State officials in human rights, and the adjustment of domestic legislation so as to give effect to the undertakings set forth in the Covenant. The State party must not only adopt measures of protection, but also positive measures in all areas so as to achieve the effective and equal empowerment of women. States parties must provide information regarding the actual role of women in society so that the Committee may ascertain what measures, in addition to legislative provisions, have been or should be taken to give effect to these obligations, what progress has been made, what difficulties are encountered and what steps are being taken to overcome them.

States parties are responsible for ensuring the equal enjoyment of rights without any discrimination. Articles 2 and 3 mandate States parties to take all steps necessary, including the prohibition of discrimination on the ground of sex, to put an end to discriminatory actions, both in the public and the private sector, which impair the equal enjoyment of rights. Inequality in the enjoyment of rights by women throughout the world is deeply embedded in tradition, history and culture, including religious attitudes. The subordinate role of women in some countries is illustrated by the high incidence of prenatal sex selection and abortion of female foetuses. States parties should ensure that traditional, historical, religious or cultural attitudes are not used to justify violations of women's right to equality before the law and to equal enjoyment of all Covenant rights. States parties should furnish appropriate information on those aspects of tradition, history, cultural practices and religious attitudes which jeopardize, or may jeopardize, compliance with article 3, and indicate what measures they have taken or intend to take to overcome such factors.

In order to fulfil the obligation set forth in article 3, States parties should take account of the factors which impede the equal enjoyment by women and men of each right specified in the Covenant. To enable the Committee to obtain a complete picture of the situation of women in each State party as regards the implementation of the rights in the Covenant, this general comment identifies some of the factors affecting the equal enjoyment by women of the rights under the Covenant and spells out the type of information that is required with regard to these rights. The equal enjoyment of human rights by women must be protected during a state of emergency (art. 4). States parties which take measures derogating from their obligations under the Covenant in time of public emergency, as provided in article 4, should provide information to the Committee with respect to the impact on the situation of women of such measures and should demonstrate that they are non-discriminatory. Women are particularly vulnerable in times of internal or international armed conflicts. States parties should inform the Committee of all measures taken during these situations to protect women from rape, abduction and other forms of gender-based violence. In becoming parties to the Covenant, States undertake, in accordance with article 3, to ensure the equal right of men and women to the enjoyment of all civil and political rights set forth in the Covenant, and in accordance with article 5, nothing in the Covenant may be interpreted as implying for any State, group or person any right to engage in any activity or perform any act aimed at the destruction of any of the rights provided for in article 3, or at limitations not covered by the Covenant.

Moreover, there shall be no restriction upon or derogation from the equal enjoyment by women of all fundamental human rights recognized or existing pursuant to law, conventions, regulations or customs, on the pretext that the Covenant does not recognize such rights or that it recognizes them to a lesser extent. When reporting on the right to life protected by article 6, States parties should provide data on birth rates and on pregnancy- and childbirth-related deaths of women. Gender-disaggregated data should be provided on infant mortality rates. States parties should give information on any measures taken by the State to help women prevent unwanted pregnancies, and to ensure that they do not have to undergo life-threatening clandestine abortions.

States parties should also report on measures to protect women from practices that violate their right to life, such as female infanticide, the burning of widows and dowry killings. The Committee also wishes to have information on the particular impact on women of poverty and deprivation that may pose a threat to their lives. To assess compliance with article 7 of the Covenant, as well as with article 24, which mandates special protection for children, the Committee needs to be provided information on national laws and practice with regard to domestic and other types of violence against women, including rape. It also needs to know whether the State party gives access to safe abortion to women who have become pregnant as a result of rape. The States parties should also provide the Committee with information on measures to prevent forced abortion or forced sterilization. In States parties where the practice of genital mutilation exists information on its extent and on measures to eliminate it should be provided.

The information provided by States parties on all these issues should include measures of protection, including legal remedies, for women whose rights under article 7 have been violated. Having regard to their obligations under article 8, States parties should inform the Committee of measures taken to eliminate trafficking of women and children, within the country or across borders, and forced prostitution. They must also provide information on measures taken to protect women and children, including foreign women and children, from slavery, disguised, *inter alia*, as domestic or other kinds of personal service. States parties where women and children are recruited, and from which they are taken, and States parties where they are received should provide information on measures, national or international, which have been taken in order to prevent the violation of women's and children's rights.

States parties should provide information on any specific regulation of clothing to be worn by women in public. The Committee stresses that such regulations may involve a violation of a number of rights guaranteed by the Covenant, such as: article 26, on non-discrimination; article 7, if corporal punishment is imposed in order to enforce such a regulation; article 9, when failure to comply with the regulation is punished by arrest; article 12, if liberty of movement is subject to such a constraint; article 17, which guarantees all persons the right to privacy without arbitrary or unlawful interference; articles 18 and 19, when women are subjected to clothing requirements that are not in keeping with their religion or their right of self-expression; and, lastly, article 27, when the clothing requirements conflict with the culture to which the woman can lay a claim.

With regard to article 9, States parties should provide information on any laws or practices which may deprive women of their liberty on an arbitrary or unequal basis, such as by confinement within the house. As regards articles 7 and 10, States parties must provide all information relevant to ensuring that the rights of persons deprived of their liberty are protected on equal terms for men and women. In particular, States parties should report on whether men and women are separated in prisons and whether women are guarded only by female guards. States parties should also report about compliance with the rule that accused juvenile females shall be separated from adults and on any difference in treatment between male and female persons deprived of liberty, such as access to rehabilitation and education programmes and to conjugal and family visits. Pregnant women who are deprived of their liberty should receive humane treatment and respect for their inherent dignity at all times, and in particular during the birth and while caring for their newborn children; States parties should report on facilities to ensure this and on medical and health care for such mothers and their babies.

As regards article 12, States parties should provide information on any legal provision or any practice which restricts women's right to freedom of movement, for example the exercise of marital powers over the wife or of parental powers over adult daughters; legal or de facto requirements which prevent women from travelling, such as the requirement of consent of a third party to the issuance of a passport or other type of travel documents to an adult woman. States parties should also report on measures taken to eliminate such laws and practices and to protect women against them, including reference to available domestic remedies. States parties should ensure that alien women are accorded on an equal basis the right to submit arguments against their expulsion and to have their case reviewed, as provided in article 13. In this regard, they should be entitled to submit arguments based on gender-specific violations of the Covenant such as those mentioned in paragraphs 10 and 11 above.

States parties should provide information to enable the Committee to ascertain whether access to justice and the right to a fair trial, provided for in article 14, are enjoyed by women on equal terms with men. In particular, States parties should inform the Committee whether there are legal provisions preventing women from direct and autonomous access to the courts; whether women may give evidence as witnesses on the same terms as men; and whether measures are taken to ensure women equal access to legal aid, in particular in family matters. States parties should report on whether certain categories of women are denied the enjoyment of the presumption of innocence under article 14, paragraph 2, and on the measures which have been taken to put an end to this situation.

The right of everyone under article 16 to be recognized everywhere as a person before the law is particularly pertinent for women, who often see it curtailed by reason of sex or marital status. This right implies that the capacity of women to own property, to enter into a contract or to exercise other civil rights may not be restricted on the basis of marital status or any other discriminatory ground. It also implies that women may not be treated as objects to be given, together with the property of the deceased husband, to his family. States must provide information on laws or practices that prevent women from being treated or from functioning as full legal persons and the measures taken to eradicate laws or practices that allow such treatment. States parties must provide information to enable the Committee to assess the effect of any laws and practices that may interfere with women's right to enjoy privacy and other rights protected by article 17 on the basis of equality with men.

An example of such interference arises where the sexual life of a woman is taken into consideration in deciding the extent of her legal rights and protections, including protection against rape. Another area where States may fail to respect women's privacy relates to their reproductive functions, for example, where there is a requirement for the husband's authorization to make a decision in regard to sterilization; where general requirements are imposed for the sterilization of women, such as having a certain number of children or being of a certain age, or where States impose a legal duty upon doctors and other health personnel to report cases of women who have undergone abortion. In these instances, other rights in the Covenant, such as those of articles 6 and 7, might also be at stake. Women's privacy may also be interfered with by private actors, such as employers who request a pregnancy test before hiring a woman.

States parties should report on any laws and public or private actions that interfere with the equal enjoyment by women of the rights under article 17, and on the measures taken to eliminate such interference and to afford women protection from any such interference. States parties must take measures to ensure that freedom of thought, conscience and religion, and the freedom to adopt the religion or belief of one's choice - including the freedom to change religion or belief and to express one's religion or belief - will be guaranteed and protected in law and in practice for both men and women, on the same terms and without discrimination. These freedoms, protected by article 18, must not be subject to restrictions other than those authorized by the Covenant and must not be constrained by, *inter alia*, rules requiring permission from third parties, or by interference from fathers, husbands, brothers or others.

Article 18 may not be relied upon to justify discrimination against women by reference to freedom of thought, conscience and religion; States parties should therefore provide information on the status of women as regards their freedom of thought, conscience and religion, and indicate what steps they have taken or intend to take both to eliminate and prevent infringements of these freedoms in respect of women and to protect their right not to be discriminated against. In relation to article 19, States parties should inform the Committee of any laws or other factors which may impede women from exercising the rights protected under this provision on an equal basis. As the publication and dissemination of obscene and pornographic material which portrays women and girls as objects of violence or degrading or inhuman treatment is likely to promote these kinds of treatment of women and girls, States parties should provide information about legal measures to restrict the publication or dissemination of such material.

States are required to treat men and women equally in regard to marriage in accordance with article 23, which has been elaborated further by General Comment No. 19 (1990). Men and women have the right to enter into marriage only with their free and full consent, and States have an obligation to protect the enjoyment of this right on an equal basis. Many factors may prevent women from being able to make the decision to marry freely. One factor relates to the minimum age for marriage. That age should be set by the State on the basis of equal criteria for men and women. These criteria should ensure women's capacity to make an informed and uncoerced decision. A second factor in some States may be that either by statutory or customary law a guardian, who is generally male, consents to the marriage instead of the woman herself, thereby preventing women from exercising a free choice. Another factor that may affect women's right to marry only when they have given free and full consent is the existence of social attitudes which tend to marginalize women victims of rape and put pressure on them to agree to marriage.

A woman's free and full consent to marriage may also be undermined by laws which allow the rapist to have his criminal responsibility extinguished or mitigated if he marries the victim. States parties should indicate whether marrying the victim extinguishes or mitigates criminal responsibility and, in the case in which the victim is a minor, whether the rape reduces the marriageable age of the victim, particularly in societies where rape victims have to endure marginalization from society. A different aspect of the right to marry may be affected when States impose restrictions on remarriage by women that are not imposed on men. Also, the right to choose one's spouse may be restricted by laws or practices that prevent the marriage of a woman of a particular religion to a man who professes no religion or a different religion. States should provide information on these laws and practices and on the measures taken to abolish the laws and eradicate the practices which undermine the right of women to marry only when they have given free and full consent. It should also be noted that equality of treatment with regard to the right to marry implies that polygamy is incompatible with this principle.

Polygamy violates the dignity of women. It is an inadmissible discrimination against women. Consequently, it should be definitely abolished wherever it continues to exist. To fulfil their obligations under article 23, paragraph 4, States parties must ensure that the matrimonial regime contains equal rights and obligations for both spouses with regard to the custody and care of children, the children's religious and moral education, the capacity to transmit to children the parent's nationality, and the ownership or administration of property, whether common property or property in the sole ownership of either spouse. States parties should review their legislation to ensure that married women have equal rights in regard to the ownership and administration of such property, where necessary. Also, States parties should ensure that no sex-based discrimination occurs in respect of the acquisition or loss of nationality by reason of marriage, of residence rights, and of the right of each spouse to retain the use of his or her original family name or to participate on an equal basis in the choice of a new family name.

Equality during marriage implies that husband and wife should participate equally in responsibility and authority within the family. States parties must also ensure equality in regard to the dissolution of marriage, which excludes the possibility of repudiation. The grounds for divorce and annulment should be the same for men and women, as well as decisions with regard to property distribution, alimony and the custody of children. Determination of the need to maintain contact between children and the non-custodial parent should be based on equal considerations. Women should also have equal inheritance rights to those of men when the dissolution of marriage is caused by the death of one of the spouses. In giving effect to recognition of the family in the context of article 23, it is important to accept the concept of the various forms of family, including unmarried couples and their children and single parents and their children, and to ensure the equal treatment of women in these contexts.

Single-parent families frequently consist of a single woman caring for one or more children, and States parties should describe what measures of support are in place to enable her to discharge her parental functions on the basis of equality with a man in a similar position. The obligation of States parties to protect children (art. 24) should be carried out equally for boys and girls. States parties should report on measures taken to ensure that girls are treated equally to boys in education, in feeding and in health care, and provide the Committee with disaggregated data in this respect. States parties should eradicate, both through legislation and any other appropriate measures, all cultural or religious practices which jeopardize the freedom and well-being of female children. The right to participate in the conduct of public affairs is not fully implemented everywhere on an equal basis. States parties must ensure that the law guarantees to women the rights contained in article 25 on equal terms with men and take effective and positive measures to promote and ensure women's participation in the conduct of public affairs and in public office, including appropriate affirmative action.

Effective measures taken by States parties to ensure that all persons entitled to vote are able to exercise that right should not be discriminatory on the grounds of sex. The Committee requires States parties to provide statistical information on the percentage of women in publicly elected office, including the legislature, as well as in high-ranking civil service positions and the judiciary. Discrimination against women is often intertwined with discrimination on other grounds such as race, colour, language, religion, political or other opinion, national or social origin, property, birth or other status. States parties should address the ways in which any instances of discrimination on other grounds affect women in a particular way, and include information on the measures taken to counter these effects. The right to equality before the law and freedom from discrimination, protected by article 26, requires States to act against discrimination by public and private agencies in all fields.

Discrimination against women in areas such as social security laws as well as in the area of citizenship or rights of non-citizens in a country violates article 26. The commission of so-called "honour crimes" which remain unpunished constitutes a serious violation of the Covenant and in particular of articles 6, 14 and 26. Laws which impose more severe penalties on women than on men for adultery or other offences also violate the requirement of equal treatment. The Committee has also often observed in reviewing States parties reports that a large proportion of women are employed in areas which are not protected by labour laws and that prevailing customs and traditions discriminate against women, particularly with regard to access to better paid employment and to equal pay for work of equal value. States parties should review their legislation and practices and take the lead in implementing all measures necessary to eliminate discrimination against women in all fields, for example by prohibiting discrimination by private actors in areas such as employment, education, political activities and the provision of accommodation, goods and services.

States parties should report on all these measures and provide information on the remedies available to victims of such discrimination. The rights which persons belonging to minorities enjoy under article 27 of the Covenant in respect of their language, culture and religion do not authorize any State, group or person to violate the right to the equal enjoyment by women of any Covenant rights, including the right to equal protection of the law. States should report on any legislation or administrative practices related to membership in a minority community that might constitute an infringement of the equal rights of women under the Covenant and on measures taken or envisaged to ensure the equal right of men and women to enjoy all civil and political rights in the Covenant. Likewise, States should report on measures taken to discharge their responsibilities in relation to cultural or religious practices within minority communities that affect the rights of women. In their reports, States parties should pay attention to the contribution made by women to the cultural life of their communities.

THE ENJOYMENT OF ALL ECONOMIC, SOCIAL AND CULTURAL RIGHTS

The equal right of men and women to the enjoyment of all human rights is one of the fundamental principles recognized under international law and enshrined in the main international human rights instruments. The International Covenant on Economic, Social and Cultural Rights (ICESCR) protects human rights that are fundamental to the dignity of every person. In particular, this Covenant provides for the equal right of men and women to the enjoyment of the rights it articulates. This provision is founded on Article 1, paragraph 3, of the United Nations Charter and the Universal Declaration of Human Rights. Except for the reference to ICESCR, it is identical to the International Covenant on Civil and Political Rights (ICCPR), which was drafted at the same time.

The travaux préparatoires state was included in the Covenant, as well as in ICCPR, to indicate that beyond a prohibition of discrimination, "the same rights should be expressly recognized for men and women on an equal footing and suitable measures should be taken to ensure that women had the opportunity to exercise their rights .... Moreover, even if overlapped with, it was still necessary to reaffirm the equality rights between men and women. That fundamental principle, which was enshrined in the Charter of the United Nations, must be constantly emphasized, especially as there were still many prejudices preventing its full application". Unlike article 26 of ICCPR, of ICESCR are not stand-alone provisions, but should be read in conjunction with each specific right guaranteed under part III of the Covenant.

ICESCR provides for a guarantee of non-discrimination on the basis of sex among other grounds. This provision, and the guarantee of equal enjoyment of rights by men and women, is integrally related and mutually reinforcing. Moreover, the elimination of discrimination is fundamental to the enjoyment of economic, social and cultural rights on a basis of equality. The Committee on Economic, Social and Cultural Rights (CESCR) has taken particular note of factors negatively affecting the equal right of men and women to the enjoyment of economic, social and cultural rights in many of its general comments, including those on the right to adequate housing, the right to adequate food, the right to education, the right to the highest attainable standard of health, and the right to water. The Committee also routinely requests information on the equal enjoyment by men and women of the rights guaranteed under the Covenant in its list of issues in relation to States parties' reports and during its dialogue with States parties.

Women are often denied equal enjoyment of their human rights, in particular by virtue of the lesser status ascribed to them by tradition and custom, or as a result of overt or covert discrimination. Many women experience distinct forms of discrimination due to the intersection of sex with such factors as race, colour, language, religion, political and other opinion, national or social origin, property, birth, or other status, such as age, ethnicity, disability, marital, refugee or migrant status, resulting in compounded disadvantage.

CONCEPTUAL FRAMEWORK

Equality

The essence of ICESCR is that the rights set forth in the Covenant are to be enjoyed by men and women on a basis of equality, a concept that carries substantive meaning. While expressions of formal equality may be found in constitutional provisions, legislation and policies of Governments, also mandates the equal enjoyment of the rights in the Covenant for men and women in practice. The enjoyment of human rights on the basis of equality between men and women must be understood comprehensively. Guarantees of non-discrimination and equality in international human rights treaties mandate both de facto and de jure equality. De jure (or formal) equality and de facto (or substantive) equality are different but interconnected concepts.

Formal equality assumes that equality is achieved if a law or policy treats men and women in a neutral manner. Substantive equality is concerned, in addition, with the effects of laws, policies and practices and with ensuring that they do not maintain, but rather alleviate, the inherent disadvantage that particular groups experience. Substantive equality for men and women will not be achieved simply through the enactment of laws or the adoption of policies that are, prima facie, gender-neutral. In implementing, States parties should take into account that such laws, policies and practice can fail to address or even perpetuate inequality between men and women because they do not take account of existing economic, social and cultural inequalities, particularly those experienced by women.

States parties must respect the principle of equality in and before the law. The principle of equality in the law must be respected by the legislature when adopting laws, by ensuring that those laws further equal enjoyment of economic, social and cultural rights by men and women. The principle of equality before the law must be respected by administrative agencies, and courts and tribunals, and implies that those authorities must apply the law equally to men and women.

Non-discrimination

The principle of non-discrimination is the corollary of the principle of equality. Subject to what is stated below on temporary special measures, it prohibits differential treatment of a person or group of persons based on his/her or their particular status or situation, such as race, colour, sex, language, religion, political and other opinion, national or social origin, property, birth, or other status, such as age, ethnicity, disability, marital, refugee or migrant status. Discrimination against women is "any distinction, exclusion or restriction made on the basis of sex which has the effect or purpose of impairing or nullifying the recognition, enjoyment or exercise by women, irrespective of their marital status, on a basis of equality of men and women, of human rights and fundamental freedoms in the political, economic, social, cultural, civil or any other field" Discrimination on the basis of sex may be based on the differential treatment of women because of their biology, such as refusal to hire women because they could become pregnant; or stereotypical assumptions, such as tracking women into low-level jobs on the assumption that they are unwilling to commit as much time to their work as men.

Direct discrimination occurs when a difference in treatment relies directly and explicitly on distinctions based exclusively on sex and characteristics of men or of women, which cannot be justified objectively. Indirect discrimination occurs when a law, policy or programme does not appear to be discriminatory, but has a discriminatory effect when implemented. This can occur, for example, when women are disadvantaged compared to men with respect to the enjoyment of a particular opportunity or benefit due to pre-existing inequalities. Applying a gender-neutral law may leave the existing inequality in place, or exacerbate it.

Gender affects the equal right of men and women to the enjoyment of their rights. Gender refers to cultural expectations and assumptions about the behaviour, attitudes, personality traits, and physical and intellectual capacities of men and women, based solely on their identity as men or women. Gender-based assumptions and expectations generally place women at a disadvantage with respect to substantive enjoyment of rights, such as freedom to act and to be recognized as autonomous, fully capable adults, to participate fully in economic, social and political development, and to make decisions concerning their circumstances and conditions. Gender-based assumptions about economic, social and cultural roles preclude the sharing of responsibility between men and women in all spheres that is necessary to equality.

Temporary special measures

The principles of equality and non-discrimination, by themselves, are not always sufficient to guarantee true equality. Temporary special measures may sometimes be needed in order to bring disadvantaged or marginalized persons or groups of persons to the same substantive level as others. Temporary special measures aim at realizing not only de jure or formal equality, but also de facto or substantive equality for men and women. However, the application of the principle of equality will sometimes require that States parties take measures in favour of women in order to attenuate or suppress conditions that perpetuate discrimination. As long as these measures are necessary to redress de facto discrimination and are terminated when de facto equality is achieved, such differentiation is legitimate.

STATES PARTIES' OBLIGATIONS

General legal Obligations

The equal right of men and women to the enjoyment of economic, social and cultural rights is a mandatory and immediate obligation of States parties. The equal right of men and women to the enjoyment of economic, social and cultural rights, like all human rights, imposes three levels of obligations on States parties - the obligation to respect, to protect and to fulfil. The obligation to fulfil further contains duties to provide, promote and facilitate sets a non-derogable standard for compliance with the obligations of States parties as set out of ICESCR.

Specific legal obligations

Obligation to respect

The obligation to respect requires States parties to refrain from discriminatory actions that directly or indirectly result in the denial of the equal right of men and women to their enjoyment of economic, social and cultural rights. Respecting the right obliges States parties not to adopt, and to repeal laws and rescind, policies, administrative measures and programmes that do not conform with the right protected. In particular, it is incumbent upon States parties to take into account the effect of apparently gender-neutral laws, policies and programmes and to consider whether they could result in a negative impact on the ability of men and women to enjoy their human rights on a basis of equality.

Obligation to protect

The obligation to protect requires States parties to take steps aimed directly at the elimination of prejudices, customary and all other practices that perpetuate the notion of inferiority or superiority of either of the sexes, and stereotyped roles for men and women. States parties' obligation to protect under ICESCR includes, inter alia, the respect and adoption of constitutional and legislative provisions on the equal right of men and women to enjoy all human rights and the prohibition of discrimination of any kind; the adoption of legislation to eliminate discrimination and to prevent third parties from interfering directly or indirectly with the enjoyment of this right; the adoption of administrative measures and programmes, as well as the establishment of public institutions, agencies and programmes to protect women against discrimination.

States parties have an obligation to monitor and regulate the conduct of non-State actors to ensure that they do not violate the equal right of men and women to enjoy economic, social and cultural rights. This obligation applies, for example, in cases where public services have been partially or fully privatized.

Obligation to fulfill

The obligation to fulfill requires States parties to take steps to ensure that in practice, men and women enjoy their economic, social and cultural rights on a basis of equality. Such steps should include:

- To make available and accessible appropriate remedies, such as compensation, reparation, restitution, rehabilitation, guarantees of non-repetition, declarations, public apologies, educational programmes and prevention programmes;
- To establish appropriate venues for redress such as courts and tribunals or administrative mechanisms that are accessible to all on the basis of equality, including the poorest and most disadvantaged and marginalized men and women;
- To develop monitoring mechanisms to ensure that the implementation of laws and policies aimed at promoting

the equal enjoyment of economic, social and cultural rights by men and women do not have unintended adverse effects on disadvantaged or marginalized individuals or groups, particularly women and girls;

- To design and implement policies and programmes to give long-term effect to the economic, social and cultural rights of both men and women on the basis of equality. These may include the adoption of temporary special measures to accelerate women's equal enjoyment of their rights, gender audits, and gender-specific allocation of resources;
- To conduct human rights education and training programmes for judges and public officials;
- To conduct awareness-raising and training programmes on equality for workers involved in the realization of economic, social and cultural rights at the grass-roots level;
- To integrate, in formal and non-formal education, the principle of the equal right of men and women to the enjoyment of economic, social and cultural rights, and to promote equal participation of men and women, boys and girls, in schools and other education programmes;
- To promote equal representation of men and women in public office and decision-making bodies;
- To promote equal participation of men and women in development planning, decision-making and in the benefits of development and all programmes related to the realization of economic, social and cultural rights.

SPECIFIC EXAMPLES OF STATES PARTIES' OBLIGATIONS

A cross-cutting obligation and applies to all the rights contained to 15 of the Covenant. It requires addressing gender-based social and cultural prejudices, providing for equality in the allocation of resources, and promoting the sharing of responsibilities in the family, community and public life. The examples provided in the following paragraphs may be taken as guidance on the ways in which article 3 applies to other rights in the Covenant, but are not intended to be exhaustive.

The Covenant requires States parties to safeguard the right of everyone to the opportunity to gain a living by work which is freely chosen or accepted and to take the necessary steps to achieve the full realization of this right. Implementing, in relation to article 6, requires inter alia, that in law and in practice, men and women have equal access to jobs at all levels and all occupations and that vocational training and guidance programmes, in both the public and private sectors, provide men and women with the skills, information and knowledge necessary for them to benefit equally from the right to work. The Covenant requires States parties to recognize the right of everyone to enjoy just and favourable conditions of work and to ensure, among other things, fair wages and equal pay for work of equal value requires, inter alia, that the State party identify and eliminate the underlying causes of pay differentials, such as gender-biased job evaluation or the perception that productivity differences between men and women exist. Furthermore, the State party should monitor compliance by the private sector with national legislation on working conditions through an effectively functioning labour inspectorate.

The State party should adopt legislation that prescribes equal consideration in promotion, non-wage compensation and equal opportunity and support for vocational or professional development in the workplace. Finally, the State party should reduce the constraints faced by men and women in reconciling professional and family responsibilities by promoting adequate policies for childcare and care of dependent family members. The Covenant requires States parties to ensure the right of everyone to form and join trade unions of his or her choice, requires allowing men and women to organize and join workers' associations that address their specific concerns. In this regard, particular attention should be given to domestic workers, rural women, women working in female-dominated industries and women working at home, who are often deprived of this right.

The Covenant requires that States parties recognize the right of everyone to social security, including social insurance, and to equal access to social services. Implementing, requires, inter alia, equalizing the compulsory retirement age for both men and women; ensuring that women receive the equal benefit of public and private pension schemes; and guaranteeing adequate maternity leave for women, paternity leave for men, and parental leave for both men and women. Article 10, paragraph 1, of the Covenant requires that States parties recognize that the widest possible protection and assistance should be accorded to the family, and that marriage must be entered into with the free consent of the intending spouses.

Implementing article 3, in relation to article 10, requires States parties, inter alia, to provide victims of domestic violence, who are primarily female, with access to safe housing, remedies and redress for physical, mental and emotional damage; to ensure that men and women have an equal right to choose if, whom and when to marry - in particular, the legal age of marriage for men and women should be the same, and boys and girls should be protected equally from practices that promote child marriage, marriage by proxy, or coercion; and to ensure that women have equal rights to marital property and inheritance upon their husband's death. Gender-based violence is a form of discrimination that inhibits the ability to enjoy rights and freedoms, including economic, social and cultural rights, on a basis of equality.

States parties must take appropriate measures to eliminate violence against men and women and act with due diligence to prevent, investigate, mediate, punish and redress acts of violence against them by private actors. Article 11 of the Covenant requires States parties to recognize the right of everyone to an adequate standard of living for him/herself and his/her family, including adequate housing(para. 1) and adequate food (para. 2). Implementing article 3, in relation to article 11, paragraph 1, requires that women have a right to own, use or otherwise control housing, land and property on an equal basis with men, and to access necessary resources to do so. Implementing article 3, in relation to article 11, paragraph 2, also requires States parties, inter alia, to ensure that women have access to or control over means of food production, and actively to address customary practices under which women are not allowed to eat until the men are fully fed, or are only allowed less nutritious food.

Article 12 of the Covenant requires States parties to undertake steps towards the full realization of the right of everyone to the enjoyment of the highest attainable standard of physical and mental health. The implementation of article 3, in relation to article 12, requires at a minimum the removal of legal and other obstacles that prevent men and women from accessing and benefiting from health care on a basis of equality. This includes, inter alia, addressing the ways in which gender roles affect access to determinants of health, such as water and food; the removal of legal restrictions on reproductive health provisions; the prohibition of female genital mutilation; and the provision of adequate training for health-care workers to deal with women's health issues.

Article 13, paragraph 1, of the Covenant requires States parties to recognize the right of everyone to education and in paragraph 2 (a) stipulates that primary education shall be compulsory and available free to all. Implementing article 3, in relation to article 13, requires, inter alia, the adoption of legislation and policies to ensure the same admission criteria for boys and girls at all levels of education. States parties should ensure, in particular through information and awareness-raising campaigns, that families desist from giving preferential treatment to boys when sending their children to school, and that curricula promote equality and non-discrimination. States parties must create favourable conditions to ensure the safety of children, in particular girls, on their way to and from school.

Article 15, paragraph 1 (a) and (b), of the Covenant require States parties to recognize the right of everyone to take part in cultural life and to enjoy the benefits of scientific progress. Implementing article 3, in relation to article 15, paragraph 1 (a) and (b), requires, inter alia, overcoming institutional barriers and other obstacles, such as those based on cultural and religious traditions, which prevent women from fully participating in cultural life, science education and scientific research, and directing resources to scientific research relating to the health and economic needs of women on an equal basis with those of men.

IMPLEMENTATION AT THE NATIONAL LEVEL

Policies and Strategies

The most appropriate ways and means of implementing the right under article 3 of the Covenant will vary from one State party to another. Every State party has a margin of discretion in adopting appropriate measures in complying with its primary and immediate obligation to ensure the equal right of men and women to the enjoyment of all their economic, social and cultural rights. Among other things, States parties must, integrate into national plans of action for human rights appropriate strategies to ensure the equal right of men and women to the enjoyment of economic, social and cultural rights. These strategies should be based on the systematic identification of policies, programmes and activities relevant to the situation and context within the State, as derived from the normative content of article 3 of the Covenant and spelled out in relation to the levels and nature of States parties' obligations referred to in paragraphs 16 to 21 above.

The strategies should give particular attention to the elimination of discrimination in the enjoyment of economic, social and cultural rights. States parties should periodically review existing legislation, policies, strategies and programmes in relation to economic, social and cultural rights, and adopt any necessary changes to ensure that they are consonant with their obligations under article 3 of the Covenant. The adoption of temporary special measures may be necessary to accelerate the equal enjoyment by women of all economic, social and cultural rights and to improve the de facto position of women. Temporary special measures should be distinguished from permanent policies and strategies undertaken to achieve equality of men and women.

States parties are encouraged to adopt temporary special measures to accelerate the achievement of equality between men and women in the enjoyment of the rights under the Covenant. Such measures are not to be considered discriminatory in themselves as they are grounded in the State's obligation to eliminate disadvantage caused by past and current discriminatory laws, traditions and practices. The nature, duration and application of such measures should be designed with reference to the specific issue and context, and should be adjusted as circumstances require. The results of such measures should be monitored with a view to being discontinued when the objectives for which they are undertaken have been achieved. The right of individuals and groups of individuals to participate in decision-making processes that may affect their development must be an integral component of any policy, programme or activity developed to discharge governmental obligations under article 3 of the Covenant.

Remedies and accountability

National policies and strategies should provide for the establishment of effective mechanisms and institutions where they do not exist, including administrative authorities, ombudsmen and other national human rights institutions, courts and tribunals. These institutions should investigate and address alleged violations relating to article 3 and provide remedies for such violations. States parties, for their part, should ensure that such remedies are effectively implemented.

Indicators and benchmarks

National policies and strategies should identify appropriate indicators and benchmarks on the right to equal enjoyment by men and women of economic, social and cultural rights in order to effectively monitor the implementation by the State party of its obligations under the Covenant in this regard. Disaggregated statistics, provided within specific time frames, are necessary to measure the progressive realization of economic, social and cultural rights by men and women, where appropriate.

VIOLATIONS

States parties must fulfill their immediate and primary obligation to ensure the equal right of men and women to the enjoyment of economic, social and cultural rights. The principle of equality between men and women is fundamental to the enjoyment of each of the specific rights enumerated in the Covenant. Failure to ensure formal and substantive equality in the enjoyment of any of these rights constitutes a violation of that right. Elimination of de jure as well as de facto discrimination is required for the equal enjoyment of economic, social and cultural rights.

Failure to adopt, implement and monitor effects of laws, policies and programmes to eliminate de jure and de facto discrimination with respect to each of the rights enumerated in articles 6 to 15 of the Covenant constitutes a violation of those rights. Violations of the rights contained in the Covenant can occur through the direct action of, failure to act or omission by States parties, or through their institutions or agencies at the national and local levels. The adoption and undertaking of any retrogressive measures that affect the equal right of men and women to the enjoyment of the all the rights set forth in the Covenant constitutes a violation of article 3.

WOMEN'S RIGHT TO FOOD AS A HUMAN RIGHT

Across the world, women are treated unequally and less value is placed on their lives because of their sex. Women's differential access to power and control of resources is central to this discrimination in all institutional spheres, i.e. the household, community, market, and state. Within the household women and girls can face discrimination in the sharing out of household resources including food, sometimes leading to higher malnutrition and mortality indicators for women. Because of their lower social and economic status, as well as their physiological needs, women are often more vulnerable to nutritional problems. Poor female nutrition early in life reduces learning potential, increases reproductive and maternal health risks, and lowers productivity. This situation contributes to women's diminished ability to gain access to other assets later in life and undermines attempts to eliminate gender inequalities.

In essence, women with poor nutrition are caught in a vicious circle of poverty and under nutrition. Considering the role women have in the household, with regard to food production, food preparation and child care, gender inequality in access to and control of resources may well result in misallocation of scarce resources, increased health care costs, lowered productivity, and poor human development trends. Investment in women's nutrition returns to improving household nutrition and overall human development capacity for a country. In September 2000, the Millennium Development Goals marked a significant step towards the achievement of fundamental human rights by setting 8 priority objectives, among them: promoting gender equality and empowering women.

INSTRUMENTS PROTECTING WOMEN'S RIGHT TO FOOD

International standards

Efforts to consider food as a human right date back to the early years of the United Nations (UN). Sensitivity to the problem was visible even prior to the establishment of the UN when, in January 1941, American President Franklin D. Roosevelt, in his "State of the Union" address, since known as the 'Four Freedoms' speech, coined the notion of 'freedom from want'. Roosevelt's vision provided an important basis for the drawing up of the Universal Declaration of Human Rights (UDHR), through which the right to food achieved formal recognition in international law.

"Everyone has the right to a standard of living adequate for the health and well-being of himself and his family, including food...". Thus the UDHR, adopted the United Nations (UN) General Assembly in 1948. Furthermore "everyone is entitled to all the rights and freedoms set forth in this Declaration, without distinction of any kind, such as race, colour, sex, language, religion, political or other opinion, national or social origin, property, birth or other status". Being a declaration of principles, a so called 'soft law act', the UDHR does not create binding obligations. However, it can be argued that the solemn nature and significance of the UDHR, and the broad consensus it received among States, reflects a strong desire to respect the principles contained therein. To the extent that such desire was confirmed by the practice of States, the UDHR could be considered customary international law, containing binding rules for States.

Eighteen years after the UDHR, the ICESCR, to date ratified by 156 States, marked a significant positive step, making the right to food a rule of binding international law for the States Parties. The ICESCR deepened the right to food concept. Article 11, which can be considered the core provision with regard to the right to food and its protection under international law, confirms "the right to adequate food", adding "the fundamental right of everyone to be free from hunger". Referring to "freedom from hunger" meant that the ICESCR deepened the right to food concept. Article 11, which can be considered the core provision with regard to the right to food and its protection under international law, confirms "the right to adequate food", adding "the fundamental right of everyone to be free from hunger".

Referring to "freedom from hunger" meant that the state would commit itself to ensuring that its people did not starve, at the very least. In this way, the right to be free from hunger was closely related to the right to life as spelled out for instance in article 3 of the UDHR, article 6 of the International Covenant on Civil and Political Rights (ICCPR) and article 6 of the Convention on the Rights of the Child (CRC). "The States Parties to the present Covenant undertake to guarantee that the rights enunciated in the present Covenant will be exercised without discrimination of any kind as to race, colour, sex, language, religion, political or other opinion, national or social origin, property, birth or other status" and in article 3 "The States Parties to the present Covenant undertake to ensure the equal right of men and women to the enjoyment of all economic, social and cultural rights set forth in the present Covenant".

Protecting the right to food for all in a non-discriminatory manner, implies giving particular attention to women, leading to what is known as *positive discrimination/affirmative action*. In General Comment 11, the Committee on Economic, Social and Cultural Rights (CESCR) explains: "The adoption of temporary special measures intended to bring about *de facto* equality for men and women and for disadvantaged groups is not a violation of the right to non-discrimination, so long as such measures do not lead to the maintenance of unequal or separate standards for different groups, and provided they are not continued after the objectives for which they were taken have been achieved."

The Committee further stressed the importance of giving "particular attention to the need to prevent discrimination in access to food or resources for food. This should include: guarantees of full and equal access to economic resources, particularly for women, including the right to inheritance and the ownership of land and other property, credit, natural resources and appropriate technology; measures to respect and protect self-employment and work which provides a remuneration ensuring a decent living for wage earners and their families (as stipulated in article 7 (a) (ii) of the Covenant); maintaining registries on rights in land (including forests)."

The Convention on the Rights of the Child (CRC), adopted by the UN in 1989, affirms, in article 24: "States Parties recognise the right of the child to the enjoyment of the highest attainable standard of health. States Parties shall pursue full implementation of this right and, in particular, shall take appropriate measures...to combat disease and malnutrition, including within the framework of primary health care, through, inter alia, the application of readily-available technology and through the provision of adequate, nutritious food". Furthermore, at article 27: "States Parties recognize the right of every child to a standard of living adequate for the child physical, mental, spiritual, moral and social development". This provision recalls the wording of article 25 of the Universal Declaration of Human Rights, and of article 11 of the International Covenant on Economic, Social and

Cultural Rights and it spells out States obligations with particular regard to nutrition, clothing and housing.

A particular dimension of the right to food is that of armed conflict. International Humanitarian Law (IHL) deals with this issue through provisions in the Geneva Conventions of 1949 and their Optional Protocols. Although IHL does not, proclaim the right to food as such, it sets out rules to protect access to food and prohibit denial of food, as a preventive function, as well as rules related to humanitarian assistance for the civilian population. In particular, article 54 of Additional Protocol I regarding the protection of objects indispensable for the survival of the civilian population, states: "Starvation of civilians as a method of warfare is prohibited...". According to the 1998 Rome Statute of the International Criminal Court, "Intentionally using starvation of civilians as a method of warfare by depriving them of items indispensable to their survival, including wilfully impeding relief supplies as provided for under the Geneva Conventions, is a war crime when committed in international armed conflicts."

There are food related provisions in article 55 of the Fourth Geneva Convention, with regard to ensuring food to the population of occupied territories, and in article 49 relative to prohibition of displacement which contributes to starvation. Other relevant provisions can be found in the Convention Against Torture and Other Cruel, Inhumane or Degrading Treatment or Punishment (1984), which forbids starvation as a form of torture; and in the Convention on the Prevention and Punishment of the Crime of Genocide (1948). Article 2 of the Convention on the Suppression and Punishment of the Crime of Apartheid (1973) refers to the infliction of serious bodily harm and any form of torture or degrading treatment or punishment (including intentional starvation) as "inhumane acts".

The right to food in this sense becomes also a civil and political right, in addition to being an economic, social and cultural right. With particular regard to women, the Declaration on the Protection of Women and Children in Emergency and Armed Conflicts states, at article 6: "Women and children belonging to the civilian population and finding themselves in circumstances of emergency and armed conflict in the struggle for peace, self-determination, national liberation and independence, or who live in occupied territories, shall not be deprived of shelter, food, medical aid or other inalienable rights, in accordance with the provisions of the UDHR, the ICCPR, the ICESCR, the Declaration of the Rights of the Child or other instruments of international law."

Other relevant provisions are those in the ILO Conventions – for instance the Convention (No.111) concerning Discrimination in Respect of Employment and Occupation, 1958 and the Convention (No.100) concerning Equal Remuneration for Men and Women Workers for Work of Equal Value, 1951 - which if on the one hand do not specifically tackle the right to food, on the other, they cover issues related to it, such as for instance access to resources. Gender-specific provisions have been adopted also in instruments relating to issues such as environment and sustainable development: the Rio Declaration on Environment and Development, the Johannesburg Declaration on Sustainable Development and the Convention to Combat Desertification.

Moreover the international community solemnly affirmed its commitment to gender equality and women's empowerment at the Fourth World Conference on Women, in September 1995 (Beijing Declaration and Platform for Action), at the World Food Summits in 1996 and 2002. Most recently, women's rights in food issues have been reaffirmed in the Voluntary Guidelines on the Progressive Implementation of the Right to Adequate Food in the context of National Food Security (hereinafter Right to Food Guidelines), adopted by the FAO Council in November 2004. The document – which is voluntary in nature but which at the same time builds on international law and provides guidance on implementation of already existing bligations – encourages a gender perspective throughout its provisions and stresses equal rights of women, as well as special protection for pregnant women and mothers.

Overall, international law appears to provide a substantive legal framework for the protection of women's rights and for their right to food in particular. Surely some provisions are more developed than others due to a number of factors, historical circumstance and geopolitical and social contexts during times of adoption in *primis*. However, considering the fact that *de facto* protection of women's rights is so weak compared to *de iure* protection, the question arises: Where is the gap? What is missing? It could be argued that, in some cases, the law does not make sufficient provision to engage state actors or to empower individuals. International ruling must be followed by the national incorporation of norms, which need to be further elaborated and implemented according to domestic contexts.

Efforts should be made at the national level to build the legal capacity of right-holders to demand that their rights be respected and, at the same time, to build the capacity of duty-bearers to fulfil their obligations.

A close look at CEDAW

The instrument that deals more comprehensively with women's rights is the Convention on the Elimination of All Forms of Discrimination against Women. The Convention creates binding legal obligations to pursue "by all appropriate means and without delay, a policy of eliminating discrimination against women". (article 2) It also constitutes a powerful advocacy and awareness-raising tool to increase women's knowledge of their rights and capacity to claim these rights. Although the Convention does not specifically refer to the right to food as such, it protects women's equal access to land, credit, income and social security or safety nets, which are all essential elements for the full realization of the right to food.

The articles that can be seen as being most related to food are article 12 and article 14. In article 12: "...States Parties shall ensure to women appropriate services in connection with pregnancy, confinement and the post-natal period, granting free services where necessary, as well as adequate nutrition during pregnancy and lactation." In article 14.2: "States Parties shall take all appropriate measures to eliminate discrimination against women in rural areas in order to ensure, on a basis of equality of men and women, that they participate in and benefit from rural development and, in particular, shall ensure to such women the right: to enjoy adequate living conditions, particularly in relation to housing, sanitation, electricity and water supply, transport and communications."

These two articles refer to the right to food in dealing with two particular situations where women's vulnerability is high: pregnancy and rural livelihoods. Together with the rest of the norms condemning discrimination throughout the Convention, the two articles can be seen as providing a solid structure for the protection of women's right to food. However, something is missing. Is that a specific article on the right to food? Would that make a difference? Is the gap merely in implementation or could the Convention have provided for more? One aspect that could be stressed more in relation to violation of women's right to food is cultural food habits, which in many countries hamper women's enjoyment of the right to food on an equal footing with men.

We refer to household contexts where for instance women eat last or others where women are not allowed to eat certain foods, available only to men. In this regard, it should be noted that a number of reservations have been made to the Convention by Governments entering it on the grounds of culture and custom, by which much of the protection guaranteed by the Convention becomes meaningless. There is, of course, a need to protect culture and differences but that should not lead to the persistence of discrimination, or to violating human rights principles that are universal and overcome any cultural relativism. It should also be noted that within the context of economic, social and cultural rights, including the right to food, the obligation of non-discrimination is one of immediate effect and is not, therefore, limited by the provision of progressive realization applied to other obligations under the ICESCR (article 2.2).

Furthermore, the right to equality and non discrimination – recognized in UDHR, ICESCR and ICCPR, is considered in international law as having the character of ius cogens, status made explicit in the ICCPR where at article 4 it is stated that even when the life of a nation is threatened by a public emergency, although the parties may take steps derogating from certain obligations under the Covenant, such measures may not involve discrimination solely on the grounds of race, colour, sex, language, religion or social origin.

National protection

Quite apart from international law, a number of national Constitutions today protect the right to food, either through direct mention of the right (explicit recognition) or by including food as part of a broader right, such as health or an adequate standard of living, social security or minimum wage (implicit recognition).

At the national level, since the adoption of CEDAW, there has been significant progress in the recognition and implementation of the human rights of women and the right to food. The legal framework for equality has been strengthened in many countries, ensuring that *de iure* equality for women is now better established. Constitutions in many countries include provisions guaranteeing equality on the grounds of sex. Legislation prohibiting discrimination in general and with regard to specific areas, such as employment, has become a standard component of regulatory framework. Many countries have repealed discriminatory provisions in civil, penal and personal status codes to bring them into conformity with the Convention. New laws have been adopted to create protection and remedies for women.

Numerous laws prohibit discrimination and provide for equality of women, and States are required to act with due diligence to prevent, investigate and punish discrimination and violence against women committed by the State or private actors. Many countries have adopted national plans of action and established institutional machinery to follow up the Beijing Platform for Action. More generally, legislative reforms have brought about changes in family law (towards equality between spouses and full legal capacity of married women) in succession law (toward joint titling and the elimination of discriminatory norms in relation to access to land in agrarian reform programmes). In some cases, discrimination has been prohibited with specific regard to access to credit and to the exercise of self employment economic activities.

Moreover, women's legal status has been improved by judicial decisions declaring the unconstitutionality of discriminatory norms. However, in many countries the implementation of legislation protecting women's rights is constrained by entrenched cultural practices, lack of legal awareness, limited access to courts and lack of resources. These implementation problems are generally stronger in rural areas. In these cases, effective interventions to improve women's legal status need to include not only legislative reform but also steps to bridge the gap between law and practice. Often, socio-cultural practices have affected the application of statutory legislation. In some countries, discrimination is reflected in customary law and in others the existence of a pluralist system challenges women's right to food. However, even in cases where the law is comprehensive, and gender equality is established *de iure*, women continue to suffer from *de facto* discrimination: legal equality does not always amount to substantive equality. Normative content of the right to adequate food.

There has been considerable progress in understanding the meaning of the right to food, in developments that started in the 1980s and accelerated in the follow-up to the WFS of 1996, which called for the clarification of the right to food in Objective 7.4 of the Plan of Action. The seminal work of Mr Asbjørn Eide as Special Rapporteur of the Sub- Commission on the Prevention of Discrimination and Protection of Minorities in the 1980s had a positive influence but, given the global geopolitics, was perhaps somewhat before its time. In the follow-up to the WFS, the human rights community and FAO cooperated in achieving better understanding of the right to food and considering better ways of implementing it.

Efforts to clarify the right to food culminated in the adoption by the Committee on Economic, Social and Cultural Rights of

General Comment 12, which is generally considered to constitute an authoritative interpretation of article 11 of ICESCR. General Comment 12 affirms that the right to adequate food is indivisibly linked to the inherent dignity of the human person and is indispensable for the fulfilment of other human rights. According to General Comment 12, the realization of the right to adequate food requires: "the availability of food in a quantity and quality sufficient to satisfy the dietary needs of individuals, free from adverse substances, and acceptable within a given culture"; and "the accessibility of such food in ways that are sustainable and that do not interfere with the enjoyment of other human rights" (para 8). By "accessibility" the CESCR refers to both economic and physical accessibility.

The former relates to financial costs associated with the acquisition of food which should be such that the attainment and satisfaction of other basic needs are not threatened or compromised. The latter refers to food being physically accessible to everyone, including vulnerable people (para 13). General Comment 12 also provides guidance as to the implementation of the right to adequate food, looking into States' obligations. This particular aspect will be dealt with in the next section. The Special Rapporteur on the Right to Food elaborated on this definition and stated: "The right to food is the right to have regular, permanent and free access, either directly or by means of financial purchases, to quantitatively and qualitatively adequate and sufficient food corresponding to the cultural traditions of the people to which the consumer belongs, and which ensures a physical and mental, individual and collective, fulfilling and dignified life free of fear.

State obligations

Considering that States alone are Parties to the ICESCR, they are ultimately accountable for compliance with it and primarily responsible for the full realization of the right to food for all persons within their territory. Under international law, States have both progressive and immediate obligations to realize the rights contained in the Covenant. Under the terms of the ICESCR, "Each State Party to the present Covenant undertakes to take steps, individually and through international assistance and co-operation, especially economic and technical, to the maximum of its available resources, with a view to achieving progressively the full realization of the rights recognized in the present Covenant by all appropriate means, including particularly the adoption of legislative measures" (article 2.1).

The emphasis on "progressive realization" is due to the multifaceted nature of economic, social and cultural rights and to resource constraints. However steps towards achieving the full realization of these rights must be taken within reasonable time and should be deliberate, concrete and targeted. Regarding the way in which to achieve results, States have a margin of discretion in deciding on the most appropriate measures under given circumstances. States should take steps to the maximum of available resources, meaning that where resources are available, they should be used to enable people to exercise their rights, and not get diverted to other fields.

Furthermore, article 11.2 describes specific obligations pertaining particularly to the right to food: from improving methods of production, conservation and distribution to dissemination of knowledge and reforming the agrarian system. It should be noted that under this provision States must not only work towards the realization of the right to food, but also guarantee the fundamental right to be free from hunger - the only right qualified as 'fundamental' in the Covenant. This particular right guarantees protection against starvation at the very least, and is in this sense interpreted as referring to the minimum essential for people's survival. States obligation to ensure the right to freedom from hunger is of immediate effect and thus not subject to the condition of progressive realization.

General Comment 12 further examined the obligations emanating from the Covenant and in particular identified three types of obligations: to respect, protect and fulfil (facilitate and provide). In the light of women's right to food, which is the subject of this paper, the obligation to respect the right to food means that the State is obliged to refrain from doing anything that impedes women's existing access to food, water, land, income or other resources. The obligation to protect the right to food for women means that the State is obliged to protect women from all forms of discrimination by non-State actors, including discrimination in the workplace, in the private sphere, and in access to resources.

The obligation to fulfill the right to food for women means that Governments have a positive obligation to create an enabling environment to ensure that women have sufficient access to resources to be able to feed themselves and, as a final resort, to support women who, for reasons beyond their control, cannot feed themselves.

This positive obligation means that the State must take concrete positive action to improve the substantive equality of women and to challenge norms, traditions and customary laws that legitimate discrimination and violence against women, including within the family and within the household, particularly in relation to the allocation of food.

WOMEN, HUMAN RIGHTS AND INTERNATIONAL HUMANITARIAN LAW

The development in the last 50 years of the principles that comprise human rights law has had a major impact on international humanitarian law and indeed on international law generally. In more recent years, the movement for recognition of the equal rights of women has been exerting its own influence on human rights law and to some effect. In 1979, for example, the international community adopted the Convention on the Elimination of All Forms of Discrimination against Women (CEDAW), to which 155 States are now party.

Consideration is currently being given to the adoption of an Optional Protocol that will allow for individual and group complaints to be brought before the CEDAW Committee. Governmental and non-governmental organizations have increasingly focused on women's human rights.

As a result, a wide range of studies, reports and recommendations on various aspects of the issue is available. The topic of women is thus firmly established on the international human rights agenda. So much human suffering in today's world occurs, however, in situations of armed conflict, where to a large extent human rights are in abeyance, leaving individuals to rely solely on the protection offered by international humanitarian law. And women are major victims in these situations.

There is now evidence, moreover, that women experience conflict in a different way to men, a phenomenon that is confirmed by those working in the field. This distinctive experience, although its effects differ widely across cultures depending upon the role of women in each society, is related to the particular vulnerability of this group when armed conflict breaks out. War exacerbates the inequalities that exist in different forms and to varying degrees in all societies, and women make up 70 per cent of the world's population living in poverty.

They are, moreover, generally disadvantaged in terms of education and are considerably less mobile because of their traditional role in caring for others. Perhaps most significantly, women are generally excluded from access to power structures and participation in decision-making with regard to armed conflict. They are therefore unable to draw attention to the particular difficulties they experience in conflict situations and, moreover, are powerless to recommend any preventive action.

Against that background, the present article considers the extent to which the focus on women's human rights and the advances made in the protection of women under human rights law has had an impact on international humanitarian law. As will become apparent, this impact can be seen primarily in developments regarding the criminalization and punishment of sexual violence against women in armed conflicts. Broader consideration has yet to be given to the question of women, armed conflict and humanitarian law.

THE PROVISIONS OF THE LAW OF ARMED CONFLICT RELATING TO WOMEN AT THE TIME OF THE ADOPTION OF THE UNIVERSAL DECLARATION OF HUMAN RIGHTS

There were occasional references to the protection of women in some of the earliest documents of the law of armed conflict. For example, Article XLVII of the Lieber Code punished those responsible for the rape of inhabitants of a hostile country. Until recently, however, sexual violence against women was never taken seriously. Rape was not listed as a war crime at Nuremberg, despite the high incidence of sexual violence during the Second World War. Indictments before the Tokyo Tribunal did contain charges of rape and some individuals were convicted for their failure to ensure that subordinates complied with the law. Moreover, the occupying powers included rape as a war crime in the charters of their national courts set up to try offences committed in Germany, although no prosecutions were ever undertaken on this basis. Generally, however, rape and sexual violence against women were regarded as an inevitable aspect of armed conflict and seldom if ever prosecuted. The four 1949 Geneva Conventions, which at the time of their adoption were the major instruments protecting the victims of armed conflict (and with their two 1977 Protocols remain so today), contain some 19 provisions that are specifically relevant to women.

The scope of these rules is somewhat limited and many of them are in fact designed to protect children. Overall, the aim of the Conventions is to provide special protection for pregnant women, nursing mothers and mothers in general and to address the vulnerability of women to sexual violence in times of armed conflict. Significantly, Article 27(2) of the Fourth Geneva Convention contains the first provision specifically dealing with rape and requires that "women shall be especially protected against any attack on their honour, in particular against rape, enforced prostitution, or any form of indecent assault". Although this article constitutes a long overdue recognition that rape is unacceptable in times of armed conflict, the extent and gravity of the practice are not acknowledged since the provision falls outside the system of grave breaches of international humanitarian law (under this system States are obliged to seek out and punish persons responsible for failing to observe certain designated provisions of the Conventions). Article 27(2) has also been criticized on the grounds that, like many of the provisions relating to women, it categorizes rape as an attack on the victim's honour and thus does not reflect the seriousness of the offence of sexual violence.

Apart from the protection afforded under such articles, which is clearly valuable as far as it goes, any indication that the difficulties women experience in armed conflicts might be distinctive and encompass wider issues than their roles as mothers and victims of sexual violence is not discernible in the provisions of the Geneva Conventions. To what extent were the provisions of the 1977 Protocols relating to women influenced by the human rights movement? The movement to bring about further improvements in international humanitarian law that culminated in the adoption by States of the 1977 Protocols owed a great deal to developments in the area of human rights. Gerald Draper wrote that progress in the law of armed conflict "had come perilously close to stagnation before the impact of the movement for a regime of human rights was brought to bear". As early as 1956, the ICRC had completed a set of Draft Rules for the limitation of dangers incurred by the civilian population in time of war. No action was taken on these rules.

The question of further revision of the law of armed conflict was shelved by the international community until the work on human rights in peacetime undertaken by the United Nations Commission on Human Rights and the UN General Assembly began to expand logically into concern for human rights in armed conflict. The International Conference on Human Rights held in Tehran in 1968 can be seen as a watershed in this relationship. The final outcome of these initiatives was the adoption of the two 1977 Protocols, which have a distinct human rights flavour. The Protocols merge the respective principles of the so-called law of The Hague and law of Geneva and focus on the protection of civilians.

What is the approach of the Protocols to women victims of armed conflict? Does the emphasis on protection that underpinned the negotiations leading up to the adoption of these instruments and is reflected in their final text extend to recognition of the distinctive difficulties women experience in times of armed conflict? Overall, the approach to women remains unchanged in the provisions of the Protocols. The focus continues to be on protection for pregnant women and mothers. In the context of sexual violence, Article 76 of Protocol I contains the important comprehensive provision specifically protecting women against rape, although this practice is still not designated as a grave breach. There is no recognition, either in the travaux préparatoires or in the provisions themselves, of the other distinctive problems women face in armed conflicts.

WOMEN AND HUMAN RIGHTS

It would be misleading to represent the existing body of human rights law as a satisfactory regime from the perspective of women. Commentators have convincingly demonstrated the limitations of this law, which does not adequately take into account the reality of women's experience of the world. However, it is in the context of human rights law rather than humanitarian law that more progress has been made in recognizing and attempting to meet the as yet unaddressed needs of women. This attention to women's human rights has had substantial implications for international humanitarian law. Indeed, the fact that violence against women and strategies to contain it have been the focus of much of the work of human rights agencies concerned with this group has led to a consideration of the issue in connection with armed conflicts, where so much of the violence against women occurs. What have been some of the results of this work?

The 1993 Vienna Declaration and Programme of Action, adopted by the United Nations World Conference on Human Rights, confirmed that "violations of the human rights of women in situations of armed conflict are violations of the fundamental principles of human rights and humanitarian law" and that they require a "particularly effective response". The Programme of Action also stressed that "the equal status of women and the human rights of women" should be "integrated into the mainstream of United Nations system-wide activity" and "form an integral part of United Nations human rights activities." This growing movement to address the problem saw the adoption by the General Assembly in December 1993 of the Declaration on the Elimination of Violence Against Women. The Declaration expressly recognizes that women in situations of armed conflict are especially vulnerable to violence.

Another important development in the context of women and human rights during armed conflicts has been the appointment of Special Rapporteurs with mandates covering certain aspects of women's experience of armed conflict. In 1994 the United Nations Commission on Human Rights appointed Radhika Coomaraswamy as the Special Rapporteur on violence against women, with a mandate covering situations of armed conflict. In January 1998 the Special Rapporteur submitted her report on the subject, in which she recommended, in the context of international wars, that the Geneva Conventions be re-examined and re-evaluated so as to "incorporate developing norms against women during armed conflict". Additionally, in 1995 the United Nations Sub-Commission on Prevention of Discrimination and Protection of Minorities appointed Linda Chavez as Special Rapporteur on the situation of systematic rape, sexual slavery and slavery-like practices during periods of armed conflict. The Fourth UN World Conference on Women, held in Beijing in 1995, recognized the seriousness of armed conflict and its impact on the lives of women.

The Beijing Declaration referred to the determination of the participating States to "ensure respect for international law, including humanitarian law, in order to protect women and girls in particular". The Conference's Platform for Action identified women and armed conflict as one of the twelve critical areas of concern to be addressed by Member States, the international community and civil society. A remedial strategy identified in the Platform was to "increase the participation of women in conflict resolution at decision-making levels and protect women living in situations of armed and other conflicts or under foreign domination".

The process of identifying women's particular difficulties and demonstrating the failure of the law to acknowledge them is thus considerably more advanced within human rights bodies than within organizations focusing solely on armed conflict. Of course action plans, recommendations and proposals need to be implemented if they are to be of lasting value. Progress is slow and at times disheartening. There are, however, positive signs. Of particular significance in this context is the very effective work at the grass roots level of the UN High Commissioner for Refugees in relation to refugee women. All these efforts, whilst groundbreaking in nature, have focused almost exclusively on sexual violence. The broader context of the problem has been largely ignored. However, an exception to this limited view is evident, for example, in the work of the Economic and Social Council, particularly in relation to Palestinian women and children in occupied territories.

THE IMPACT ON INTERNATIONAL HUMANITARIAN LAW OF DEVELOPMENTS IN WOMEN'S HUMAN RIGHTS

There is no doubt that the work of human rights organizations has had a considerable impact on the approach taken to the protection of women in times of armed conflict. A change of emphasis over recent years can be discerned in the work of the ICRC in this context. The protection of women victims of conflict has always been part of the ICRC's mandate. Traditionally, however, women have been subsumed under the general category of civilians or under the separate category of "women and children". This has occurred despite the fact that the needs of these various categories of victims are not identical. Over the years, the ICRC has been active in attempts to mitigate the horrors of conflict for women. For example, efforts were made during the Second World War to ensure the lawful treatment of women prisoners of war. In the post-war period as well, from time to time the ICRC made efforts to ensure that women were treated humanely in various conflict situations.

However, in the context of sexual violence – the most obvious way in which women experience conflict – the silence was deafening, despite the appalling reality of this practice in all armed struggles. The invisibility of women and sexual violence rapidly came to an end with the events that took place during the armed conflict in the former Yugoslavia. Although sexual violence against women had been on the agenda of human rights bodies for some years, it was this conflict that galvanized the international community into action and led to the most significant development of humanitarian law attributable to the growing emphasis on women's human rights: the inclusion of rape within the system of grave breaches. In 1993, as a response to the findings of widespread violations of international humanitarian law in the former Yugoslavia, including rape and many other forms of sexual violence against women, the Security Council set up the International Criminal Tribunal for the former Yugoslavia (ICTY) to prosecute persons responsible for such acts.

One of the issues to be resolved was the place of rape within the Statute of the ICTY. In 1992, in the context of what constituted a grave breach of international humanitarian law, the ICRC had declared that the phrase common to the Geneva Conventions and their Protocols, "wilfully causing great suffering or serious injury to body or health", obviously covered not only rape but also any other attack on a woman's dignity. This added weight to the argument that prevailed with the Commission of Experts set up by the Security Council to consider the question of the establishment of the ICTY, namely that rape and other sexual assaults, although not specifically designated as grave breaches in the Conventions and Protocols, constituted "torture or inhumane treatment" and acts that "wilfully caused great suffering or serious injury to body or health" and were thus punishable as grave breaches under the Conventions. In the Statute of the ICTY, however, rape is only specifically punishable as a crime against humanity and, to constitute such a crime, it must be directed against the civilian population as a whole: for it to occur on an individual basis is not sufficient.

The practice of the Office of the Prosecutor has nevertheless been to charge defendants with sexual violence as a war crime and a grave breach. Although the precedential value of the ICTY is limited both by its origin as a Security Council measure and by its geographical scope, the normative effect of these initiatives is much more widespread. Consequently, it will now be difficult to maintain that rape and various forms of sexual violence against women committed in international armed conflicts are not grave breaches of treaty rules. This is a major development of humanitarian law and it can be attributed to the growing recognition that women's human rights call for the prosecution of crimes of sexual violence committed in armed conflicts. Doubts have nevertheless been expressed, in the context of the Rwandan conflict, as to whether the Yugoslav experience indicates a lasting reversal of the long tradition of silence and inaction in relation to sexual violence against women in armed conflicts.

The Special Rapporteur on Violence Against Women, after hearing of the levels of sexual violence in the Rwandan conflict was, in her words, "absolutely appalled that the first indictment on the grounds of sexual violence at the International Tribunal for Rwanda (ICTR) was issued only in August 1997, and then only after heavy international pressure from women's groups". Despite these reservations, the criminalization of sexual violence against women in internal armed conflicts by the Statute of the ICTR is an important development, and owes much to the work of human rights activists and commentators. International humanitarian law has traditionally distinguished between international and internal armed conflicts, concentrating on the former. However, the redrawing of the boundaries of human rights law has been integral to the implementation of women's human rights and the influence of this approach is now being felt in humanitarian law. Any consideration of violence against women naturally encompasses international and internal armed conflicts without distinction (an increasingly unreal division in any context).

The Statute of the ICTR reflects this view by providing both that rape is punishable as a crime against humanity and that the practice falls within the Tribunal's jurisdiction since, in common with enforced prostitution and indecent assault, it is specifically designated as a crime under Articl e 3 common to the Geneva Conventions. Breaches of Article 3, the so-called "mini code" for internal armed conflicts, have traditionally not been regarded as constituting war crimes. Further developments in humanitarian law relating to the enforcement of the provisions protecting women against sexual violence have their genesis in the Yugoslav conflict and the practice of the ICTY. It has long been recognized in the context of women's human rights that, to be effective, any enforcement regime for prohibitions on sexual violence in armed conflicts must incorporate procedural reforms. This view is slowly gaining broader acceptance within the international community and some progress has been made in taking into account the particular concerns of women in the prosecution of sexual offences.

Such matters as the anonymity of witnesses and victims in trials for sexual assault and provision for their support and counseling have been addressed by the ICTY However, these changes have not been readily accepted. For example, there is a perceived conflict between the demands of a fair trial and the protection of women as victims and witnesses. The two are not necessarily inconsistent: what is required is an appropriate balance between them. Recognition has also been given to the importance of equal gender distribution in the composition of enforcement tribunals and their support staff. The scrutiny by human rights groups of sexual violence against women in armed conflicts has translated into a new perception that such acts must be addressed by mainstream bodies dealing with the enforcement of international humanitarian law. The inclusion, within the definition of war crimes and as serious violations of Article 3 common to the Geneva Conventions, of several forms of sexual violence against women was considered during the negotiations of the Statute for the International Criminal Court.

Other issues of concern to women in relation to the enforcement process in general were also discussed in this context, such as the gender balance of the Court, protection for witnesses and victims, and the investigation of crimes of sexual violence. The Commission on the Status of Women, at its March 1988 meeting called on States to support these initiatives in relation to the future International Criminal Court. The ICRC has given increasing recognition to the fact that the situation of women in armed conflicts poses distinctive challenges for humanitarian law. In 1993 the Final Declaration of the International Conference for the Protection of War Victims expressed alarm at "the marked increase in acts of sexual violence directed notably against women and children" and reiterated that "such acts constituted grave breaches of international humanitarian law".

In 1995 the 26th International Conference of the Red Cross and Red Crescent adopted by consensus a resolution dealing separately with sexual violence against women, which condemned this practice, reaffirmed that rape in the conduct of hostilities was a war crime and highlighted the importance of enforcing the relevant provisions and the need to train those involved in such processes. Moreover, there is growing acknowledgement of the broader nature of the problem, which has not previously been apparent in the work of human rights bodies. For example, recent ICRC publications emphasize that armed conflict exacerbates inequalities which already exist in different forms and to varying degrees in all societies.

After years on the fringe of human rights law, the topic of women and human rights is nowadays gaining increasing respect as a separate area of concern within the mainstream of international law. Moreover, although women's human rights are very much in the developmental stage as regards both framework and substance, each passing year sees the further elaboration of their guiding principles. Yet the new concern being paid to women's human rights and the impact, albeit small, that the issue has so far made on humanitarian law have not led to the general acknowledgement that women's human rights warrant a special place within the field of international humanitarian law. This is, however, only a matter of time. Let us hope that such acknowledgement, when it comes, will be accompanied by a reassessment of humanitarian law that takes into account the actual ways in which women experience armed conflict.

SUBJUGATION OF WOMEN RIGHTS

Human rights as an issue occupies centre stage in contemporary public debate. Part of the debate on Human rights is about the origin and significance of the notion itself. Changes in a society demand changes in the way of maintaining social order. The techniques of social control are also adjusted to changed situations, as no system of social control works perfectly. People often deviate from social and legal norms, although non-conformity varies greatly in form and frequency. Though deviation is perceived as a threat to social stability yet attitude towards deviants keeps on changing with change in beliefs in the causes of deviant behaviour in general and crime in particular. Almost every day there are chilling instances of violence, ethnic cleansing, heinous torture, child abuse, man slaughter and several other human rights violations. Despite the adoption of the Universal Declaration Human Rights (1948) and special covenants provided for the rights of children, women and disabled, crimes continue unhindered and unabated.

SUBJUGATION OF WOMEN

Violence affects the lives of millions of women worldwide, in all socio-economic and educational classes. It cuts across cultural and religious barriers, impeding the right of women to participate fully in society. Violence against women takes a dismaying variety of forms, from domestic abuse and rape to child marriages and female circumcision. All are violations of the most fundamental human rights.

In India women constitute nearly fifty percent of our population. Women are denied human rights from the cradle to the grave. Infanticide is rampant in certain parts of the country where the birth of a girl child is not welcome. Nearly forty-one percent of the women abroad play an active role in the production process. In India the situation leaves much to be desired. Sexual abuse and flesh trade are gnawing evils, which threaten the existence of women as independent entities.

KINDS OF VIOLENCE AGAINST WOMEN

Domestic violence

Violence against women in the family occurs in developed and developing countries alike. It has long been considered a private matter by bystanders – including neighbors', the community and government. But such private matters have a tendency to become public tragedies.

Traditional practices

In many countries, women fall victim to traditional practices that violate their human rights. The persistence of the problem has much to do with the fact that most of these physically and psychologically harmful customs are deeply rooted in the tradition and culture of society.

Female genital mutilation

According to the World Health Organization, 85 million to 115 million girls and women in the population have undergone some form of female genital mutilation and suffer from its adverse health effects.

Son preference

Son preference affects women in many countries, particularly in Asia. Its consequences can be anything from foetal or female infanticide to neglect of the girl child over her brother in terms of such essential needs as nutrition, basic health care and education. In India, some women choose to terminate their pregnancies when expecting daughters but carry their pregnancies to term when expecting sons. According to reports from India, genetic testing for sex selection has become a booming business, especially in the country's northern regions. Indian gender-detection clinics drew protests from women's groups after the appearance of advertisements suggesting that it was better to spend $38 now to terminate a female foetus than $3,800 later on her dowry. A study of amniocentesis procedures conducted in a large Bombay hospital found that 95.5 per cent of foetuses identified as female were aborted compared with a far smaller percentage of male foetuses.

Dowry-related violence and early marriage

Dowry is the greatest crime against women. 'Are our daughters and sisters for sale? Women are virtually sold into the marriage market. Huge dowries are still demanded even when the girl can supplement the man's income. In such a milieu, a woman enjoys no rights because she is a woman. In some countries, weddings are preceded by the payment of an agreed-upon dowry by the bride's family. Failure to pay the dowry can lead to violence. In India, an average of five women a day is burned in dowry-related disputes – and many more cases are never reported. Early marriage, especially without the consent of the girl, is another form of human rights violation. Early marriage followed by multiple pregnancies can affect the health of women for life.

VIOLENCE IN THE COMMUNITY

Rape

Rape is a weapon to subjugate women. The woman is safe nowhere. Justice prides herself on being blind to everything but the truth - yet as far as rape is concerned; the facts paint a different picture. Rape can occur anywhere, even in the family, where it can take the form of marital rape or incest. It occurs in the community, where a woman can fall prey to any abuser. It also occurs in situations of armed conflict and in refugee camps.

Sexual Assault Within Marriage

In many countries sexual assault by a husband on his wife is not considered to be a crime: a wife is expected to submit. It is thus very difficult in practice for a woman to prove that sexual assault has occurred unless she can demonstrate serious injury.

Sexual Harassment

Sexual harassment in the workplace is a growing concern for women. Employers abuse their authority to seek sexual favours from their female co-workers or subordinates, sometimes promising promotions or other forms of career advancement or simply creating an untenable and hostile work environment. Women who refuse to give in to such unwanted sexual advances often run the risk of anything from demotion to dismissal. *But in recent years more women have been coming forward to report such practices* – Some taking their cases to court. In a significant judgment of Vishakha v. State of Rajasthan, the Supreme Court laid down exhaustive guidelines for preventing sexual Harassment of working women in their place of work until legislation is enacted for this Purpose.

Prostitution and Trafficking

Many women are forced into prostitution either by their parents, husbands or boyfriends – or as a result of the difficult economic and social conditions in which they find themselves. They are also lured into prostitution, sometimes by "mail-order bride" agencies that promise to find them a husband or a job in a foreign country. As a result, they very often find themselves illegally confined in brothels in slavery-like conditions where they are physically abused and their passports withheld. Most women initially victimized by sexual traffickers have little inkling of what awaits them. They generally get a very small percentage of what the customer pays to the pimp or the brothel owner. Once they are caught up in the system there is practically no way out, and they find themselves in a very vulnerable situation. Since prostitution is illegal in many countries, it is difficult for prostitutes to come forward and ask for protection if they become victims of rape or want to escape from brothels. Customers, on the other hand, are rarely the object of penal laws.

Violence Against Women Migrant Workers

Female migrant workers typically leave their countries for better living conditions and better pay – but the real benefits accrue to both the host countries and the countries of origin. For home countries, money sent home by migrant workers is an important source of hard currency, while receiving countries are able to find workers for low-paying jobs that might otherwise go unfilled. But migrant workers themselves fare badly, and sometimes tragically. Many become virtual slaves, subject to abuse and rape by their employers.

Pornography

Another concern highlighted is pornography, which represents a form of violence against women that "glamorizes the degradation and maltreatment of women and asserts their subordinate function as mere receptacles for male lust".

VIOLENCE PERPETRATED OR CONDONED BY STATES

Custodial Violence Against Women

Violence against women by the very people who are supposed to protect them – members of the law enforcement and criminal justice systems – is widespread. Women are physically or verbally abused; they also suffer sexual and physical torture. According to Amnesty International, thousands of women held in custody are routinely raped in police detention centre worldwide. In the Mathura Case. - The judgment did not distinguish between consent and forcible submission. Correspondingly the judgments in Bhanwari Devi and a few other cases were unjust and in favor of the accused. Governments agreed to adopt and implement national legislation to end violence against women and to work actively to ratify all international agreements that relate to violence against women. They agreed that there should be shelters, legal aid and other services for girls and women at risk, and counseling and rehabilitation for perpetrators. Governments also pledged to adopt appropriate measures in the field of education to modify the social and cultural patterns of conduct of men and women. And the Platform called on media professionals to develop self-regulatory guidelines to address violent, degrading and pornographic materials while encouraging non-stereotyped, balanced and diverse images of women.

IMPACT OF SEXUAL HARASSMENT ON WOMEN

To understand the impact of sexual harassment on women one must listen to the account of its victims as no one conveys the meaning and truth of sexual harassment better than the women who have endured it. In response to the question "What kind of emotional response does eve teasing /sexual harassment evoke in you", not a single woman ticked the category of "indifferent". The survey of the Gender Study Group shows that most women felt disgusted, insulted and scared by any sort of harassment. Women often internalise male perceptions of sexual harassment and blame themselves for having brought on the harassment. They not only doubt the validity of their own experiences but begin to believe that they themselves must be 'abnormal', 'cheap', 'indecent' or deserving the violence that comes their way.

Most respondents, men and women, described 'verbal harassment' as eve teasing and contrasted this with 'physical harassment' which has been seen as sexual harassment. They described eve teasing as relatively harmless behaviour committed usually by strangers, while sexual harassment would be grievous committed by acquaintances or men in positions of institutional power. In addition, most men and women described eve teasing as isolated incidents while sexual harassment would typically be repetitive and sustained over a long period of time. Many respondents said that they felt extreme anger, frustration and helplessness at not being able to do anything about the harassment.

Many women having faced this behaviour also said that they find it difficult to trust or have friendships with men. In response to the question "Has sexual harassment /eve teasing affected your academic/personal development in any way?' 45% of women stated that sexual harassment on Delhi campus roads has affected their personal or academic development in one way or another. Many women have found a way of handling these situations by changing their personalities but at one level these changes are also forced by the circumstances over which they have no control, and has left some of them bitter.

Authority Structures

Despite gross instances of sexual harassment in the past the Delhi University administration has not treated sexual harassment as a serious problem which has traumatic consequences for the women. The university administrators do not want to recongnize the magnitude of the problem of sexual harassment faced by women in the University, everyday. The general attitude of the administration has by and large been one that either disbelieves the victim or blames her for 'provoking harassment'. By treating sexual harassment as 'normal' the administration has systematically legimatised the sexist violence women face in the University.

Police

A great deal of cynicism exists regarding police action. Women said that even when they have gone ahead to complain to the police nothing has been done about it. In our survey 20.2% women hostellers said that they have faced sexual harassment from policemen, this includes staring, winking and lewd comments. The problem of harassment can be sorted out only if the hostel and university authorities and the police work together in tackling it.

Need for a policy on Sexual Harassment

The suggestions made by the Wad Committee have been included in the report. Some of its important provisions are:

Till the time legislation is passed, the university should frame appropriate statutes for dealing with cases of harassment. The university should appoint a committee of three women teachers to inquire into serious charges of harassment. If this committee records prima facie findings of guilt, the person responsible should be suspended in anticipation of disciplinary proceedings. The Disciplinary Enquiry should be headed b a retired judge and should be associated by one woman member, not connected with the University.

Women need to strategize about their safety and not simply ' avoid going out in the late evening alone'. Some strategies that women could use in case of Street Harassment are:

- Ignore as a strategy.
- Scream for help.
- Lash out.
- Push the person away and hit them with slippers / bags.
- Use self-defense mechanisms e.g. kick them off balance.
- Note down the number and features of the vehicle.

It is a mater of concern that 91.7% of the women hosteller respondents reported having faced harassment on the campus. This report came out in 1996, however nothing concrete has still been done to tackle this problem. It is about time that the university authorities, the teachers associations and various student bodies take responsibility and through open discussions take a political stand, which would ensure action to make the campus safer for its women students. It is important that we question our own perceptions on the issue of harassment, before we can bring about any change.

LAW ON SEXUAL HARASSMENT

Undeterred by the absence of legislation covering the issue of Sexual Harassment at the Workplace, the Supreme Court has laid down the necessary guidelines and norms in, Vishaka v. State of Rajasthan, for the protection of the fundamental rights of women, violated, as a result of Sexual Harassment at Work. The Court has emphasised that the guidelines and norms being laid down by it had to be duly observed at all workplaces or other institutions until a legislation is enacted for this purpose and that these should be treated as law under Art 141 of the Constitution. These guidelines are in accordance with the recommendations and conventions of various international organisations like the ILO and the European Communities.

Commission

The European Communities Commission has emphasised worldwide that the most effective method of combating with this menace is to develop and implement a preventive policy at the enterprise level. Taking their recommendations into considerations, the Supreme Court have laid down the following guidelines: Preventive steps: The employers should take appropriate steps to prevent sexual harassment. These include:

a. Express prohibition of sexual harassment at the workplace should be notified, published and circulated in appropriate ways.
b. The rules/regulations of government and public bodies relating to conduct and discipline should include rules/ regulations prohibiting sexual harassment and provide for appropriate penalties in such rules against the offender.
c. Appropriate work conditions should be provided in respect of work, leisure, health and hygiene to further ensure that there is no hostile environment towards women at workplaces and no woman employee should have some reasonable grounds to believe that she is disadvantaged in connection with her employment.

Criminal Proceedings

Where such conduct amounts to a specific offence under the Indian Penal Code or under any other law, the employer shall initiate appropriate action in accordance with law by making a complaint with the appropriate authority. In order to ensure that the victims are not discriminated against, while dealing with complaints of sexual harassment, the victims should have the option to seek transfer of the perpetrator or their own transfer.

Disciplinary action

Where such conduct amounts to misconduct in employment as defined by the relevant service rules, disciplinary action should be initiated by the employer in accordance with these rules.

Complaint Mechanism

Whether or not such conduct constitutes an offence under law or a breach of the service rules, a complaint mechanism should be created in the organisation for redress of the complaint made by the victim.

Complaints Committee

A complaint mechanism should provide for a Complaints Committee. The Complaints Committee should be headed by a woman and not less than half of its members should be women. Further, to prevent the possibility of any undue influence from senior levels, the Committee should involve a third party, either NGO or any other body familiar with the issue of sexual harassment.

Workers initiative

Employees should be allowed to raise issues of sexual harassment in workers meetings and other appropriate forums.

Awareness

Awareness of the rights of female employees in this regard should be created in particular by prominently notifying the guidelines.

Third party harassment

Where sexual harassment occurs as a result of an act or omission by any third party or outsider, the employer and person in charge will take all steps necessary and reasonable to assist the affected person in terms of support and preventive action. The Supreme Court has held in Apparel Export Promotion Council V. A.K. Chopra, that in any case involving charge of sexual harassment or attempt to sexually molest, the courts are required to examine the broader probabilities of the case and not get swayed by insignificant discrepancies or narrow technicalities or the dictionary meaning of the expression 'molestation'.

The Court also held that the statement of the victim must be appreciated in the background of the entire case. Notwithstanding the availability of potential remedies under labour or criminal or tort laws to a victim of sexual harassment, it is now widely accepted that the most effective way of combating with this menace is to situate the primary remedy against sexual harassment in the Sex Discrimination Law itself.

DOWRY DEATH

It is sad that even today the numbers of dowry deaths in India are so high. Due to the unfulfillment of demands of dowry, many women die at the hands of their in-laws in both rural and urban India. But there i s something that can be done about it. Section 304 B was introduced in the Indian Penal Code in order to strictly deal with and punish the offence of Dowry Death. It was a new offence created with effect from November 19, 1986 by insertion of the provision in the Indian Penal Code providing for a more stringent offence, than provided by Section 498A of the same Act, which deals with punishment for cruelty by husband and his relatives. The ingredients necessary for the application of Section 304B are:

- When the death of a woman is caused by any burns or bodily injury, or occurs under unusual circumstances.
- And the aforesaid two facts spring within 7 years of the girl's marriage.
- And soon before her death, she was subjected to cruelty or harassment by her husband or her relative,
- And this is in connection with the demand for dowry.

If these conditions exist, it would constitute a dowry death, and the husband and/or his relatives shall be.deemed to have caused her death. For the purposes of this sub section, dowry shall have the same meaning as in Section 2 of the Dowry Prohibition Act, 1961. The definition of 'Dowry' includes any property or valuable security given or agreed to be given either directly or indirectly:

- By one party to a marriage to the other party to the marriage; or
- By the parents of either party to a marriage or by any other person, to either party to the marriage or to any other person at or before or any time after the marriage in connection with the marriage of the said parties.

Section 304 B also provides that whoever commits a dowry death shall be punished with imprisonment for a term which shall not be less than 7 years but which may extend to imprisonment for life. It is true that in criminal jurisprudence the benefit of the doubt is extendable to the accused. This concept of 'benefit of doubt' has an important role to play but within the confines of the stringency of laws. Since the cause of death of a married woman was to occur not in normal circumstances but as a dowry death, for which the evidence was not easily available, as it is mostly confined within the four walls of a house, namely the husband's house, where all likely accused reside, the amendments brought in the concept of deemed dowry death by the husband or the relatives.

In cases of dowry deaths and suicides, circumstantial evidence plays an important role and inferences can be drawn on the basis of direct or indirect evidence. This section lays down stringent provisions by shifting the burden onto the accused by bringing in the deemed clause. According to Section 8-A of the 1961 Act, which came into force for taking or abetting any dowry, the burden to explain is placed on such person against whom the allegation of committing the offence is made. Similarly, under Explanation to Section 113 B of the Indian Evidence Act, there is a presumption that a death caused within 7 years of marriage is a dowry death. In Ashok Kumar vs. State of Rajasthan where the post mortem report indicated that the smell of kerosene was there in the body and even the burnt hair was smelling of kerosene, it was held that this fact ruled out the statement of the husband's sister that the deceased was the victim of the accidental burning while making tea and also ruled out the remotest possibility of an accident.

The demand for dowry is itself punishable if the other ingredients of Section 304 B are established. In case of Pawan Kumar vs. State of Haryana, the facts were that a few days after the marriage, there was a demand for a scooter and fridge, which when not being met led to repetitive taunts and maltreatment. The wife finally committed suicide. The Court stated that Section 4 of the Dowry Prohibition Act deals with the penalty of demanding dowry. This makes it clear that even the mere demand for dowry was punishable.

The Court thus concluded that the persistent demands for scooter, fridge etc made from the bride after marriage or from her parents, would constitute to be in connection with the marriage and it would be a case of demand of dowry within the meaning of the Section 304 B IPC. It is not always necessary that there be any agreement for dowry. The Court also held that the facts proved cruelty in connection with dowry demand. In Akula Ravinder vs. State of A.P it was held that death must be proved to be one out of the course of nature and the mere fact that the deceased was young and death was not accidental is not sufficient to establish that death must have occurred otherwise than under normal circumstances.

BRIDE BURNING & LAWS IN INDIA

Today, Indian society is surrounded with many problems such as unemployment, illiteracy, population growth, terrorism, etc. Among these problems, a problem which is deep rooted in Indian society is the problem of dowry system. It has become the every day news item, no day passes away when we don't hear news relating to dowry death or dowry harassment. The irony lies in the fact that women in India are worshipped in the form of shakti, she is burned and harassed by her in-laws every day in one part of the nation or the other. Dowry, in ordinary sense, refers to money, gifts, goods or estate that wife brings to her husband in marriage.

The dowry has a long history in Europe, South Asia, Africa and other parts of the world. The system of dowry is deep rooted in the Indian society since the early days of the history. This system prevailed in ancient Indian society, in ancient period dowry was the part of the ritual of kanyadan which was very different from modern- dowry. Among the eight types of marriages recognized by smritis, it was only in the Brahma marriage that father gave away his daughter, with such gifts and presents as he could afford, to a man of superior character.In the medieval period, the dowry, which was earlier regarded as dakshina (gift offered willingly), became an evil, father in order to marry her daughter had to offer money demanded by groom's family. In medieval times, the dowry system had engulfed the society at alarming rate, though it was practiced in the aristocratic and royal families.

The extra ordinary pride which rich people took in their ancestry was mainly responsible for this development. The youth of the bluest blood were preferred as sons-in-law by a large member of peoples, as a consequence of which their value increased in the market. The evil, which targeted the aristocratic and royal families in the ancient and the medieval period, in the British and modern period it engulfed the entire society. In the present era, it is in the most disastrous form. Women are harassed, beaten and face every kind of cruelty if she is unable to fulfill the demand of dowry and the harassment goes to such an extent that they are burned to death.

The most glaring example is of a lady Pooja Chauhan, who was so harassed by her-in laws because of dowry, which compelled her to parade in semi nude condition on the road of Rajkot to seek the justice. While greed may be the apparent causes for dowry demands some more suitable and unconscious motivations could also motivates this evil system such as:

1. Aspiration to marry in the High and Rich family.
2. Pressure of the caste system.

3. Social Custom
4. Marriage system.
5. False notion of social status and
6. Vicious Circle.

ANTI- DOWRY LAWS

The attempt to eradicate the evil system of dowry through the mechanism of the law dates as far back the Sindh Leti Deti Act of 1939. After independence of India only two states, namely, Bihar and Andhra Pradesh enacted legislation restraining the dowry system. But as the incidence of dowry ascended at high rate, need for the central legislation became essential and as a result, the first national anti-dowry legislation popularly known as the Dowry Prohibition Act was passed in 1961, and this Act applies to all the communities in India. However, the Act proved quite ineffective, which demanded changes in this toothless piece of legislation. With a view to remedy the inherent weakness of the Dowry Prohibition Act, this Act was amended in the year 1984 and again in the year 1986 to make the provisions of the Act more stringent and stricter than before and also to make its implementation effective.

Law Commission 91st report 1983, recommended certain several provisions in IPC, Cr. PC and Indian Evidence Act to combat this social evil. In IPC section 498-A was added which made cruelty by the husband or his relatives punishable with imprisonment up to three years and sections 304-B was added to the IPC by Criminal Law Amendment Act, passed in 1986 which provides that where the death of a woman is caused by any burns or bodily or occurs otherwise than under normal circumstances within seven years of her marriage and it is shown that immediately before her death she was harassed and put to cruelty by her husband or any relative of the husband in connection with demand for dowry, such death shall be called as dowry death; and sub-section (2) provides punishment with a minimum of seven years which may extend to imprisonment for life. Section 174 and 176 of CrPC, deals with the investigations and inquires into the causes of unnatural deaths, by the police and magistrate respectively. The Amendment Act 1983 makes it mandatory for the police officer to send the body for post-mortem examination if the death of the woman occurred with in seven years of marriage as a result of suicide or under other suspicious circumstances. A new section 113-B was added in the Indian Evidence Act which deals with the burden of proof in dowry deaths according to which the Court has to presume that a dowry death was caused by the person who is shown to have subjected the woman to cruelty or harassment soon before her death.

Judicial Efforts

Apart from the efforts of legislature, judiciary is also playing an important role in combating and eradicating the evil dowry system from the Indian society. In case of Kundula Bala Subrahmaniam V State of A.P., the Supreme Court gave some indications in dealing with the case of dowry related violence. The Apex Court observed that such cases ought to be dealt with in a more realistic manner and criminals should not be allowed to escape on account of procedural technicalities or insignificant lacunae in the evidence and the courts are expected to be sensitive in cases involving crime against women. In case of Stree Atyachar Virodhi Parishad V. Dilip Nathumal Chordia, The supreme Court observed, 'We are referring to these provisions only to emphasize that it is not enough if the legal order with the sanction above moves forward for protection of women and preservation of societal values.'

The criminal justice system must equally respond to the needs and notions of the society. The investigating agency must display a live concern. The Court must also display greater sensitivity to criminality and avoid on all courts 'soft justice'. In a number of decisions the Supreme Court has shown practical approach in dealing with bride burning cases, some cases are as follows: State (Delhi Admn.) V Laxman Kumar, State of Punjab V. Amarjit Singh, Subrahmanyam V. State of A.P. and Sarojini V State of M.P., which reflect this approach of the Apex Court.

RISE OF DOWRY VIOLENCE DESPITE OF LAWS

The legal and judicial efforts to eradicate the evil system of dowry failed to make any remarkable break in alarming rise of this dowry system. The National Crime Records statistics show that there have been over 58,000 incidents of dowry harassment and over 67, 000 dowry murders in the year 2005, and as per national crime Bureau, in the year 1994- there were 4,935 dowry deaths and 25,946 cases of dowry harassment, this shows that in the sort span of ten years dowry related crimes accelerated at a very high speed. It may be said that approximately 56,000 dowry deaths and more than 40,000 cases of dowry harassment takes place every where. Moreover, cases which occur in privacy of husband's house are much more and go unreported.

RISE OF DOWRY VIOLENCE DESPITE OF LAWS

The legal and judicial efforts to eradicate the evil system of dowry failed to make any remarkable break in alarming rise of this dowry system. The National Crime Records statistics show that there have been over 58,000 incidents of dowry harassment and over 67,000 dowry murders in the year 2005 and as per national crime bureau in the year 1994, there were 4,935 dowry deaths and 25,946 cases of dowry harassment. this shows that in the sort span of the years dowry related crimes accelerated at a very high speed. It may be said that approximately 50,000 dowry deaths and more than 40,000 cases of dowry harassment takes place every where. Moreover, cases which occur in privacy of husband's house are much more and go unreported.

6

The Violence against Women Act and International law's Enhancement

An important issue pending before the U.S. Supreme Court is whether Congress has constitutionally based power to enact the Violence Against Women Act (VAWA). Although some have focused on congressional power under the Commerce Clause, treaty-based and customary international law concerning fundamental human rights of women, coupled with other provisions of the Constitution, also provide an enhancement of congressional power to enact the VAWA. This essay identifies a purpose of the VAWA as partly to protect human rights of women to freedom from gender-based violence. The essay also identifies constitutionally-based enhancement of congressional power to implement international law.

VAWA'S PURPOSE

INTERNATIONAL LEGAL AND DOMESTIC MEDIA BACKGROUNDS

In 1994, prior to enactment of the VAWA, the Declaration on the Elimination of Violence Against Women recognized gender-based violence as a matter of serious concern to the international community. Also in 1994, and prior to enactment of the VAWA, the U.N. Commission on Human Rights appointed a Special Rapporteur on Violence Against Women to assure more adequate implementation of the human rights of women to freedom from violence. Previously, there had also been global attention to domestic violence as a matter of significant international concern and as a serious human rights infraction.

In 1993 and 1994, domestic media in the United States also brought attention to the fact that domestic violence against women involves human rights violations, and several articles expressly noted that drafts of the VAWA would aid in protecting women's human rights to freedom from gender-based violence. Congress, and especially the Executive branch as a key participant in the international legal process, could not have been unaware of such attention, the human rights dimension of domestic violence against women, or the purpose of the draft legislation in part to protect human rights of women. Indeed, there are several recognitions of the interface between human rights and domestic violence against women in statements of congresspersons in 1993 as well as the human rights-protecting nature of the proposed VAWA, as noted below.

CONGRESSIONAL AND EXECUTIVE RECOGNITIONS

Part of the Violence Against Women Act contains provisions enabling battered immigrant women to obtain protections, thus evidencing a congressional purpose in part to address problems of domestic violence involving transnational processes or contexts in which immigrants in this country have a need for special domestic legal protections. These and other parts of the Act applying more broadly to women tend to serve human rights of the victims of domestic violence, as recognized by the Executive Branch. Importantly, during the first U.S. Report to the Human Rights Committee of the International Covenant on Civil and Political Right on U.S. compliance with obligations under the treaty to ensure respect for relevant human rights and to enact appropriate legislation, the Executive assured the international body that the Violence Against Women Act was a measure undertaken in part to comply with and execute such treaty obligations.

Prominent mention of the VAWA in the first U.S. report to the Human Rights Committee serves not merely to evidence our continuing national commitment to human rights, but also to underscore congressional and Executive resolve to avoid friction with the international community with respect to U.S. compliance with human rights treaty obligations. Bonnie J. Campbell, Director of the Violence Against Women Office of the U.S. Department of Justice, also confirmed that domestic violence is "now... recognized as a violation of our human rights..." and that the VAWA is an example of U.S. legislation designed to address human rights violations against women. Indeed, one express purpose of the Civil Rights for Women Act, which is part of the VAWA, is "to protect the civil rights of victims of gender motivated violence... by establishing a Federal civil rights cause of action for victims of crimes of violence motivated by gender," and there is express recognition that "all persons within the United States shall have the right to be free from crimes of violence motivated by gender."

In 1994, the Senate Foreign Relations Committee recommended that the Senate give advice and consent to ratification of the Convention on the Elimination of All Forms of Discrimination Against Women, while noting that the treaty "requires broad regulation of private conduct, in particular under Articles 2, 3 and 5," and stating that the U.S. will not take "action with respect to private conduct except as mandated by the Constitution and laws of the United States." Thus, the Senate Committee's report to the Senate contemplated U.S. legislation to implement certain treaty-based human rights protections against private conduct involving violence against women, and the VAWA had been enacted just three weeks earlier.

The year prior to the enactment of the Violence Against Women Act was marked by significant recognition by various congresspersons of the human rights aspects of domestic violence against women.

In their preview of the 103rd Congress, Senators Dole and Lott referred to "provisions regarding violence against women" in their "crime bill" and to "The Sexual Assault Prevention Act of 1993, which would also be introduced in the House by Congresswoman Susan Molinari, and which is a comprehensive response to violence against women, both on the streets, and in the home, "while also decrying similar and additional human rights violations by Slobodan Milosevic in Bosnia. Representative Christopher Smith affirmed the relationship between violent abuses of human rights and "violence against women (including rape and wife beating)" in Nicaragua. Senator DeConcini also spoke of the need for "appointment of a special U.N. rapporteur on gender discrimination and violence against women and the strengthening of implementation procedures under the Convention for the Elimination of All Forms of Discrimination Against Women" as part of a "human rights agenda into the next century" Senator Pell spoke of serious human rights violations in East Timor involving "discrimination and violence against women."

Senator Boxer spoke of human rights atrocities in Bosnia-Herzegovina "with a specific focus on acts of violence against women," adding: "As you know well, Madam President... we are working together to stop the violence against women in this country and around the world...." Later that year, Senator Pressler spoke of human rights violations in Africa, including "violence against women... in particular, wife beating...;"Representative Snowe introduced bills addressing "women's human rights," including "violence against women," and "special needs of refugee women and children;"and Senator Pell stressed the need for the Human Rights Commission to "appoint a special rapporteur on violence against women ...who should investigate human rights violations including battering in the family, rape, female infanticide, `honor killings,' `dowry murder,' and other violence related to traditional and customary practices. "While addressing violent crime control, H.R. 4092 (which was termed the "Violent Crime Control and Law Enforcement Act of 1994"), and "The Sexual Assault Prevention Act," each addressing violence against women, certain congresspersons noted relevant hearings by the Congressional Human Rights Caucus, presumably indicating some interface with human rights concerns.

In July of 1993, during the Senate Judiciary Committee's confirmation hearing concerning Ruth Bader Ginsburg as Supreme Court Justice, Judge Ginsburg spoke of human rights of women to equality before the law and, in response, Senator Biden addressed "the Violence Against Women Legislation which he had drafted and been fighting to get passed for three years now... and stated that he wanted to make it clear the purpose of that... is to break down the barriers that continue to exist in the unequal application of the law," thus recognizing a broad human rights purpose of what would become the Violence Against Women Act. More specifically, in June, Senator Biden had proclaimed that "violence that primarily targets women" would be addressed in the proposed VAWA, which treats gender-based violence as a hate crime, and openly recognized "violence against women as a human rights issue" that would be met in part by the new legislation.

JUDICIAL RECOGNITION

At least one federal court, while finding that a plaintiff's claim under the Violence Against Women Act was valid, has recognized that "a woman's basic human right to be free from rape, including in the workplace, was "obviously" not first created by the VAWA," and the court "therefore" would not entertain argument that there were "`no constitutional rights at issue here,... only a statutory one.'" The constitutionally-based power of Congress to enact legislation implementing either treaties or customary international law, even with respect to matters otherwise closely connected to interests of states within the United States, is well known. Article I, Section 8, Clause 10 (the Offenses Clause) of the Constitution expressly confirms congressional power to enact legislation defining and punishing offenses under the law of nations, and Clause 18 (the Necessary and Proper Clause) expressly confirms congressional power to enact any laws necessary and proper to carry into execution such a power as well as all other powers vested by the Constitution in the Government of the United States or any department or officer thereof. The treaty power is one such power.

Among the many cases recognizing congressional power to implement treaty-based rights or obligations is Missouri v. Holland. In that case, the Court recognized the power of Congress to enact legislation to protect ducks "as a necessary and proper means to execute the powers of the Government" in connection with the treaty power. The Court also expressly noted that "the great body of private relations usually fall within the control of the State, but a treaty may override its power;" "most of the laws of the United States are carried out within the States...;" and, especially in view of the express mandate of the Supremacy Clause that "all Treaties... shall be supreme Law of the Land," the Tenth Amendment is no barrier to congressional implementation of treaties. Certainly if congressional power is enhanced by a treaty and the treaty power in order to protect ducks it can also be enhanced to protect women.

Another interesting case recognizing enhancement of congressional power to regulate private conduct occurring within states by reason of relevant treaties is the earlier case of United States v. Haun. In Haun, Justice Campbell, sitting on circuit, ruled that congressional legislation to suppress the slave trade was supported by several treaties and was a valid exercise of power under Article I, Section 8, Clauses 3, 10, and 18, even though importation of slaves had already occurred and punishable acts took place within the limits of the states. While addressing international legal precepts, Justice Campbell also declared that President Jefferson unquestionably "supposed that something beyond a regulation of commerce was concerned" when it was recognized that Congress "might interpose their authority constitutionally to withdraw the citizens of the United States from all further violations of human rights which have been so long continued on the unoffending inhabitants of Africa." Importantly, it was also a recognition by a President and Supreme Court Justice that private individuals can violate human rights of other individuals.

Addressing the power of Congress to implement customary international law and enact legislation reaching private conduct, the Supreme Court noted in United States v. Arjona that "the law of nations requires every national government to use `due diligence' to... punish those who within its own jurisdiction counterfeit the money of another nation" and that others have a reciprocal right to demand compliance. The Court recognized that states within the United States are not prevented from punishing the same violations of customary international law, but also noted:

A right secured by the law of nations to a nation, or its people, is one the United States as the representative of this nation are bound to protect. Consequently, a law which is necessary and proper to afford this protection is one that Congress may enact, because it is one that is needed to carry into execution a power conferred by the Constitution on the Government of the United States... and "as a means of performing a duty" which the law of nations has imposed on them as part of their international obligations.

Congress, in enacting the statute in question, had not mentioned its power or purpose to implement international law, but the Court declared that it was not necessary that the offense "be declared in the statute itself to be `an offence against the law of nations'... if the thing made punishable is one which the United States are required by their international obligations to use due diligence to prevent and such being the case, there is no more need of declaring in the statute that it is such an offence than there would be in any other criminal statute to declare that it was enacted to carry into execution any other particular power...."

The Court also noted that no such purpose had been expressed in the statutes punishing violations of neutrality, but it had never been supposed that they were thus invalid. More generally, the Supreme Court has affirmed that federal courts can "discern some legislative purpose or factual predicate that supports the exercise of... power" to enact federal legislation whether or not any power or a different power is mentioned. In any event, with respect to the VAWA, a human rights purpose is clearly discernable.

Another case recognizing the role of customary international legal obligations in enhancing congressional power to regulate conduct of private individuals is Finzer v. Barry. In Finzer, customary and treaty-based obligations to protect foreign embassies and personnel were stressed as supporting congressional power to enact legislation under the Offences Clause, and it was recognized that "since the founding of our nation adherence to the law of nations... has been regarded as a fundamental and compelling national interest," adding: "it is also clear that the founders... explicitly gave Congress the power to enforce adherence to the standards of the law of nations...."

It is also certain that human rights were of fundamental importance to the Founders and were partly what out nation and much of the Bill of Rights, including the Ninth Amendment, were founded upon. As Chief Justice Marshall affirmed, our federal courts "are established to decide on human rights."

In view of the above, it is clear that Congress has power under the Constitution to enact the Violence Against Women Act partly to better effectuate the human rights of women to freedom from domestic violence. It is also evident that this was partly the purpose of the legislation. Choice and power of our national political branches to effectuate international law, especially in view of the Supremacy Clause, provide an overriding constitutional propriety of the VAWA regardless of the reach of the commerce power.

HUMAN RIGHTS AND SEXUAL ORIENTATION IN INTERNATIONAL LAW

International human rights law and the lesbian and gay rights movement have grown up together in the years since World War II. Both are still developing. Both are evolving from western initiatives to a world-wide presence. The founding documents of international human rights law are the United Nations Charter of 1945, the Universal Declaration of Human Rights of 1948, the European Convention on Human Rights of 1950, and the two basic United Nations human rights treaties of 1966, the International Covenant on Civil and Political Rights and the International Covenant on Economic, Social and Cultural Rights. The six "core" United Nations human rights treaties include, as well, the conventions on racial discrimination, women, torture and children. Does this international system recognize the rights of lesbians, gay men, bisexuals and transgendered people? None of the international human rights instruments mentioned make any reference to "sexual orientation" or "gender identity."

A general approach to discrimination has not been characteristic of international human rights law. Instead there are treaties and programs dealing with discrimination on the basis of race and sex, and concerns with specific groups such as refugees, cultural minorities, indigenous peoples and migrant workers. Only through invoking provisions on personal privacy and certain general provisions on equality have lesbians and gay men been able to gain some recognition. The International Covenant on Civil and Political Rights, has a broad guarantee of equality. The European Convention on Human Rights has a new general equality provision.

By the end of the 20th century concern with discrimination on the basis of sexual orientation had gained sufficient recognition:

- In national legal systems,
- In the European human rights system and various European institutions,
- In actions of the United Nations treaty bodies, special procedures and working groups,
- In initiatives of the UN High Commissioner for Human Rights, and
- In the work of important Non-Governmental Organizations that it had become realistic to say that the issue was now a part of a broad international human rights agenda,

though progress often continues to be contested.

For gays and lesbians the United Nations system, at the moment, is partly open and partly closed. The story begins in Europe.

THE EUROPEAN CONVENTION ON HUMAN RIGHTS

The first breakthrough came in the 1981 decision of the European Court of Human Rights in Dudgeon v United Kingdom. The United Kingdom had decriminalised gay male sexual activity in England and Wales in 1967. Criminal prohibitions were still in place in Northern Ireland. Jeffrey Dudgeon, an activist with the Northern Ireland Gay Rights Association, challenged the law. Since the European Convention on Human Rights did not have a general equality provision it was necessary to find a specific right in the convention that had been denied. The Court ruled that the law violated Dudgeon's right to respect for his private life. Dudgeon was a very good test case. The United Kingdom could not claim that the law was necessary for the "protection of health or morals", justifications allowed in the Convention. It had repealed the same law in England and Wales.

As well, the law was not being enforced, something that is true in almost every country that continues to have a criminal prohibition. The law was out of step with the laws in other European states, a fact that strongly influenced the Court. The United Kingdom wanted to loose. Public opinion in Northern Ireland was evenly divided. Reform was stalled by the strong opposition of conservative Protestants. The Court decision made law reform politically possible. After Dudgeon the European Court of Human Rights ruled against similar laws in Norris v Ireland in 1988 and in Modinos v Cyprus in 1993. While the European human rights system started well with the Dudgeon decision in 1981, gays and lesbians lost all subsequent cases except those identical to Dudgeon. In frustration, the International Lesbian and Gay Association (ILGA) decided in 1990 to press for an additional protocol to the Convention to expressly prohibit discrimination on grounds of sexual orientation. There seemed no other way to make progress. But, without any change to the Convention, the Commission and Court changed direction in the late 1990s.

In Sutherland v United Kingdom in 1997 the European Commission of Human Rights applied privacy reasoning to strike down an unequal age of consent for homosexual and heterosexual acts, reversing earlier decisions. The Commission noted changed medical views on homosexuality, and observed that the law "might inhibit efforts to improve the sexual health of young homosexual and bisexual men." The Court came to the same conclusion in January, 2003, in a case from Austria. The Austrian Constitutional Court had said the law was designed to protect a young, maturing person "from developing sexually in the wrong way." The European Court found scientific support for the proposition that sexual orientation was determined before puberty, undercutting any justification based on protecting youth...the Court reiterates that sexual orientation is a concept covered by art 14. Just like differences based on sex, differences based on sexual orientation require particularly serious reasons by way of justification.

In other cases criminal laws against sado-machocistic acts were upheld, criminal laws against group sex were struck down, and a ban on lesbian and gay organizations that have members who are under 19 was upheld. The United Kingdom's ban on homosexuals in the military was successfully challenged in the 1999 decisions in Smith and Lustig-Prean. The government conceded that the ban interfered with the right of individuals to respect for their private lives, but claimed justification. The Court ruled that the military concerns with "operational effectiveness" were based "solely upon the negative attitudes of heterosexual personnel..." these attitudes, even if sincerely felt by those who expressed them, ranged from stereotypical expressions of hostility to those of homosexual orientation, to vague expressions of unease about the presence of homosexual colleagues. To the extent that they represent a predisposed bias on the part of a heterosexual majority against a homosexual minority, these negative attitudes cannot, of themselves, be considered by the Court to amount to sufficient justification for the interferences with the applicants' rights outlined above, any more than similar negative attitudes towards those of a different race, origin or colour.

A key part of the argument against the ban was the inconsistency of the policy on homosexuals with the policies designed to ensure the successful integration of women and racial minorities in the armed forces.

As in Dudgeon, the Court looked to changed practices in other countries:

The Court notes the evidence before the domestic courts to the effect that the European countries operating a blanket legal ban on homosexuals in their armed forces are now in a small minority. It considers that, even if relatively recent, the Court cannot overlook the widespread and consistently developing views and associated legal changes to the domestic laws of Contracting States on this issue...

The Court concluded that the discrimination was not "necessary in a democratic society", a requirement for any justification under Article 8. The Court held that the hallmarks of a democratic society included "pluralism, tolerance and broadmindedness..."

The Court had ruled that respect for personal privacy required non-discrimination in employment. Respect for privacy, paradoxically, allows homosexuals to be open about their sexual orientation without the fear of loosing their jobs. Arguably all forms of discrimination on the basis of sexual orientation or gender identity are covered by this expansive interpretation of privacy rights. For many years the Commission did not recognize lesbian and gay families. In December, 1999, in the da Silva Mouta case, the Court found a breach of Article 8 in a case where a man had lost custody of his child on the basis of his homosexuality. He had been granted parental access only on the condition that he hide his orientation. This was the first family rights case to be won. The Court noted that the denial of access on the part of the gay father was based on sexual orientation, and ruled that this was "a distinction which cannot be tolerated under the Convention".

In February, 2002, in the Frette case, the Court ruled that France could refuse to allow gays and lesbians to adopt children. Three judges said there were significant divisions within the scientific community about the possible consequences for children being brought up by one or more homosexual parents. One judge held that adoption rights did not come within the Convention. Three judges dissented. As a result, there was no majority reasoning. A new case is re-examining adoption issues. In July, 2003, in the Karner case, the Court upheld successor tenancy rights for same-sex partners, which Austrian law recognized for a spouse or an unmarried "life companion." The claim for survivor rights in relation to rent-controlled tenancies had been won earlier in landmark equality cases in New York and the United Kingdom. The decision of the Austrian Supreme Court had limited "life companion" to a heterosexual companion, on the basis that this would have been the intent of the legislators in 1974 when the language was adopted. The Austrian government argued that the goal was to protect the family "in the traditional sense."

The Court spoke very clearly:

...very weighty reasons have to be put forward before the Court could regard a difference in treatment based exclusively on the ground of sex as compatible with the Convention ... Just like differences based on sex, differences based on sexual orientation require particularly serious reasons by way of justification...

A goal of supporting the 'traditional family' did not require the denial of homosexual equality. Transsexual rights have now been supported by the Court. In July 2002 the Court rejected some of its earlier decisions and ordered the United Kingdom to change the information on Christine Goodwin's birth certificate. In the twenty first century the right of transsexuals to personal development and to physical and moral security in the full sense enjoyed by others in society cannot be regarded as a matter of controversy requiring the lapse of time to cast clearer light on the issues. In short, the unsatisfactory situation in which post-operative transsexuals live in an intermediate zone as not quite one gender or the other is no longer sustainable. ...society may reasonably be expected to tolerate a certain inconvenience to enable individuals to live in dignity and worth in accordance with the sexual identity chosen by them at great personal cost. The breach was not simply of the right of privacy, but also of the right to marry.

The Court ruled that Christine Goodwin, a male to female transsexual, had the right to marry a man. In June, 2003, in van Kuck, the Court held that those German courts had violated privacy rights by interpreting a health insurance contract between a transsexual woman and a private insurance company as not requiring reimbursement for the costs involved in gender reassignment. A broad equality provision has been added to the European Convention. The text of the twelfth protocol to the Convention was approved in 1999, adding a general ban on discrimination, comparable to that in the International Covenant on Civil and Political Rights. It came into force on April 1, 2005. At that point, however, only 11 European countries had ratified the protocol, not including France, Germany or the United Kingdom. While "sexual orientation" is not specifically mentioned in the text, it is referred to in the explanatory report. It will clearly be treated as a prohibited ground of discrimination. The changed attitude in the European Court of Human Right makes the protocol simply a confirmation of recent decisions on sexual orientation and gender identity.

THE COUNCIL OF EUROPE AND THE EUROPEAN UNION

The basic European institutions are the Council of Europe and the European Union. The first is a broad political organisation responsible for the European Convention on Human Rights. States seeking membership in the European Union must first ratify the European Convention on Human Rights and join the Council of Europe. To begin this process, it is now necessary for states to repeal any anti-homosexual criminal laws, have an equal age of consent for sexual activity and prohibit discrimination.

The landmark developments have been:

1981 - The report to the Parliamentary Assembly of the Council of Europe on "Discrimination Against Homosexuals". The report led to a set of resolutions (a) calling on the World Health Organisation to remove homosexuality from its list of diseases (which has occurred), (b) urging member states to decriminalise homosexual acts and apply equal ages of consent for homosexual and heterosexual acts, and (c) seeking equal treatment for lesbians and gay men in employment.

1983 - In a resolution on HIV/AIDS the Parliamentary Assembly reaffirmed...its unshakeable attachment to the principle that each individual is entitled to have his privacy respected and to self-determination in sexual matters. 1989 - both the Parliamentary Assembly of the Council of Europe and the European Parliament addressed the rights of transsexuals, prompted, it seems, by the negative decision of the European Court of Human Rights in the Rees case. The Council of Europe published reports on transsexual issues, in 1995 and 2000.

1993 - In the groundbreaking Roth report, the Committee on Civil Liberties of the European Parliament reported on equality issues for lesbians and gay men. In response to the report, the European Parliament, in February, 1994, called for (a) decriminalisation, (b) an equal age of consent, (c) equal social benefits, (d) inheritance and housing rights, (e) state action against homophobic violence, (f) anti-discrimination laws, (g) equal state funding for homosexual social and cultural organizations, (h) access to marriage or an "equivalent legal framework" and (i) equal adoption rights.

1997 - The Treaty of Amsterdam authorized the EU Council to act against discrimination on the basis of sexual orientation, but only if it acted unanimously and in response to a proposal from the Commission.

2000 - The Parliamentary Assembly of the Council of Europe restated now familiar calls for decriminalization, an equal age of consent, anti-discrimination laws and registration for same-sex relationships. It added some subjects: (a) refugee status for persons facing persecution on the basis of sexual orientation, (b) immigration rights for the same-sex partners of nationals, and (c) educational programs against homophobia, particularly in schools, the medical profession, the armed forces and the police.

Responding to these decisions, the Committee of Ministers of the Council of Europe in September, 2001, indicated some support, and specifically rejected "cultural" arguments:

Homosexuality can still give rise to powerful cultural reactions in some societies or sectors thereof, but this is not a valid reason for governments or parliaments to remain passive. On the contrary, this fact only underlines the need to promote greater tolerance in matters of sexual orientation.

2000 – The EU Council adopted the Employment Equality Directive, 2000/78/EC, which bars discrimination in employment on a number of grounds, including sexual orientation. The EU established a Group of Independent Experts on sexual orientation discrimination. They completed a detailed report on the implementation of the sexual orientation part of the equality directive in late 2004.

2000 - The European Union Charter of Fundamental Rights was proclaimed by the Parliament, Council and Commission of the European Union on December 7th, 2000, in Nice, France. Article 21 prohibits discrimination on a number of grounds, including sexual orientation.

2002 - Peter Schieder, the President of the Parliamentary Assembly of the Council of Europe, accepted the role of honorary patron of the European conference of the International Lesbian and Gay Association, meeting in Lisbon in October, 2002.

2002 - The European Parliament criticized Egypt's prosecution of 50 men as homosexuals, following up on an earlier resolution of November 2001, when the men were first arrested and charged. A further resolution in April, 2003, called on Egypt to "stop persecuting gays and to prohibit discrimination on grounds of sexual orientation..."

2003 – The European Court of Justice confirmed an earlier ruling that discrimination against transsexuals is a form of discrimination on the basis of sex, and prohibited by the EU treaty.

2004 – The draft European Constitution was completed, incorporating the Charter of Fundamental Rights, previously agreed upon. As before, the Charter would only apply to EU law, not to domestic law. The Constitution, which specifically committed the Union to combat discrimination based on sexual orientation, was defeated in referenda in France and the Netherlands in 2005.

2005 – The mobility directive 2004/58/EC came into force in July, 2005. It recognizes as a "family member" a same-sex partner of an EU citizen in situations where there has been a registered partnership under the laws of a member state and where registered partnerships are recognized in the law of the host country. The new directive, though limited, is the first occasion on which registered partnerships have gained recognition in EU law.

THE BUTTIGLIONE AFFAIR

In October, 2004, the incoming president of the EU Commission, Jose Manuel Barroso, named his 24 member executive team from candidates put forward by member states. For justice commissioner he chose Rocco Buttiglione of Italy, a friend of both the conservative Italian Prime Minister Silvio Berlusconi and Pope John Paul II. In hearings before the European Parliament Buttiglione was asked his position on homosexuality. He said he viewed homosexual acts as sinful, adding that this would not influence his actions as justice commissioner because such acts were not illegal. In additional comments he supported traditional roles for women. These events occurred in a period of some competition between the Parliament and the Commission. Quickly the homosexual issue became a flash point, with strong opposition building against Buttiglione.

The Parliament could not reject Buttiglione alone, but had the power to reject the full panel of commissioners proposed by President Barroso, something it had done once before on corruption issues. There was political pressure on parliamentarians to endorse Barroso's appointments, to prevent a hiatus. To appease the critics, Barroso made certain promises. He pledged to replace the existing anti-discrimination directives with a single document (which, by treating the differing grounds together, would extend the prohibition of sexual orientation discrimination beyond employment). Additionally he pledged to establish a new European human rights agency (an idea already moving forward). Opponents were not satisfied. On October 27th, Barroso withdrew his nominations in the face of almost certain rejection by the Parliament. Romano Prodi stayed in office as President on a caretaker basis.

On October 30th Buttiglione withdrew his name and Italy appointed foreign minister Franco Frattini in his place. Frattini, in questioning by members of the European Parliament, stated that same-sex partners who are legally recognized in any one of the EU member states should enjoy the same legal recognition throughout the European Union, a more progressive position than that found in the new mobility directive. In the Buttiglione affair, the issue of homosexual rights had caused an institutional crisis in the EU. The old distinction between sin and crime, which had been acceptable in public discourse in the 1950s and 1960s, was rejected. The crisis led to political promises on anti-discrimination laws and on mobility rights. It was a striking victory for GLBT equality in Europe, though promises made in the heat of battle remain to be fulfilled.

Getting into the Council of Europe and the European Union

After the end of the cold war the human rights requirements of the Council of Europe and the European Union were responsible for the rapid repeal of anti-homosexual criminal laws in Eastern Europe. No such rush of reforms has occurred in any other comparable period in any other region.

The reforms have now gone beyond decriminalisation to deal with the requirement of an equal age of consent and anti-discrimination laws. On September 7th, 1998, the European Parliament passed a resolution stating that it would not "give its consent to the accession of any country that, through its legislation or policies, violates the human rights of lesbians and gay men". It went on to criticize Austria, Bulgaria, Cyprus, Estonia, Hungary, Lithuania and Romania for unfair treatment of lesbians and gay men. Discriminatory laws were repealed in Lithuania in September, 2000, Estonia in September, 2001, Romania in December 2001, Cyprus in July, 2002, and Hungary and Bulgaria in September, 2002.

"This is a truly historic success for the human-rights policies of the European Union, for the European Parliament and for Europe's LGBT movement," said ILGA-Europe Executive Director Ailsa Spindler. "Changes which could have taken decades without international pressure have been effected in a few years." The on-going reforms led ILGA-Europe to announce that with the completion of law reform in Armenia on August 1st, 2003, Europe was free of laws banning same-sex relationships for the first time in 1,500 years. For the first time in many centuries, and probably since the enactment of Byzantine Emperor Justinian's legal code in the 6th Century AD, there will be no part of Europe where lesbians, gays and bisexuals face a threat of criminal prosecution simply because of their love for a person of the same sex. While the process of repealing laws banning same-sex relationships goes back two hundred years to the Napoleonic Code, the major changes have come about in the last half-century; in 1950 two-thirds of today's 48 European countries still criminalized relations between women and between men, or between men only.

Organisation for Security and Co-operation in Europe

The OSCE arose out of the Helsinki Accord of 1975, in which representatives of the two cold-war military alliances, the Warsaw Pact and the North Atlantic Treaty Organization, agreed to a set of security and human rights provisions. The OSCE has created a number of specialized institutions as well as holding meetings on various issues. Representatives of the International Lesbian and Gay Association have been active at meetings of the OSCE, beginning in 1980 when the OSCE was still a "Conference" not an "Organisation". A key ILGA representative, Kurt Krickler of Vienna, states:

ILGA has been participating as an NGO in the Human Dimension of the OSCE since the Moscow meeting in 1991. Since 1993, we have been presenting oral statements to the Human Dimension, reporting positive developments in participating States with regards to the respect of the human rights of lesbians and gay men but also reminding non-complying States to honour their commitments entered not only under the OSCE process but also under the International Covenant on Civil and Political Rights and the European Human Rights Convention.

The Final Report of the 1993 CSCE Implementation Meeting on Human Dimension Issues held in Warsaw included the following sentences:

Participants point out to groups which were not "national minorities" but which none the less suffered discrimination, including women, homosexuals, migrant workers, and conscientious objectors...

It was pointed out that CSCE commitments in the area of non-discrimination cover homosexuals as well. Suggestions were made that discriminatory State policies against homosexuals, and criminalizing legislation, should be eliminated. The Parliamentary Assembly of the OSCE met in Ottawa, Canada, in July, 1995. The Assembly passed a declaration that called on member States...to ensure that all persons belonging to different segments of their population be accorded equal respect and consideration in their constitutions, legislation and administration and that there be no subordination, explicit or implied, on the basis of ethnicity, race, colour, language, religion, sex, sexual orientation, national or social origin or belonging to a minority. The reference to sexual orientation was included at the initiative of Danish parliamentarians. It passed by a large majority, over protests from Bulgarian members.

FUNDING DECISIONS BY EUROPEAN INSTITUTIONS

The European Commission funded summer courses in lesbian and gay studies in Utrecht in 1989, in Essex in 1991, and again in Utrecht in 1995. The courses were organised by a number of European universities, including the Department of Gay and Lesbian Studies at the University of Utrecht in the Netherlands. European Union funding resulted in the production and publication in 1993 of two significant studies, "Lesbian Visibility" and "Homosexuality: A European Community Issue". The Democracy Programme of the European Union is designed to support economic and political reform in former eastern-bloc States. In 1994 the Programme funded an anti-discrimination project of ILGA involving work with seven lesbian and gay organisations in Estonia, Latvia, Lithuania and Russia. A number of the annual conferences of the International Lesbian and Gay Youth Organisation have received funding from the European Youth Foundation (Council of Europe) and the Commission of the European Union. Since December, 2000, ILGA-Europe, the European regional organization of the International Lesbian and Gay Association, has been receiving core funding from the European Commission under a program supporting organizations fighting discrimination at the European level. This support has led to the publication of a quarterly newsletter and the hiring of staff.

EUROPEAN FOREIGN POLICY

European Parliamentarians have looked beyond Europe. On January 23rd, 2001, a resolution of the European Parliament outlined priorities for the work of member States in the annual session of the United Nations Commission on Human Rights. Among other things, the parliament called for states to support measures to protect homosexuals against degrading and inhumane treatment. In April, 2001, the Parliament condemned the outbreak of homophobia within the ruling party of Namibia. In February, 2002, 127 MEPs signed an appeal to President Hosni Mubarak calling for the release of 23 Egyptians convicted and imprisoned for participating in a gay party. French President Chirac raised the issue directly with President Mubarak during his visit to Paris, February 9th, 2002.

In July 2001, the European Parliament adopted its annual report on the Union's foreign policy towards third countries. It called upon the "eighty countries in the world which still prohibit homosexuality in their domestic law to change this legislation without delay" and "urges those States which impose the death penalty on homosexuals to stop doing so immediately." The Netherlands has included financial support for lesbian and gay organisations in its foreign policy. It has provided funding to lesbian and gay groups in Costa Rica, El Salvador, Malaysia, Nicaragua and Zimbabwe, and funding for a regional conference in the Caribbean.

In 2003 it granted 170,000 Euros to a Ukrainian group, enough to allow the purchase of an office and salaries for four employees. Other states have made grants supporting lesbian and gay equality in developing states as part of their international promotion of human rights, including Australia, Canada, Denmark and Norway. But often they have recognized potential problems in such funding, and at least hesitated. A Canadian funded human rights workshop took three years to be approved, in spite of significant backing from figures in the ruling Liberal Party. The European Parliament does not include sexual orientation equality conditionality in their development assistance agreements with Third World states.

THE UNITED NATIONS

Sexual orientation issues are recognized in some parts of the large UN system and rejected in others. Progress has occurred in (a) treaty bodies, (b) world conferences, (c) the work of special rapporteurs, (d) the activities of working groups, and (e) the concerns of important non-governmental organizations.

CONSULTATIVE STATUS

The United Nations Economic and Social Council can grant 'consultative status' to non-governmental organizations, allowing them limited rights of participation in UN human rights meetings. The International Lesbian and Gay Association, ILGA, was granted consultative status in July, 1993, after an earlier refusal. Now there was an ongoing lesbian and gay voice within the United Nations. How was ILGA able to gain consultative status? Western states were determined to have Human Rights Watch accredited, over the objections of a number of states, particularly China and Cuba. For the first time decisions on accrediting NGOs, both in the NGO committee and in the Economic and Social Council itself, were done by majority vote, not by consensus. For the first time individual states did not have a veto. Because of that change, and because of the absence of delegates from developing countries at key meetings, ILGA was accredited as an innocent bystander during the fight over Human Rights Watch. Western states were pleased, but the accreditation of ILGA was something of a fluke. ILGA representatives made statements in the 1993 and 1994 sessions of the Sub-Commission and in the 1994 session of the Commission on Human Rights.

In 1994 right-wing forces in the United States found an issue to attack ILGA's accreditation at the United Nations. Of ILGAs 350 members, one was a highly controversial US organization that supported consensual "man-boy love." United States Senator Jesse Helms used that affiliation to block US funding to various international organizations if ILGA remained accredited at the UN. ILGA responded to the controversy by expelling three organizations from membership in June, 1994. Investigations by the United States concluded that there were other problematic ILGA members. On the basis of that information ECOSOC suspended ILGA in September, 1994. ILGA went on to draft a new constitution that committed the organization to the support of international human rights standards, including those in the Convention on the Rights of the Child. But the NGO committee of the Economic and Social Council repeatedly delayed dealing again with the question of ILGA, in spite of the wording of the suspension resolution and frequent ILGA requests. Letters and telephone calls went unanswered.

In January, 2002, the NGO Committee of the Economic and Social Council finally reconsidered the issue of ILGA's status. Germany, France, the United States, Romania, Chile and Bolivia voted in favour of consultative status. Canada, though not a member of the committee, lobbied strongly in favor of ILGA. Sudan, Pakistan, Tunisia, Libya, China, Senegal, Ethiopia and Russia voted against. Cuba, India, Colombia, Turkey and Algeria abstained. On April 30th the full Economic and Social Council confirmed the committee's decision by a vote of 29 to 17, with seven abstentions. Opposition in the Council to ILGA was led by Egypt, where the criminal convictions of homosexual men had garnered international publicity in 2001.

Other active opponents were Iran, Qatar, Sudan, Uganda and Zimbabwe. Active support came from western states, though Spain broke ranks with EU members to vote against ILGA. As a result, no organization representing gay, lesbian, bisexual or transgendered people presently has consultative status at the United Nations. No such organization has the ability to attend the regular meetings of the UN Charter bodies concerned with human rights, such as the Commission on Human Rights. A number of non-governmental organizations with consultative status now support lesbian and gay equality rights, including Amnesty International and Human Rights Watch. Lesbian and gay spokespeople have been able to speak in the UN Commission on Human Rights in recent years, accredited by various organizations that have consultative status.

WORLD CONFERENCES

The World Conference on Human Rights

Three lesbian and gay non-governmental organizations were accredited by the United Nations World Conference on Human Rights, held in Vienna in 1993. Participation was not limited to organizations accredited by the Economic and Social Council, for there were few such organizations in the developing world. Vienna was the first time that lesbian and gay organizations were recognized at a UN event. Six statements were made by lesbian and gay activists either in the plenary session or in the main committee. In addition, the representatives participated in the meetings of the NGO parallel conference. Five governments made positive references to lesbian and gay issues at Vienna: Australia, Austria, Canada, Germany and the Netherlands. Singapore was the only state to make a negative comment. In a statement pointedly titled "The Real World of Human Rights" Singapore described most human rights as "still essentially contested concepts."

The statement went on:

Singaporeans, and people in many other parts of the world do not agree, for instance, that pornography is an acceptable manifestation of free expression or that homosexual relationships is just a matter of lifestyle choice. Most of us will also maintain that the right to marry is confined to those of the opposite sex. The draft final conference statement had an equality paragraph condemning discrimination on listed grounds. In the drafting committee Canada proposed adding "sexual orientation" to the list. In response the paragraph was rewritten as a general, open-ended prohibition of discrimination, without a list.

The Fourth World Conference on Women

The Fourth World Conference on Women was held in Beijing in September, 1995. Canada and other states worked to have references to "sexual orientation" included in the final conference statement. In a preparatory conference in Vienna in October, 1994, Canada proposed a paragraph addressing discrimination against women on multiple grounds, such as sex and race, sex and disability, sex and sexual orientation. This "diversity paragraph," as it came to be known, was included in the draft text without opposition or discussion. At the New York preparatory meeting in March-April, 1995, Canada again proposed the paragraph. The paragraph along with much of the draft was "bracketed", indicating that there was no consensus on the wording. At the New York meeting several delegations, including South Africa, Canada, Israel and the European Union, proposed wording that referred to "sexual orientation." Lesbians were visible at the Conference in Beijing and at the NGO Forum in nearby Huairou. There was a 'lesbian tent' at the Forum and a lesbian march on September 5th. Eleven explicitly lesbian or lesbian and gay organisations were accredited to the conferences.

Two Canadian women unfurled a banner "Lesbian Rights are Human Rights" in the main conference hall. Security guards hastily intervened. At the beginning of the Beijing Conference there were four references to "sexual orientation" in the draft "Platform of Action". The four references were considered together in a drafting committee meeting that stretched into the early morning of the final day, Friday, September 15th, ending after 4 a.m. After an hour of debate on sexual orientation, the chair, Ms. Patricia Licuanan, commented that this had been the first substantive discussion of the subject in any United Nations forum. She said it required much more discussion, but given the division, the references would be omitted. Thirty-three States indicated their support for the references. Twenty States indicated opposition. The diplomatic preference for consensus decision-making prevailed. A fight on the floor in the closing plenary was avoided.

Five years after the Beijing conference, a special UN General Assembly session in June, 2000, revisited women's equality issues. Again the debate was intense, and again there was no consensus on adding "sexual orientation" even in a sentence that was drafted as a factual comment:

The turning point came in the wee hours of Thursday morning, the first of two all-night negotiating sessions, when Western nations continued insisting that expanded homosexual rights be listed among the document's accomplishment. The section noted measures taken "by a growing number of countries...to prohibit discrimination on the basis of sexual orientation."

"We cannot accept that language," said a delegate from Senegal. A Syrian delegate agreed: "There's no way we can accept a document tonight with the phrase 'sexual orientation.'" Delegates from Nicaragua and Kuwait said they could not accept "sexual orientation," an undefined term, as a human right. ...

Then the blowup came. Western delegations are "holding the women of the world hostage to one term, 'sexual orientation,'" when their real needs are clean water and help in overcoming illiteracy, said the Pakistan delegate. The International Service for Human Rights recorded the outcome:

The two most contentious issues were abortion and sexual orientation. A significant source of opposition came from Catholic and Islamic countries, including the Holy See, Nicaragua, Pakistan, Libya, Sudan, Iraq and Iran. Delegates from these countries blocked the use of the term "sexual orientation" from the final draft document and prevented it from being used even in a passage highlighting non-discrimination laws in various countries. In their closing statements, representatives of Norway, New Zealand, Canada and the European Union, stated their disappointment in the lack of language against discrimination based on sexual orientation and reaffirmed their commitment to anti-discrimination laws.

The General Assembly Special Session on HIV/AIDS

In June, 2001, the United Nations General Assembly held a Special Session on HIV/AIDS. Two questions arose. Would a speaker from the International Gay and Lesbian Human Rights Commission (IGLHRC), a US-based NGO, be allowed to speak at a UN sponsored workshop preceding the Special Session? Secondly, would the final statement of the Session mention homosexuals or sexual orientation? The Iranian Ambassador feared that the Session would turn into an opportunity for certain forces in the Western world to push the envelope in areas where there is cultural sensitivity, ideological sensitivity, ethical sensitivity.

Karen Kaplan, a staff person with IGLHRC, was included in the workshop by the Assembly President, then banned at the request of Egypt, Iran, Libya, Malaysia, Morocco, Pakistan, Saudi Arabia, Sudan and Syria. A motion to reinstate her was made by Canada, backed by the European Union, Australia, New Zealand, Argentina, Norway, Chile, Iceland and others. The United States did not co-sponsor the motion, but voted in favor. On the 24th, the issue of approving Kaplan was debated for over two hours, delaying the opening of the Session. Islamic states sought unsuccessfully on Monday to block a U.S.-based gay rights group from participating in a panel, delaying for hours a major U.N. General Assembly session on AIDS. The nations, from Malaysia to Syria, many represented by the Organization of Islamic Conference, tried to deny the assembly a quorum after it was clear they would lose a vote. But Assembly President Harri Holkeri of Finland refused to rule that a threatened walkout meant there was no quorum and said delegates could not speak in the assembly and then say they were not there. "We have had the presence of the majority of members here in the plenary," he said.... The Islamic nations were backed by Cuba, China, Russia and Belarus as well as Nigeria, Tanzania, Burkina Faso, Cameroon, Congo, Kenya, Mali, Senegal, Haiti and El Salvador. In the end, Karen Kaplan spoke at the workshop.

A Catholic-Muslim-Evangelical alliance was active. Lamani [a Moroccan diplomat representing the Organization of the Islamic Conference] said he was first approached by U.S. Christian non-governmental organizations, or NGOs, at the special session of the U.N. General Assembly on AIDS in New York in June 2001. Liberal Western activists and governments, he said, had offended the religious and cultural sensitivities of Islamic countries by proposing that a final conference declaration include explicit references to the need to protect prostitutes, intravenous drug users and "men who have sex with men" from contracting AIDS. "It was totally unacceptable for us," Lamani said. "The Vatican and so many NGOs came to us saying this is exactly the same position we are defending."

The final document approved by the Special Session made no mention of homosexuals, or the phrase "men who have sex with men," a phrase commonly used in HIV/AIDS prevention work. A last-minute compromise on the declaration came after

Western nations reluctantly agreed to drop language specifically naming groups vulnerable to the disease including homosexuals and prostitutes because it was offensive to some Muslim nations. Instead of mentioning "men who have sex with men," the new language refers to those who are at risk due to "sexual practice." Prostitutes are referred to as those vulnerable to infection due to "livelihood," and prisoners as those made vulnerable through "institutional location."

One Western diplomat, however, said the compromise text represented a victory for the Western camp. "The language of the declaration is not perfect because it does not contain any reference to sexual orientation," the diplomat stressed. "But the reference to homosexuals was a cut-off point for the Muslim group of countries." Europe was left in isolation after coalitions of Latin American and African countries as well as the United States failed to back its position, the diplomat said. But the Western camp was successful in imposing a paragraph on "cultural obstacles" relating to education, prevention and treatment of AIDS, he said, noting that the Islamic group had been persuaded to go along with it. Moreover, the text recognizes "women's rights over their sexuality." "It's a great victory for the European Union and a defeat for Egypt and Iran," said the diplomat, noting that "on a scale of one to three, we notched up two and a half."

THE WORLD CONFERENCE ON RACISM

The UN World Conference on Racism, Racial Discrimination, Xenophobia and Related Intolerance, was held in Durban, South Africa, August 31st to September 6th, 2001. Preparatory meetings developed a Draft Declaration and Programme of Action that included one reference to "sexual orientation" in another diversity-style paragraph. We recognize that certain persons and groups may experience other forms of discrimination on the basis of their gender, age, disability, genetic condition, language, religion, sexual orientation, economic status or social origin, and that in addition they may experience acts of racism, racial discrimination, xenophobia and related intolerance. We note that this situation can result in such persons being victims of multiple forms of discrimination, and stress that special attention should be given to the elaboration of strategies, policies and programmes, which may include affirmative action, for such persons.

A fight occurred over whether ILGA would be accredited to the conference. Malaysia, in the name of the Organization of the Islamic Conference, objected to ILGA's accreditation. The bitter fight in June over IGLHRC was repeated. On July 30th, 2001, a vote was held on ILGA, resulting in a 43-43 tie, defeating accreditation. The countries supporting ILGA were Western and Latin American States, but also Japan. The countries opposing were African and Islamic states, including Indonesia, Malaysia and Pakistan, plus China, India, Mongolia, Nepal, Singapore, Sri Lanka, and Vietnam. Abstainers included Cuba, the Philippines, Russia, South Africa, and Thailand. Many of the votes were not consistent with positions of those states taken in previous votes involving accreditation or the inclusion of references to sexual orientation. In spite of ILGA being barred, many lesbian and gay representatives participated at the parallel conference.

The opening speech of Secretary-General Kofi Annan on August 21st, 2001, referred to various grounds for discrimination – race, nationality, ethnicity, religion, gender, descent, citizenship and particular groups – refugees, migrants, migrant workers, indigenous peoples. The speech addressed the most divisive issues - the conflict between Israel and Palestine, and possible reparations for slavery. But, he said, by omission, discrimination on the basis of sexual orientation was not yet a United Nation's human rights concern.

Homosexuals again got no mention in the final conference declaration. But the document has an open-ended statement on equality and non-discrimination. There are three ways in which it can be interpreted as covering discrimination on the basis of sexual orientation, though those words are not included. It also speaks of goals of "tolerance, pluralism and respect for diversity," language used by the European Court of Human Rights to support homosexual equality rights.

TREATY BODIES

Six of the human rights treaties that operate under United Nations sponsorship have committees established to monitor state compliance with the provisions of the treaty. The Human Rights Committee is the UN treaty body responsible for monitoring state compliance with the International Covenant on Civil and Political Rights. Individuals from states that have signed the Optional Protocol to the treaty can make direct 'communications' to the Committee, alleging state violations of treaty provisions. The first decision of the Committee on lesbian and gay rights occurred in 1982 in Hertzberg v. Finland. Finnish penal law prohibited the public encouragement of "indecent behaviour" between persons of the same sex. This provision led to regulations and policies against radio and television programs dealing with homosexuality. Two programs had been censored and a third had been prosecuted, unsuccessfully, under Finnish penal law. Article 19 (3) of the Covenant on Civil and Political Rights provides that the right of freedom of expression can be limited to protect "public health or morals."

Finland argued that the restrictions in Finnish law reflected prevailing moral conceptions. The Committee considered asking for the transcripts of the two censored programs, noting that only by such an examination could it determine whether the programs simply contained factual information on issues relating to homosexuality. Apparently willing to assume that the programs could have been wholly factual, the Committee ruled in favor of Finland. It has to be noted, first, that public morals differ widely. There is no universally applicable common standard. Consequently, in this respect, a certain margin of discretion must be accorded to the responsible national authorities. The Committee finds that it cannot question the decisions of the responsible organs of the Finnish Broadcasting Company that radio and TV are not appropriate forums to discuss issues related to homosexuality, as far as a programme could be judged as encouraging homosexual behaviour. According to article 19 (3), the exercise of the rights provided for in article 19 (2) carries with it special duties and responsibilities for those organs. As far as radio and TV programmes are concerned, the audience cannot be controlled. In particular, harmful effects on minors cannot be excluded.

Norwegian academic Torkel Opsahl was joined by two other members of the Committee, in dissenting from this reasoning:

Under Article 19(2) and subject to article 19(3), everyone must in principle have the right to impart information and ideas - positive or negative about homosexuality and discuss any problem relating to it freely, through any media of his choice and on his own responsibility.

Moreover, in my view the conception and contents of the 'public morals' referred to in article 19(3) are relative and changing. State-imposed restrictions on freedom of expression must allow for this fact and should not be applied so as to perpetuate prejudice or promote intolerance. It is of special importance to protect freedom of expression as regards minority views, including those that offend, shock or disturb the majority. Therefore even if such laws as paragraph 9(2) of chapter 20 of the Finnish Penal Code may reflect prevailing moral conceptions, this is not in itself sufficient to justify it under article 19(3). It must also be shown that the application of the restriction is 'necessary'. In 1994 the Human Rights Committee decided Toonen v Australia, a case with strong similarities to Dudgeon v. United Kingdom. The Toonen decision, like the Dudgeon decision for Europe, marked a foundational recognition of gay and lesbian rights within the United Nations human rights system.

Nicholas Toonen, like Jeffrey Dudgeon, was a gay rights activist. Tasmania, like Northern Ireland, retained old criminal prohibitions on homosexual activity. All other Australian jurisdictions had decriminalised. The government of Australia, like that of the United Kingdom, sought the repeal of the law. As in Northern Ireland, the law in Tasmania was not enforced in practice. As in Northern Ireland opinion in Tasmania was divided on law reform. As in Northern Ireland, opposition was led by intemperate reactionaries. Elected representatives were quoted as saying that gay men were "no better than Saddam Hussein" and that people were "15 times more likely to be murdered by a homosexual than a heterosexual" Toonen argued privacy rights and equality rights. Article 17 of the International Covenant on Civil and Political Rights bars "arbitrary or unlawful interference" with privacy. Article 26 prohibits discrimination on any ground such as race, colour, sex, language, religion, political or other opinion, national or social origin, property, birth or other status.

There were two equality arguments. The discrimination was on the basis of "sexual orientation" which, it was argued, would come within the phrase "other status". As well the law discriminated on the basis of "sex" by applying only to male homosexual activity. By ignoring lesbians, the law followed a criminal law tradition that denied women's sexuality. Tasmania argued that the law was partly motivated by a concern to check the spread of HIV/AIDS. But Australia, the World Health Organisation and UN bodies all agreed that criminal prohibitions aimed at gay men made it more difficult to organise effective programs to prevent HIV infection. Tasmania also argued a moral basis for the prohibition. Australia conceded that "domestic social mores may be relevant to the reasonableness of an interference with privacy", while asserting a general Australian view that discrimination on the basis of sexual orientation was wrong.

The Committee followed the rulings of the European Court of Human Rights in Dudgeon, Norris and Modinos in finding that the Tasmanian law violated Toonen's right to privacy. They easily rejected Tasmania's arguments on HIV/AIDS and turned to the issue of a moral justification for the law in a passage which clearly departs from the spirit of the majority ruling in the earlier decision Hertzberg v. Finland:

The Committee cannot accept that for the purposes of article 17 of the Covenant, moral issues are exclusively a matter of domestic concern, as this would open the door to withdrawing from the Committee's scrutiny a potentially large number of statutes interfering with privacy. It further notes that with the exception of Tasmania, all laws criminalizing homosexuality have been repealed throughout Australia and that, even in Tasmania, it is apparent that there is no consensus as to whether Sections 122 and 123 should not also be repealed. Considering further that these provisions are not currently enforced, which implies that they are not deemed essential to the protection of morals in Tasmania, the Committee concludes that the provisions do not meet the "reasonableness" test in the circumstances of the case, and that they arbitrarily interfere with Mr. Toonen's right under article 17, paragraph 1.

The Committee dealt briefly with the issue of equality rights:

The State party has sought the Committee's guidance as to whether sexual orientation may be considered an "other status" for the purposes of article 26. The same issue could arise under article 2, paragraph 1, of the Covenant. The Committee confines itself to noting, however, that in its view the reference to "sex" in articles 2, paragraph 1, and 26 is to be taken as including sexual orientation.

The Committee was not saying that the exclusive focus on male activity constituted discrimination on the basis of "sex." Nor did it place "sexual orientation" within the phrase "other status." The Committee held that "sex" included "sexual orientation." Discrimination against homosexuals can only operate with reference to the sex of individuals and the sex of the people they desire. The idea that discrimination on the basis of sexual orientation is a form of discrimination on the basis of sex had not been widely accepted before the Toonen decision. Since the Toonen decision, the Human Rights Committee has included a concern with anti-homosexual criminal laws in its review of the reports required periodically of all State parties on compliance with the Covenant. India, for example, is now open to Committee criticism for maintaining a colonial-era criminal prohibition. The Committee has criticized the United States over anti-homosexual criminal laws. Other treaty bodies now deal with sexual orientation issues.

The U.N. Human Rights Committee has repeatedly concluded that laws criminalizing same-sex sodomy constitute discrimination based on sexual orientation. The U.N. Committee on Torture and the U.N. Working Group on Arbitrary Detention condemned Egypt's gender-neutral "debauchery" law as constituting discrimination on the basis of sexual orientation. Similarly the U.N. Committee on the Rights of the Child has analyzed disparities in age-of-consent laws between same and different-sex partners as sexual orientation discrimination. The concerns go beyond criminal laws. In concluding observations on Poland in November, 2004, the Human Rights Committee stated:

The State Party should provide appropriate training to law enforcement and judicial officials in order to sensitise them to the rights of sexual minorities. Discrimination on the ground of sexual orientation should be specifically prohibited in Polish law.

In 2000 the Committee on Economic, Social and Cultural Rights, the UN treaty body monitoring compliance with the International Covenant on Economic, Social and Cultural Rights, issued Comment 14 on the right to health. Such comments are issued periodically by various treaty bodies to explain their interpretation of particular provisions in their treaty. Following the logic of the Toonen case, Comment 14 interpreted the non-discrimination wording in article 2 (2) as prohibiting discrimination on the basis of "sexual orientation." In July, 2002, the Human Rights Committee considered the issue of same-sex marriage in the case of Joslin v. New Zealand. New Zealand courts had rejected the claim of two lesbian couples, both raising children, for access to marriage.

The Human Rights Committee rested its decision on the wording of section 23(2):

The right of men and women of marriageable age to marry and to found a family shall be recognized.

This is the only provision in the Covenant using gendered terms, referring to "men and women". The Committee held that this drafting limited the right to marry to opposite sex couples. A separate concurring opinion by two Committee members added that in some circumstances there might be a valid claim of denial of equality under section 26 for same sex couples, repeating the ruling from Toonen that discrimination on the basis of sexual orientation was included in the prohibition of discrimination on the basis of "sex."

Contrary to what was asserted by the State party (para. 4.12), it is the established view of the Committee that the prohibition against discrimination on grounds of "sex" in article 26 comprises also discrimination based on sexual orientation. And when the Committee has held that certain differences in the treatment of married couples and unmarried heterosexual couples were based on reasonable and objective criteria and hence not discriminatory, the rationale of this approach was in the ability of the couples in question to choose whether to marry or not to marry, with all the entailing consequences.

No such possibility of choice exists for same-sex couples in countries where the law does not allow for same-sex marriage or other type of recognized same-sex partnership with consequences similar to or identical with those of marriage. Therefore, a denial of certain rights or benefits to same-sex couples that are available to married couples may amount to discrimination under article 26, unless otherwise justified on reasonable and objective criteria.

The couples submitting the complaint had not alleged specific discrimination, seeking the symbolic validation that would be given to their relationships by marriage. In August, 2003, the Human Rights Committee again considered equality issues for same-sex couples in Young v Australia. Young's long-time same-sex partner, a war veteran, died in 1999. Young applied for the pension available to married or unmarried partners of war veterans. Since the legislation expressly applied only to heterosexual couples, the pension was refused. Australia argued that factors other than sexual orientation would have justified a denial of the pension, attempting to avoid, it seems, the discrimination issue. The Committee did not accept Australia's attempt to deflect the issue, for the legislation in question clearly limited the pension to dependents in heterosexual relationships. Australia, the Committee ruled, had shown no "reasonable or objective" ground for such discrimination (and had made no attempt to do so). The application for the pension would have to be reconsidered by Australian authorities, the Committee ruled, and a decision made which did not involve discrimination on the basis of sexual orientation.

HIGH COMMISSIONER FOR HUMAN RIGHTS

The office of the High Commissioner for Human Rights was created as a result of recommendations from the Vienna World Conference on Human Rights. The High Commissioner heads the section of the UN secretariat responsible for human rights, while having a much higher profile than simply the head of a UN department. Former Irish President Mary Robinson was High Commissioner from 1997 to 2002, with a much greater visibility than her predecessor. In October, 1998, she met with leaders of the International Lesbian and Gay Association and indicated a positive interest in receiving information on human rights violations against lesbians and gay men. Earlier she had acted for Senator Norris in the challenge to Ireland's anti-homosexual criminal laws before the European Court of Human Rights.

The present High Commissioner, Louise Arbour, was supportive of lesbian and gay equality rights when she served as a judge of the Canadian Supreme Court. The office of the High Commissioner has gradually increased in importance. The high-level report on reforming the United Nations, issued in December, 2004, suggested the High Commissioner should prepare an annual report on the situation of human rights worldwide.

SPECIAL RAPPORTEURS

Over the years 'special procedures' have developed in the UN Commission on Human Rights, that is practices that have no express basis in the Charter and go beyond earlier understandings on the limits of the Commission's mandate. The Commission authorizes the appointment of 'special rapporteurs' authorized to examine particular issues. Some are 'country specific', such as the special rapporteur on human rights in North Korea. Others are 'thematic', dealing with issues like violence against women, or torture.

In the annual meeting of the Commission on Human Rights in 2001 certain delegates objected to the inclusion of cases of extrajudicial executions of sexual minorities in the report of the UN Special Rapporteur on Extrajudicial, Summary, and Arbitrary Executions. Delegates argued that the special Rapporteur had overstepped her mandate by addressing these crimes. The resolution renewing her mandate was stripped of language explicitly recognizing that sexual minorities were vulnerable to extrajudicial executions.

This incident came a couple of months before a letter was circulated by the office of the High Commissioner for Human Rights indicating that six special rapporteurs appointed by the UN Commission on Human Rights "were interested in receiving information on sexual minority issues falling within their respective mandates..." The six are the Special Rapporteur on extrajudicial executions, the Special Rapporteur on violence against women, the Special Rapporteur on torture, the Special Rapporteur on the independence of judges and lawyers, the Special Rapporteur on freedom of expression, and the Special Representative of the Secretary-General on human rights defenders. The annual reports of these independent experts may now contain information on sexual orientation issues, if such information comes to the rapporteur's attention. As well the rapporteur may investigate specific cases. This development meant that by 2001 two parts of the United Nations system had institutionalized a concern with sexual minority issues - the treaty bodies and the Special Rapporteurs.

The Special Rapporteur on Extrajudicial, Summary and Arbitrary Executions, Asma Jahangir, was the first to include individual cases of severe persecution of members of sexual minorities in her reports to the Human Rights Commission; a decision that led to accusations by members of the Commission that she had overstepped her mandate. Since 1999, she has been systematically reviewing and investigating violations of the right to life of sexual minorities in her reports to the Commission and during her missions to various countries. Jahangir has studied issues such as the climate of impunity surrounding crimes against LGBT people, laws prescribing the capital punishment for homosexual relationships, and the link between violence and the criminalization of matters of sexual orientation. ... On 29 June 2001, the Special Rapporteur on freedom of expression, Abid Hussain, held a historic meeting with transgender activists while on official mission to Argentina. ... In November, 2001, the Special Representative on human rights defenders, Hina Jilani, met with Colombian LGBT organizations working with members of sexual minorities, people living with HIV/AIDS and sex workers during her stay in the country. That same month, the Special Rapporteur on torture, Nigel Rodley, raised the issue of torture and discrimination against sexual minorities before the UN General Assembly in New York.

The issue of the work of special rapporteurs came up again in April, 2002, at the Commission of Human Rights. The Special Rapporteur [on extrajudicial, summary or arbitrary executions] reports that she continues to receive information of persons having been subjected to death threats or extrajudicially killed due to their sexual orientation or for having advocated for the rights of sexual minorities. In this regard, urgent appeals have been sent to the Governments of Argentina, Ecuador and Mexico. A communication was also sent to the leadership of the province "Puntland" in Somalia. The urgent appeals have concerned NGOs and individuals. Pakistan, on behalf of the Organization of the Islamic Conference, moved to delete the two references to sexual orientation in the annual resolution extending the mandate of the Special Rapporteur. The motion was defeated, 28 to 15, with 9 abstentions. This reversed the hostile decision taken by the Commission in 2001.

The resolution on extrajudicial, summary and arbitrary executions, renewed periodically, continues to be the only resolution ever adopted by the Commission on Human Rights to include a reference to "sexual orientation." The report of the Special Rapporteur on health in 2004 dealt with sexual and reproductive health issues. He said these rights were central to efforts to achieve gender equality, poverty reduction, to combat HIV/AIDS and to achieve the Millennium Development Goals of the UN. ...discrimination on the grounds of sexual orientation is impermissible under international human rights law. The legal prohibition of same-sex relations in many countries, in conjunction with a widespread lack of support or protection for sexual minorities against violence and discrimination, impedes the enjoyment of sexual and reproductive health by many people with lesbian, gay, bisexual and transgender identities or conduct [referencing reports of special rapporteurs on torture and on extrajudicial executions].

Additionally, the Special Rapporteur recalls that the Human rights Committee, in Toonen v. Australia, observed: "Criminalization of homosexual activity ... would appear to run counter to the implementation of effective education programmes in respect of HIV/AIDS prevention." ...Sexual rights include the right of all persons to express their sexual orientation, with due regard for the well-being and rights of others, without fear of persecution, denial of liberty or social interference. The United States criticized the report for what it saw as a permissive stance on abortion and for suggesting that sexual orientation was within an international human rights framework. Pakistan...rejected the Special Rapporteur's conclusion that discrimination on the grounds of sexual orientation was impermissible under international human rights law and challenged the Special Rapporteur to quote exactly which article of any international human rights law convention prohibited such discrimination, According to Pakistan, the "easy" way for homosexuals, lesbians and transgender persons to avoid discrimination on the basis of sexual orientation was to "stop" engaging in non-heterosexual activity. In the words of the delegate, those of different sexual orientation should suppress their urges or "consult a medical doctor" and "get some medication." Egypt and Saudi Arabia agreed. Canada and Switzerland disagreed.

WORKING GROUPS

The Commission on Human Rights and the Sub-Commission have established a number of working groups to deal with specific issues. They typically consist of five or more members of the parent body, and meet separately from the parent body. The United Nations Working Group on Arbitrary Detention on June 21st, 2002, drew conclusions about the arrest and trail of fifty individuals in Cairo. The detention of the above-mentioned persons prosecuted on the grounds that, by their sexual orientation, they incited 'social dissension' constitutes arbitrary deprivation of liberty... This was an important development. Now three kinds of United Nations bodies - the treaty bodies, the special rapporteurs and the working groups - would be regularly examining human rights issues faced by gays and lesbians.

UN STAFF RULES

On August 4th, 2003, the organization of gay and lesbian UN employees held a panel discussion. They pointed out that the United Nations itself denied spousal benefits to same-sex partners. A UN spokesman said the secretary-general would have to move cautiously on that issue:

Member states themselves have divergent and strongly held views on this subject, so the secretary-general is carefully considering how he would forward on this issue. At the panel discussion some significant figures expressed support for dealing with gay and lesbian equality. Both Mark Malloch Brown, head of the UN Development Programme, and Peter Piot, executive director of the Joint UN Programme on HIV/AIDS, linked the ending of discrimination to the goals of their programs. The Secretary-General, Kofi Annan, issued a directive in February, 2004, extending spousal benefits to same-sex partners in those situations where the relationship was legally recognized in the staff-person's home country. The General Assembly, "pressured by the Vatican and numerous Islamic and African nations," insisted that the Secretary-General reconsider the directive. It was revised to omit the phrase "domestic partnership," but not changed in substance.

CHARTER BODIES: THE COMMISSION ON HUMAN RIGHTS AND THE SUB-COMMISSION

CRITICISMS OF THE COMMISSION AND SUB-COMMISSION

The primary UN human rights bodies established under the United Nations Charter are the Commission on Human Rights and the Sub-Commission on the Promotion and Protection of Human Rights (formerly the Sub-Commission on the Prevention of Discrimination and the Protection of Minorities). From the early 1980s, voting in the Commission has been heavily weighted against the West, and the assignment of seats is not on the basis of regional populations. Of the 53 members, 15 are from Africa, 12 from Asia, 5 from Eastern Europe, 11 from Latin America and the Caribbean and 10 from the Western group (Western Europe, the United States, Canada, Australia and New Zealand). Africa, the most homophobic continent (in terms of the statements of political leaders) has 15 votes, though the total population of the continent is less than either China or India.

Criticisms of the Commission on Human Rights are common. They were forcibly restated in the report issued in December, 2004, by the high-level group authorized by the Secretary-General to review the workings of the United Nations. It spoke of "eroding credibility and professionalism" on the part of the Commission. Standard-setting to reinforce human rights cannot be performed by States that lack a demonstrated commitment to their promotion and protection. We are concerned that in recent years States have sought membership of the Commission not to strengthen human rights but to protect themselves against criticism or to criticize others. The Commission cannot be credible if it is seen to be maintaining double standards in addressing human rights concerns.

Some observers expressed amazement that the Commission's Working Group on Situations for 2005, which reviews confidential accusations of human rights violations against states (the so called 1503 procedure), had as members Cuba, Zimbabwe and China, along with the Netherlands and Hungary. Other questionable members of the Commission for 2005 were Congo, Saudi Arabia and Sudan. And when the Brazilian resolution on sexual orientation was introduced in 2003, the Chair of the Commission represented Libya. Why the Commission is a political body, the Sub-Commission is supposed to be composed of individual experts, who, while nominated by their countries, act in a 'personal capacity.' The quality of members varies greatly, with some showing no expertise and no independence. Others are excellent.

ACTIONS OF THE COMMISSION AND SUB-COMMISSION

The only UN study on sexual orientation issues arose out of a report on prostitution, seen as a 'slavery-like practice,' done for the Sub-Commission. That report recommended an additional study on male prostitution, but the recommendation made confused references to transvestism, transsexuals and pedophilia. The resulting study, on the legal and social problems of sexual minorities, including male prostitution, was completed in 1987. There was no lesbian or gay voice within the UN system at the time. ILGA forwarded information to Mr. Fernand-Laurent, the special rapporteur, through Minority Rights Group, an accredited non-governmental organisation. The final report contained an odd mix of stereotypes and misinformation. The report attracted almost no attention. Mr. Rhenan-Segura, a member of the Sub-Commission, called the study superficial and the conclusions dubious.

He found the study to be of poor quality and said it had been received under an inappropriate agenda item, the consideration of the report of the Working Group on Slavery and Slavery-Like Practices. Such criticisms of reports are extremely rare in the diplomatic milieu of the United Nations. There were no follow up resolutions. Few at the UN remember that the report was ever done. No actions at the United Nations since then have referred back to it. The present author made the first statement as a homosexual in a United Nations forum in 1992 in the Sub-Commission. The statement was made in the name of Human Rights Advocates, a San Francisco based NGO, and the International Lesbian and Gay Association, ILGA, which did not have consultative status. Observers noted that the statement was greeted by "open hostility" on the part of some members of the Sub-Commission. A study by Special Rapporteur Danilo Turk, received by the Sub-Commission in August, 1992, addressed the issue of indicators to be used in assessing State compliance with economic, social and cultural rights. One approach, the study said, was to begin with assessing patterns of discrimination.

It went on:

To apply discrimination-oriented criteria, however, it will be necessary to devote increased attention to areas of discriminatory behaviour generally ignored at the international level, in particular the grounds of social status, income level, medical status, age, property and sexual orientation. On August 13th, 1993 Mr. Louis Joinet, the French member of the Sub-Commission, proposed that the mandate of a study on new forms of racism and xenophobia be expanded to include consideration of discrimination on the basis of sexual orientation. The proposal was not accepted. On August 24th, 1995, in the Sub-Commission Mr. Louis Joinet proposed an amendment to a resolution condemning discrimination on the basis of HIV/AIDS. The resolution mentioned nine examples of groups "suffering from disadvantaged economic, social or legal status" who were, as a result of that marginalisation, more vulnerable to the risk of HIV infection. The list did not include male homosexuals, an obvious category in the west for any such list. Mr. Joinet moved the addition of that category. The amendment was strongly opposed by two members, Ms. Warzazi and Ms. Gwanmesia.

After a somewhat heated exchange and an accusation of homophobia, the amendment was passed with ten affirmative votes, five negative votes and six abstentions. This was the first substantive resolution of the Commission or Sub-Commission to refer expressly to homosexuals. In August, 1996, representatives of Australia discussed the idea of a study on sexual orientation discrimination with several members of the Sub-Commission. There was some support, and an understanding that there would also be opposition. The matter was not raised in public sessions of the Sub-Commission. In August, 2003, a working group of the Sub-Commission drafted a document defining how it thought international human rights standards applied to transnational corporations and other business enterprises.

The document requires corporations to end any discrimination based on race, colour, sex, language, religion, political opinion, national or social origin, social status, indigenous status, disability, age or other status of the individual. The commentary attached to the draft gives as an example of an "other" status "sexual orientation." The report of the working group was approved by the Sub-Commission for consideration by the Commission.

THE BRAZILIAN RESOLUTION

The April Surprise, 2003

In April, 2003, with no advance warning, Brazil introduced a resolution "Human Rights and Sexual Orientation" in the Commission on Human Rights. The draft resolution said that the Commission

1. Expresses deep concern at the occurrence of violations of human rights all over the world against persons on the grounds of their sexual orientation;
2. Stresses that human rights and fundamental freedoms are the birthright of all human beings, that the universal nature of these rights and freedoms is beyond question and that the enjoyment of such rights and freedoms

should not be hindered in any way on the grounds of sexual orientation;

3. Calls upon all States to promote and protect the human right of all persons regardless of their sexual orientation;
4. Notes the attention given to human rights violations on grounds of sexual orientation by the special procedures in their reports to the Commission on Human Rights, as well as the treaty monitoring bodies, and encourages all special procedures of the Commission on Human Rights, within their mandates, to give due attention to the subject;
5. Requests the High Commissioner for Human Rights to pay due attention to violations of human rights on the grounds of sexual orientation;
6. Decides to continue consideration of the matter at its sixtieth session under the same agenda item.

The resolution gained 27 co-sponsors, including Australia, Canada and the countries of the European Union. Pakistan moved a "no action" motion. That procedural move was defeated, permitting consideration of the resolution itself. A number of countries had been caught off guard, and they sought direction from their home governments. No consultations had occurred with other states before the resolution was presented, a breach of standard practice. The United States delegation received instructions from Washington to abstain in any vote on the resolution. Amnesty International issued a statement of support. Amendments were proposed by Saudi Arabia, Pakistan, Egypt, Libya and Malaysia affecting all paragraphs of the draft resolution. Pakistan threatened to move a hundred more amendments.

The goal was to block any vote on the resolution. All this took place in the last days of the Commission session. The resolution and amendments were put over for consideration to the next session in 2004 by a vote of 24 to 17, with 12 abstentions. Some countries that had supported GLBT rights in votes in the past did not support the Brazilian motion in 2003, notably Argentina, Cameroon, Chile, Cuba, Peru, South Africa, the United States, Uruguay and Venezuela. Their positions may not be fixed. The GLBT Muslim organization Al-Fatiha condemned the Organization of Islamic Conference and the Vatican for using religion to justify homophobia and intolerance.

Round two - 2004

In advance of the 2004 Commission session, Pakistan, as coordinator of human rights and humanitarian issues in the Organization of the Islamic Conference, circulated a letter to other OIC missions in Geneva. It listed a set of arguments against the Brazilian resolution. The concept of "sexual orientation" has never been defined in the UN. It has hardly ever figured in a UN document. Efforts to do so have always created enormous controversy and discord. ... The list of sexual behaviour could always be expanded to include grossly errant behaviour like pedophilia. ... In our perspective sexual orientation is not a human rights issue. Instead it is related to social values and cultural norms. Individual countries need to deal with this issue within the parameters of their own social and legal systems. ... The concept of the traditional family constitutes the foundation of the human civilization.

The Holy See, which has observer status at the United Nations, also circulated its views on the Brazilian resolution. This appears to be a preliminary step to claiming equal treatment regarding "marriage" for persons of the same sex, and regarding adoption for "unisexual households." This attempt might be facilitated if a request were made to the Sub-Commission on Human Rights to undertake a study on discrimination on any grounds, including "sexual orientation." The short document dealt with marriage and adoption three times, clearly a central concern. Like the Pakistan Ambassador's letter, it argued that "sexual orientation" has not been recognized in international human rights law. Around fifty lesbian and gay activists traveled to Geneva for the 2004 session of the Commission on Human Rights to support the Brazilian resolution. No comparable lobbying effort had ever been made in the past and a number spoke in Commission sessions. The lobbyists were active and visible, organizing panel discussions during the Commission session that drew good audiences.

Argentina, Brazil, Canada, Germany and Sweden used their speeches in the 'high-level' session to state their concern with discrimination on the basis of sexual orientation. Brazil announced the launch of its "Brazil Without Homophobia" educational campaign, but did not mention the resolution. In contrast, opposition was silent or indirect. Rather ominously the Pakistani delegate concluded his statement on behalf of the OIC by stressing the need for co-operation and understanding, and warning against "efforts to create new rights not sanctioned by existing treaty law" arguing that they would be "high fractious, divisive and counterproductive." In implicit reference to the postponed resolution of Brazil on sexual orientation, the delegate asserted "attempts to develop norms which directly contradict fundamental value systems need to be avoided. No Islamic society would be able to accept any obligation which directly contradicts the basic tenets of our religion". Brazil did not reintroduce the motion in 2004. It issued a statement that more time was necessary for consultations with other states in hopes of building a consensus. The resolution was deferred to the next annual session.

Round three - 2005

In advance of the 2005 Commission session the International Commission of Jurists published a compilation of international human rights law references to sexual orientation and gender identity. It demonstrated, in over a hundred pages of detailed text, the extent to which sexual orientation issues had already been recognized in the special procedures, the treaty bodies and the refugee system. Around 60 GLBT representatives traveled to Geneva, organizing parallel panel sessions and lobbying governments. The resolution was not introduced again in 2005, ending the Brazilian initiative. The official reason given was a lack of support in the Commission. The resolution would not pass.

Both the German delegation and the NGO Human Rights Watch believed that there were probably enough votes to pass the resolution if the obstructive tactics of opposing states could be overcome. One organizer analyzed the position of various countries, concluding that approval or rejection lay with 7 states whose vote he could not predict. In contrast, a prominent opponent estimated a vote at the 2005 session of the Commission of 23 against the resolution, defeating 20 or 21 supporters, with about 11 abstentions. There have been surprises for those predicting the positions of states. Italy did not support the resolution in 2003, departing from what was otherwise an EU consensus. In 2005, South Africa indicated to local activists that it was not prepared to sponsor or support the resolution, in part, at least, to avoid undercutting its position as a leader within the African regional group.

What creates the possibility of majority support for the Brazilian resolution is a combination of votes from the West and from Latin America - plus the possibility of support from countries like South Africa, South Korea, Japan and the Philippines - and abstentions.

Understanding Brazil's actions

Given the difficulties of dealing with 'sensitive' issues within the Commission, why did Brazil make its move in 2003? And why did it back off in 2004 and 2005? It seems that the resolution had been largely the initiative of two individual Brazilian diplomats. It was consistent with positions taken by Brazil during the presidency of Fernando Henrique Cardoso, both at home and at the UN World Conference on Racism in Durban in 2001. Brazil had been a lead state in Durban in trying to get a reference to sexual orientation in the final conference statement.

The current Brazilian government of President Luis Inacio Lula da Silva, which took office in January, 2003, has been very active, internationally, but not in ways conducive to the initiative on gay and lesbian rights. Brazil has established itself as a leader of developing states at the UN and in the World Trade Organization. Brazil heads the 'G-20', which challenged the US and the EU on agricultural subsidies at the WTO ministerial meeting in Cancun, Mexico, changing the politics within the trade organization. Brazil put forward its own candidate for the post of director-general of the WTO, with support from China and India. Lula has actively sought investment from Arab states. In April, 2005, he hosted an Arab-South America summit in Brazil, with representatives of thirty-four states. The story has circulated that Egypt directly asked Brazil to drop the resolution on sexual orientation.

There are no votes for sexual orientation equality among the Arab states, and few from the members of the G-20. For Brazil, current economic and political considerations are in conflict with pursuing the equality initiative. Western states expressed a reluctance to take over sponsorship of the resolution from Brazil. The German delegation, probably the strongest supporter of the Brazilian resolution, said European sponsorship would the "kiss of death." It would polarize the issue between Western and non-Western countries, something that is already a reality within the UN.

A member of the South African delegation said that the perception of developing states was that Brazil "was being used by the EU to push the resolution" because, it said, Brazil gave no reason for the initiative. South Africa had no interest in taking over the Brazilian initiative, saying it would only support resolutions that dealt with discrimination in general, and also was focused on development issues. South Africa wanted to retain a leadership role in the African group at the UN, and support for the Brazilian resolution conflicted with that goal. To a number of participants, the goal of reducing that polarization was more important than the passage of the resolution.

Lobbying at the Commission, Without the Brazilian Resolution

While the 2005 sessions of the Commission were notable for the number of GLBT representatives trying to engage the process, opponents were oddly silent. Perhaps they knew that they had won this round. They chose to revert to silence on the issues, rather than repeating their arguments. Only one NGO made an intervention expressing concerns about sexual orientation equality (and then only in the context of the free speech implications of a specific Swedish law prohibiting the promotion of disrespect towards minorities). No State in plenary explicitly spoke against recognition of human rights based on sexual orientation, although Pakistan on behalf of the OIC (Organization of the Islamic Conference) warned against recognition of "new rights that can be contrary to religious and cultural values."

GLBT activists became engaged in a number of specific lobbying efforts during the Commission sessions in 2005. There was enthusiasm when Sweden agreed to include a reference to "gender identity" in the draft resolution on extrajudicial executions, the most obvious place in the UN system to recognize human rights abuses against transgendered individuals. But Sweden dropped the reference during bargaining on the text. Canada included a reference to "sexual orientation" in the draft text of the resolution on violence against women. Again it was dropped. Sweden and Canada have sponsored these specific resolutions for a number of years, and were concerned to get continuing support against some real opposition. Each resolution already included some controversial language (on 'honor killings' for example).

Each resolution authorizes the work of a special rapporteur. The rapporteurs can deal with issues of sexual orientation and gender identity when relevant to their mandates, with or without specific authorization. In 2005 eight rapporteurs dealt with such issues in their reports. The work of GLBT activists in the Commission in 2005 led many governments to speak in support of their goals. There were references to sexual orientation rights in the opening 'high level' segment, in the debates around special procedures, in an EU statement and in a statement by New Zealand delivered on behalf of 32 states (both current members and non-members of the Commission).

New Zealand said, in part:

Sexual orientation is a fundamental aspect of every individual's identity and an immutable part of self. It is contrary to human dignity to force an individual to change their sexual orientation, or to discriminate against them on this basis. And, it is repugnant for the State to tolerate violence committed against individuals because of their sexual orientation. ... we recognize that sexuality is a sensitive and complex issue. But we are not prepared to compromise on the principle that all people are equal in dignity, rights and freedoms. The Commission must uphold the principle of non-discrimination. We urge all States to recognize this common ground and to participate in debate. We hope this Commission will not be silent for too much longer.

Human Rights Watch noted some progress at the Commission in 2005:

Strong language on the protection of people on the grounds of sexual orientation was retained in the resolution on extra-judicial executions. However, an attempt to explicitly condemn extrajudicial killings of transgender people, a frequent phenomenon in some countries, was blocked. At the same time, the commission maintained its silence on the human rights abuses relating to sexual orientation and gender identity in other contexts, despite strong calls by non-governmental organizations for a resolution on this subject. It seems most likely that the GLBT activism at Geneva will continue. Even if there is no big issue, like the Brazilian resolution, there are on-going issues about the mandates of special rapporteurs and perhaps a goal to get an official study on sexual orientation and gender identity issues (that opponents have already identified as a move to be opposed). John Fisher, involved in the coordination of GLBT activity in 2004 and 2005, was upbeat about the most recent session of the Commission. To him the "era of invisibility is over..."

THE BOSSUYT STUDY ON DISCRIMINATION

The Sub-Commission on the Promotion and Protection of Human Rights in August, 2004, received a working paper on non-discrimination by Sub-Commission Member Emmanuel Decaux of France. Madam Warzazi, a long-standing member from Morocco, objected to a reference to sexual orientation, citing cultural and religious concerns...and asserting that the legal doctrine on this aspect of non-discrimination was not so settled as Mr. Decaux seemed to suggest. Mr Pinheiro [Brazil] disagreed; he remarked that, while cultural concerns remained a relevant factor, they should not constitute obstacles to fighting discrimination based on sexual orientation.

The Sub-Commission appointed Mr. Marc Bossuyt to undertake a full study on non-discrimination as enshrined in article 2, paragraph 2, of the International Covenant on Economic, Social and Cultural Rights. Madam Warzazi told Bossuyt to exclude any discussion of sexual orientation from the study. She said that no delegation during the Vienna World Conference on Human Rights "ever thought of sexual orientation" and that it had been "excluded" from the conference. Four other members of the Sub-Commission endorsed Madam Warzazi's comments, while two pointedly suggested that "new issues were constantly appearing" in international law. Madam Warzazi had chaired the Main Committee at Vienna, in which representatives of three accredited lesbian and gay organizations spoke. The head of the Australian government delegation personally lobbied Warzazi to allow more time for the GLBT organizations to participate, a request Warzazi rejected. And, as noted earlier, five governments made statements in plenary sessions opposing sexual orientation discrimination. Warzazi's hostility to lesbian and gay rights was clear at Vienna, making it unlikely that she would forget what had taken place.

REGIONAL TREATY-BASED HUMAN RIGHTS BODIES

In 1992 the refusal of the Government of Argentina to grant legal status to the non-governmental organisation Comunidad Homosexual Argentina was taken to the Inter-American Commission of Human Rights. The refusal had been confirmed in a decision of the Supreme Court of Argentina. Later that year the government granted legal recognition to the organisation, an act which the Commission considered an "amicable settlement" of the matter. The same problem was repeated in 1995 with the refusal of government agencies to register the Costa Rican group Abraxas and the Association of Honduran Homosexuals Against Aids. After protest, the Costa Rican organisation was registered. In 1998 a lesbian journalist in the United States was fired from her job for off-the-job political activity on behalf of lesbian and gay rights.

She petitioned the Inter-American Commission over the failure of the United States Supreme Court to review a judicial decision upholding her firing. In 1999 the Inter-American Commission ordered El Salvador to provide anti-retroviral medications to twenty-six Salvadorans whose lives were endangered by AIDS. In 1999, Marta Alvarez, a lesbian prisoner in Colombia, petitioned the Inter-American Commission for equal access to conjugal visits. In October, 2001, the Supreme Court of Colombia, in a separate case, handled by the same feminist lawyer, ordered that conjugal prison visits for a lesbian couple take place on the same basis as those for heterosexual couples. This ruling was not applied to the case of Marta Alvarez until November, 2002.

In 1995 a petition was submitted to the African Commission on Human Rights asking it to open an inquiry into Zimbabwe's laws and policies on homosexual conduct. The communication was withdrawn at the request of the country's largest lesbian and gay organisation out of concern for possible reprisals by the government. Later in 1995, a large book fair, annually held in Harare, banned a gay rights exhibit under pressure from the government. Four organisations boycotted the fair in protest. President Robert Mugabe in a speech opening the fair denounced homosexuals, saying "We do not believe they have any rights at all." Later he called for an international campaign "to oppose those who support homosexuality." He said that homosexuality was not part of African culture. Mugabe has continued to give speeches condemning homosexuals, saying they are no better than dogs or pigs.

SPECIALIZED AGENCIES

The World Health Organisation's Global Programme on AIDS was established in 1987. While the WHO constantly restates the basic proposition that HIV/AIDS is not a gay disease, it has pointed out that discrimination against gay men, women and racial minorities creates serious problems for effective HIV prevention programs. ILGA and other lesbian and gay rights organisations have participated in the various HIV/AIDS conferences organised by the WHO. ILGA has co-operated with the Global Program on AIDS in many projects. WHO supported and co-sponsored annual ILGA regional conferences for eastern and south-eastern Europe since the Prague conference in 1991. The World Health Organisation funded several research projects at the Department of Gay and Lesbian Studies at the University of Utrecht.

The 1991 Human Development Report, issued by the United Nations Development Programme, rated countries according to a "Human Freedom Index", reflecting the idea that "freedom" strengthens economic growth. The group of 77 developing states, an informal grouping within the UN membership, objected the index, for one of the forty criteria used in assessing states was whether homosexual acts were legal. Because of this opposition, the UNDP developed a new "Political Freedom Index" to replace the broader "Human Freedom Index" and stopped publishing the ratings of individual States. Refugees are defined as individuals who have a well-founded fear of persecution based on grounds of race, religion, nationality, membership of a particular social group or political opinion. The United Nations High Commissioner for Refugees has interpreted the phrase "social group" to include lesbians and gay men.

This interpretation has been accepted by decisions in many States. The first cases to gain widespread coverage occurred in Australia, Canada and the United States and involved individuals from Argentina, Brazil and China. The idea that lesbians or gay men can constitute a "social group" for refugee status no longer seems controversial and is expressly stated in the 1991 Austrian law on asylum. The issue in individual cases will be whether there is evidence establishing a well-founded fear of persecution on the part of the individual making the application, not whether lesbians or gay men constitute a 'social group.'

SUPPORT BY STATES AT THE U.N.

The following states have voted in favour of lesbian and gay rights. "A" means the state supported the original accreditation of ILGA at the United Nations either in the NGO Committee of the Economic and Social Council or in the Council itself. "B" means that the state supported wording on lesbian rights at the Fourth World Conference on Women, held in Beijing in 1995. "C" indicates the state supported lesbian and gay rights in meetings of the Organisation for Security and Co-operation in Europe. "D" means the state supported the accreditation of ILGA to the World Conference on Racism in 2001. "E" means the state supported the motion in the UN Economic and Social Council for reconsideration of ILGAs application for accreditation in April, 2002.

"F" means the state supported the inclusion of "sexual orientation" in the resolution on the Special Rapporteur on Extrajudicial Executions at the Commission on Human Rights in April, 2002. "G" means that the state supported Brazil's draft resolution in the Commission on Human Rights in April, 2003 (though the resolution never went to a vote). "H" means that they supported the New Zealand statement in the Commission on Human Rights in April, 2005 (made after it was clear that the Brazilian resolution would not be debated). Andorra (E, H), Argentina (A, H), Armenia (F,G), Australia (A,B,C,D,E,G), Austria (A,B,C,D,E,F,G,H), Barbados (B), Belarus (A), Belgium (A,B,D,F,G,H), Bolivia (B), Brazil (A,B,D,F,G), Bulgaria (A,D), Burundi (F), Cameroon (F), Canada (A,B,C,D,F,G,H), Chile (A,B,D,F,H), Colombia (B,D), Cook Islands (B), Costa Rica (A,F,G), Croatia (D,E,F), Cuba (A,B), Cyprus (H), Czech Republic (D,F,G,H), Denmark (A,B,C,D,G,H), Ecuador (F), El Salvador (D), Estonia (D), Finland (B,C,D,E,G,H), France (A,B,D,E,F,G,H), Georgia (E), Germany (A,B,D,E,F,G,H), Greece (A,B,D,G,H), Guatemala (D,F,G,H), Hungary (D,E), Iceland (H), Ireland (A,B,D,G,H), Israel (B,D), Italy (A,B,D,E,F), Jamaica (B), Japan (A,D,E,F,G), Latvia (B,D), Liechtenstein (D,G), Lithuania (D), Luxembourg (B,D,G,H), Macedonia (D), Malta (E), Mexico (A,F,G,H), Monaco (D), Netherlands (B,C,D,E,G), New Zealand (B,D,H), Norway (A,B,C,D,G,H), Peru (A,F), Poland (D,F,G),

Portugal (B,D,F,G,H), Republic of Korea (F,G,H), Romania (D,E,H), Russian Federation (A,G), San Marino (D), Slovakia (D), Slovenia (B,D,H), South Africa (B), Spain (A,B,D,F,G,H), Sweden (A,B,C,E,F,G,H), Switzerland (B,D,H), Thailand (F,G), Ukraine (A,B,C,D,G), United Kingdom (A,B,D,E,F,G,H), United States (A,B,C,D,E), Uruguay (F,H), Venezuela (F,H).

This list has some surprises. Cuba has frequently been criticised for its treatment of lesbians and gays, but it cast two positive votes internationally. During some of the years that Chile cast positive votes it still had criminal laws against male homosexual acts. Austria had discriminatory laws but a consistently positive voting record. Ireland and Russia were supportive at meetings that took place before their anti-homosexual criminal laws had been repealed. India abstained on the original ECOSOC vote to accredit ILGA, though Indian criminal law prohibits male homosexual acts. It then voted against ILGA in ECOSOC in 2002. Domestic laws or policies do not always dictate state policies in international meetings.

While the Netherlands played an early role, Australia and Canada have been the most active states in recent years, with Brazil taking a lead in 2003 at the Human Rights Commission. Australia lobbied for more speaking time for lesbian and gay organisations at the Vienna World Conference on Human Rights in 1993, as well as urging movement on sexual orientation issues in their major statement at the conference. Australia has raised lesbian and gay rights in the U.N. Commission on Human Rights. Australia introduced national legislation to implement the Human Rights Committee decision in the Toonen case. The change in government in Australia in 1996 did not alter the government's position on sexual orientation issues. Prime Minister Howard stated in February, 1996, that the two coalition parties "strongly oppose discrimination against individuals or groups on the grounds of race, gender, religion or sexuality."

His Foreign Minister, Alexander Downer stated:

I am strongly committed to individuals having the freedom to conduct their lives as they wish so long as that freedom does not impinge upon the freedom of others. I will carry out this commitment as Foreign Minister by ensuring that in its diplomatic representations abroad and in multilateral fora, Australia continues to oppose the persecution against individuals on the basis of religion, ethnic grouping or sexual preference. Canada led the campaign to have IGLHRC seated at the workshop associated with the General Assembly's Special Session on AIDS. It is also now one of the most advanced western states in terms of domestic law. The inconsistent voting patterns of Argentina, Brazil, Chile, Costa Rica, Cuba, India, Mexico, Russia, South Africa, Spain and Ukraine suggest that with effective lobbying an international gay and lesbian organization could gain "consultative status" if the organization was not tainted by controversy.

NON-GOVERNMENTAL ORGANISATIONS

The leading international lesbian and gay non-governmental organizations are ILGA and IGLHRC. ILGA, the International Lesbian and Gay Association, is a loosely organized, poorly funded federation of over 350 organizations. IGLHRC, the International Gay and Lesbian Human Rights Commission, does work comparable to Amnesty International in publishing background materials, country studies and urgent action bulletins. Neither organization has "consultative status" at the United Nations. The number of non-governmental organizations that will deal with sexual orientation issues has slowly increased, and now includes both Amnesty International and Human Rights Watch:

- In 1996 the Canadian Inter-Church Committee on Human Rights in Latin America published a report "Violence Unveiled: Repression against Lesbians and Gay Men in Latin America."
- In 1997 War on Want, based in the United Kingdom, published a report "Pride World-Wide: Sexuality, Development and Human Rights." It has begun a program of financial support for certain lesbian and gay organisations in third world countries.
- In 1998 Human Rights Watch and the International Gay

and Lesbian Human Rights Commission jointly published a report on sexual orientation and criminal law in Romania, probably the first such collaboration between a general human rights NGO and a lesbian/gay organization. In 2003 they jointly published "More Than a Name: State-Sponsored Homophobia and its Consequences in Southern Africa."

- A grouping within the World Council of Churches, begun in 2000, has taken up ILGA's call for the United Nations to commission a study on discrimination on the basis of sexual orientation.
- Amnesty International altered its mandate in August, 2001, to deal with all human rights and all forms of discrimination. Previously its work on sexual orientation issues was officially limited to cases of imprisonment, state sponsored torture or state tolerated violence. In practice it had moved beyond that mandate, a shift now officially validated. Many branches of Amnesty International have LGBT groups, including those in Thailand and the Philippines. AI members march in pride parades, call for anti-discrimination laws, and support the recognition of same-sex relationships. Amnesty organized an international human rights conference in conjunction with the Gay Games in Amsterdam and again at the Gay Games in Sydney, Australia, in 2002.
- ILGA-Europe submitted written arguments to the European Court of Human Rights in both the Frette and Karner cases, a new pattern of advocacy for the organization. These initiatives were handled by Professor Robert Wintemute, King's College, University of London, who has written widely on sexual orientation issues.
- Amnesty International U.S.A., Human Rights Watch, the Lawyers Committee for Human Rights, Interights and Minnestota Advocates for Human Rights, together with Mary Robinson, former United Nations High Commissioner for Human Rights, filed a joint amici curiae brief in the United States Supreme Court case of Lawrence

v. Texas relying on international and comparative law materials. In it's decision of June, 2003, the United States Supreme Court struck down the Texas criminal law in question which prohibited same sex acts. A brief arguing international human rights was also submitted in the Goodridge case where the highest court in Massachusetts upheld equal access to marriage.

There have been victories, and there continue to be at least temporary defeats. The decisions in Dudgeon, Norris, Modinos, Sutherland, Lustig-Prean, Karner, Goodwin, Toonen and Young were victories. In addition, international law clearly recognizes a well-founded fear of persecution on the basis of sexual orientation as qualifying individuals for refugee status. And Europe has moved to require non-discrimination rules in the laws of all members of the European Union. Lesbian and gay representatives have been able to get into important meetings such as the Vienna World Conference on Human Rights, the Beijing Conference on Women, and the Durban Conference on Racism and Xenophobia. Gay and lesbian concerns have not yet appeared in the final conference statements of any of these large UN sponsored meetings. In 2001 there were fights over participation in two major UN meetings. In both cases, some lesbian and gay participation occurred.

No gay or lesbian organizations have on-going "consultative status" at the United Nations. There are a limited but growing number of states and non-governmental organisations that speak out in favour of lesbian and gay equality rights in international meetings. International law can develop only when there have been reforms at the level of domestic legal systems. The 1996 post-apartheid constitution of South Africa was the first in the world to expressly prohibit discrimination on the basis of sexual orientation. Similar express wording was included in subsequent new constitutions in Fiji, Ecuador and Portugal. An amendment to the constitution of Switzerland bans discrimination on the basis of "form of life," a phrase intended to include sexual life. In a number of other states general constitutional guarantees of equality have been interpreted to prohibit discrimination on the basis of sexual orientation.

In the domestic legal systems of leading states human rights norms now require decriminalization, individual equality, equal spousal benefits and partner immigration rights. Significantly, these developments are no longer limited to states in the western bloc. The internationalization of sexual orientation equality rights, building on reforms at the domestic level, first occurred in the European regional system. Continuing reforms at the level of individual states - in the West and, more slowly, in Africa, Asia and Latin America - will permit sexual orientation issues to be openly addressed at the United Nations and in regional intergovernmental organizations in the years to come.

WOMEN'S SUFFRAGE

The term women's suffrage refers to the economic and political reform movement aimed at extending suffrage — the right to vote — to women. The movement's modern origins lie in France in the 18th century. Of currently existing independent countries, New Zealand was the first to give women the right to vote. However when this happened in 1893, New Zealand was a mostly self-governing colony of Britain. Similarly, the colony of South Australia enacted legislation giving women the vote in 1894. Places with similar status which granted women the vote include Wyoming Territory (1869). Other possible contenders for first "country" to grant female suffrage include the Corsican Republic, the Isle of Man (1881), the Pitcairn Islands, Franceville and Tavolara, but some of these had brief existences as independent states and others were not clearly independent. A contestant for being the first independent nation to grant the right to vote for women would be Sweden, where some women were in fact allowed to vote during the age of liberty (1718-1771), although this right was far from applying to women in general.

Voting rights for women were introduced into international law in 1948 when the UN adopted the Universal

Declaration of Human Rights. As stated in Article 21 "(1) Everyone has the right to take part in the government of his country, directly or through freely chosen representatives. (3)The will of the people shall be the basis of the authority of government; this will shall be expressed in periodic and genuine elections which shall be by universal and equal suffrage and shall be held by secret vote or by equivalent free voting procedures." Women's suffrage is also explicitly stated as a right under the Convention on the Elimination of All Forms of Discrimination Against Women, adopted by the United Nations in 1979.

Women's suffrage has been granted at various times in various countries throughout the world. In many countries women's suffrage was granted before universal suffrage, so women from certain races and social classes were still unable to vote. In medieval France and several other European countries, voting for city and town assemblies and meetings was open to the heads of households, regardless of sex. Women's suffrage was granted by the Corsican Republic of 1755 whose Constitution stipulated a national representative assembly elected by all inhabitants over the age of 25, both women (if unmarried or widowed) and men. Women's suffrage was ended when France annexed the island in 1769. The origins of the modern movement for female suffrage are to be found in France in the 1780s and 1790s in the writings of Antoine Condorcet and Olympe de Gouges, who advocated this as a right in national elections.

In 1756, Lydia Chapin Taft, also known as Lydia Taft, became the first legal woman voter in America. She voted on at least three occasions in an open New England Town Meeting, at Uxbridge, Massachusetts, with the consent of the electorate. This was between 1756 and 1768, during America's colonial period. New Jersey granted women the vote (with the same property qualifications as for men, although, since married women did not own property in their own right, only unmarried women and widows qualified) under the state constitution of 1776, where the word "inhabitants" was used without qualification of sex or race.

New Jersey women, along with "aliens...persons of color, or negroes," lost the vote in 1807, when the franchise was restricted to white males, partly in order, ostensibly at least, to combat electoral fraud by simplifying the conditions for eligibility. The Pitcairn Islands granted women's suffrage in 1838. Various countries, colonies and states granted restricted women's suffrage in the latter half of the nineteenth century, starting with South Australia in 1861. The 1871 Paris Commune granted voting rights to women, but they were taken away with the fall of the Commune and would only be granted again in July 1944 by Charles de Gaulle. In 1886 the small island kingdom of Tavolara became a republic and introduced women's suffrage.

However, in 1899 the monarchy was reinstated, and the kingdom was some years later on annexed by Italy. The Pacific colony of Franceville, declaring independence in 1889, became the first self-governing nation to practice universal suffrage without distinction of sex or color; however, it soon came back under French and British colonial rule. Unrestricted women's suffrage in terms of voting rights (women were not initially permitted to stand for election) in a self-governing colony was granted in New Zealand in the early 1890s. Following a movement led by Kate Sheppard, the women's suffrage bill was adopted mere weeks before the general election of 1893.

The self-governing colony of South Australia granted both universal suffrage *and* allowed women to stand for the colonial parliament in 1895. The Commonwealth of Australia provided this for women in Federal elections from 1902 (except Aboriginal women). The first European country to introduce women's suffrage was the Grand Duchy of Finland. The administrative reforms following the 1905 uprising granted Finnish women the right both to vote (universal and equal suffrage) and to stand for election in 1906. The world's first female members of parliament were also in Finland, when on 1907, 19 women took up their places in the Parliament of Finland as a result of the 1907 parliamentary elections.

In the years before World War I, Norway (1913) and

Denmark also gave women the right to vote, and it was extended throughout the remaining Australian states. Near the end of the war, various states gave women the right to vote, including Canada, Soviet Russia, Germany and Poland. British women over 30 had the vote in 1918, Dutch women in 1919, and American women in states that had previously denied them suffrage were allowed the vote in 1920. Women in Turkey were granted voting rights in 1926. In 1928, suffrage was extended to all British women on the same terms as men, that is, for persons 21 years old and older. One of the most recent jurisdictions to grant women full equal voting rights was Bhutan in 2008.

SUFFRAGE MOVEMENTS

No suffrage movement was a very broad one which encompassed women and men with a very broad range of views. One major division, especially in Britain, was between suffragists, who sought to create change constitutionally, and suffragettes, who were more militant. There was also a diversity of views on a 'woman's place'. Some who campaigned for women's suffrage felt that women were naturally kinder, gentler, and more concerned about weaker members of society, especially children. It was often assumed that women voters would have a civilising effect on politics and would tend to support controls on alcohol, for example.

They believed that although a woman's place was in the home, she should be able to influence laws which impacted upon that home. Other campaigners felt that men and women should be equal in every way and that there was no such thing as a woman's 'natural role'. There were also differences in opinion about other voters. Some campaigners felt that all adults were entitled to a vote, whether rich or poor, male or female, and regardless of race. Others saw women's suffrage as a way of canceling out the votes of lower class or non-white men.

7

An Insight to Women's Human Rights

The term "women's human rights" and the set of practices that accompanies its use are the continuously evolving product of an international movement to improve the status of women. In the 1980s and 1990s, women's movements around the world formed networks and coalitions to give greater visibility both to the problems that women face every day and to the centrality of women's experiences in economic, social, political and environmental issues. In the evolution of what is becoming a global women's movement, the term "women's human rights" has served as a locus for praxis, that is, for the development of political strategies shaped by the interaction between analytical insights and concrete political practices. Further, the critical tools, the concerted activism, and the broad-based international networks that have grown up around movements for women's human rights have become a vehicle for women to develop the political skills necessary for the twenty-first century. The concept of women's human rights owes its success and the proliferation of its use to the fact that it is simultaneously prosaic and revolutionary. On the one hand, the idea of women's human rights makes common sense. It declares, quite simply, that as human beings women have human rights.

Anyone would find her or himself hard-pressed to publicly make and defend the contrary argument that women are not human. So in many ways, the claim that women have human rights seems quite ordinary. On the other hand, "women's human rights" is a revolutionary notion. This radical reclamation of humanity and the corollary insistence that women's rights are human rights have profound transformative potential. The incorporation of women's perspectives and lives into human rights standards and practice forces recognition of the dismal failure of countries worldwide to accord women the human dignity and respect that they deserve-simply as human beings. A woman's human rights framework equips women with a way to define, analyze, and articulate their experiences of violence, degradation, and marginality. Finally, and very importantly, the idea of women's human rights provides a common framework for developing a vast array of visions and concrete strategies for change.

The Universal Declaration of Human Rights adopted by the United Nations General Assembly in 1948 outlines what is considered in this century to be the fundamental consensus on the human rights of all people in relation to such matters as security of person, slavery, torture, protection of the law, freedom of movement & speech, religion, and assembly, and rights to social security, work, health, education, culture, & citizenship. It clearly stipulates that these human rights apply to all equally "without distinction of any kind such as race, color, sex, language... or other status". Obviously, then, the human rights delineated by the Universal Declaration are to be understood as applying to women. However, tradition, prejudice, social, economic and political interests have combined to exclude women from prevailing definitions of "general" human rights and to relegate women to secondary and/or "special interest" status within human rights considerations.

This marginalisation of women in the world of human rights has been a reflection of gender inequity in the world at large and has also had a formidable impact on women's lives. It has contributed to the perpetuation, and indeed the condoning, of women's subordinate status. It has limited the scope of what was seen as governmental responsibility, and thus has made the process of seeking redress for human rights violations disproportionately difficult for women and in many cases outright impossible. The division between the so-called "public" has compounded the difficulties posed by women's peripheral status within international human rights mechanisms and organizations and "private" spheres prevalent in so many societies. The pervasive division of life into "public" and "private" spheres has its roots in the desire to limit the jurisdiction of the government.

In many countries, this has meant that what individuals do in the "public" sphere is subject to regulation, while activities taking place in the "private" sphere are thought to be exempt from governmental scrutiny. Since this "public" sphere is seen as the focus of interaction between state actors and citizens, abuses of that relationship have been the focus of international human rights advocacy. Of course, the status of citizen has often been exclusionary, formally or informally entailing gender, racial and socio-economic bias and privileges. Thus, for those citizens-primarily men-who predominate in public and governmental realms and who enjoy gender, racial and economic privilege, the issues of primary concern have tended to be those abuses to which they are most vulnerable-abuses of civil and political aspects of human rights such as the violation of the right to speech, arbitrary detention, torture during imprisonment, and summary execution.

While women have been able to invoke international human rights machinery when they have found themselves in such situations, some of their specifically gender experiences of such human rights abuse-for example, rape in detention-have not been visible within the prevailing definitions of abuse. This is because women have traditionally been relegated to the "private" sphere of the home and family; the typical citizen has been portrayed as male, and thus the dominant notions of human rights abuse have implicitly had a man as their archetype. A major effect of the gender nature of the public/private split is that human rights violations of women that occur between "private" individuals have been made invisible and deemed to be beyond the purview of the state. It is particularly important to note that gender is a significant factor in the decisions of governments to intervene in the so-called private sphere to prosecute human rights violations.

For example, many activities that take place in the private sphere, such as murder between siblings or the systematic enslavement African peoples in the Americas, are subject to government censure internationally. However, governments overlook much of what happens to women at the hands of men and male family members, for example domestic violence or confinement, even when there are laws against such abuse. Thus, abuses done to women in the name of family, religion, and culture have been hidden by the sanctity of the so-called private sphere, and perpetrators of such human rights violations have enjoyed immunity from accountability for their actions.

The historical emphasis on human rights abuses in the public sphere and the concomitant neglect of the human rights of women were exacerbated by the politics of the Cold War. The United Nations' human rights treaties and mechanisms developed after the horrors of World War II and consolidated during the Cold War. The purpose of many human rights organizations that developed along with them was to monitor the treatment of citizens by their governments and to ensure respect for citizens' human rights as they worked for democratic governance. As positions polarized during the Cold War, western governments attributed priority to civil and political rights, which they believed were integral to a prosperous free market economy. Meanwhile, the socio-economic rights to work, shelter, and health, for example, became identified with the socialist bloc and were thus suspect to many in the West.

Thus, human rights bodies dominated by western conceptions of human rights priorities, focused on violations within the civil and political realm-the "public" sphere. So, in addition to the obstacles for women posed by the split between so-called public and private spheres, the predominance of civil and political rights within human rights organizations eclipsed the ways in which women often do not enjoy the social and economic conditions that make possible the exercise of civil and political rights and participation in public life.

THE CONCEPT OF WOMEN'S HUMAN RIGHTS

During the United Nations Decade for Women (1976-1985), women from many geographical, racial, religious, cultural, and class backgrounds took up organizing to improve the status of women. The United Nations-sponsored women's conferences, which took place in Mexico City in 1975, Copenhagen in 1980, and Nairobi in 1985, were convened to evaluate the status of women and to formulate strategies for women's advancement. These conferences were critical venues at which women came together, debated their differences and discovered their commonalties, and gradually began learning to bridge differences to create a global movement. In the late eighties and early nineties, women in diverse countries took up the human rights framework and began developing the analytic and political tools that together constitute the ideas and practices of women's human rights. Taking up the human rights framework has involved a double shift in thinking about human rights and talking about women's lives.

Put quite simply, it has entailed examining the human rights framework through a gender lens, and describing women's lives through a human rights framework. In looking at the human rights framework from women's perspectives, women have shown how current human rights definitions and practices fail to account for the ways in which already recognized human rights abuses often affect women differently because of their gender. This approach acknowledges the importance of the existing concepts and activities, but also points out that there are dimensions within these received definitions that are gender-specific and that need to be addressed if the mechanisms, programs, and the human rights framework itself are to include and reflect the experiences of the female half of the world's population.

When people utilize the human rights framework to articulate the vast array of human rights abuses that women face, they bring clarifying analyses and powerful tools to bear on women's experiences. This strategy has been pivotal in efforts to draw attention to human rights that are specific to women that heretofore have been seen as women's rights but not recognized as "human" rights. Take, for example, the issue of violence against women.

The Universal Declaration states: "No one shall be subject to torture or to cruel, inhuman or degrading treatment or punishment." This formulation provides a vocabulary for women to define and articulate experiences of violence such as rape, sexual terrorism and domestic violence as violations of the human right not to be subject to torture or to cruel, inhuman or degrading treatment or punishment. The recognition of such issues as human rights abuses raises the level of expectation about what can and should be done about them. This definition of violence against women in terms of human rights establishes unequivocally that states are responsible for such abuse. It also raises questions about how to hold governments accountable for their indifference in such situations and what sorts of mechanisms are needed to expedite the process of redress.

APPLYING THE HUMAN RIGHTS FRAMEWORK TO WOMEN

The Universal Declaration of Human Rights defines human rights as universal, inalienable, and indivisible. In unison, these defining characteristics are tremendously important for women's human rights. The universality of human rights means that human rights apply to every single person by virtue of their humanity; this also means that human rights apply to everyone equally, for everyone is equal in simply being human. In many ways, this universality theme may seem patently obvious, but its egalitarian premise has a radical edge. By invoking the universality of human rights, women have demanded that their very humanity be acknowledged. That acknowledgement and the concomitant recognition of women as bearers of human rights-mandates the incorporation of women and gender perspectives into all of the ideas and institutions that are already committed to the promotion and protection of human rights.

The idea that human rights are universal also challenges the contention that the human rights of women can be limited by culturally specific definitions of what count as human rights and of women's role in society. The idea of human rights as inalienable means that it is impossible for anyone to abdicate her human rights, even if she wanted to, since every person is accorded those rights by virtue of being human. It also means that no person or group of persons can deprive another individual of her or his human rights. Thus, for example, debts incurred by migrant workers or by women caught up in sex trafficking can never justify indentured servitude (slavery), or the deprivation of food, of freedom of movement, or of compensation. The idea of inalienable rights means that human rights cannot be sold, ransomed, or forfeited for any reason. The idea of inalienability has also been important in negotiations over the priority given to social, religious and cultural practices in relation to human rights.

For decades, work to transform practices which are physically or psychologically damaging to women and that have often been "protected" under the rubric of religion, tradition or culture has been particularly difficult, given both the integrity of culture guaranteed by the Universal Declaration and the history of Northern domination in much of the world. Thus it was important that both the Vienna Declaration and Programs of Action from the World Conference on Human Rights held in Vienna in 1993, and the United Nations Declaration Against Violence Against Women passed by the General Assembly the same year, affirmed that in cases of conflict between women's human rights and cultural or religious practices, the human rights of women must prevail.

The indivisibility of human rights means that none of the rights that are considered to be fundamental human rights is more important than any of the others more specifically, that they are inter-related. Human rights encompass civil, political, social, economic and cultural facets of human existence; the indivisibility premise highlights that the ability of people to live their lives in dignity and to exercise their human rights fully depends upon the recognition that these aspects are all interdependent. The fact that human rights are indivisible is important for women, since their civil and political rights historically have been compromised by their economic status, by social and cultural limitations placed on their activities, and by the ever-present threat of violence that often constitutes an insurmountable obstacle to women's participation in public and political life.

The idea of indivisibility has provided women with a common framework through which to emphasize the complexity of the challenges they face, and to highlight the necessity of including women and gender conscious perspectives in the development and implementation of policy. By calling upon the indivisibility of women's human rights, women have rejected a human rights hierarchy, which places either political or civil rights or socio-economic rights as primary. Instead, women have charged that political stability cannot be realized unless women's social and economic rights are also addressed; that sustainable development is impossible without the simultaneous respect for, and incorporation into the policy process of women's cultural and social roles in the daily reproduction of life; and that social equity cannot be generated without economic justice and women's participation in all levels of political decision-making.

THE MOVEMENT FOR WOMEN'S HUMAN RIGHTS

The term "women's human rights" does not refer simply to the theoretical approaches that women have used to transform human rights concepts, programs and agendas. In addition to being instrumental in the formulation of the conceptual challenges and demands levied by women, the idea of women's human rights has had immense impact as a tool for political activism. The concept of women's human rights has opened the way for women around the world to ask hard questions about the official inattention and general indifference to the widespread discrimination and violence that women experience everyday. Whether used in political lobbying, in legal cases, in grassroots mobilization, or in broad-based educational efforts, the idea of women's human rights has been a rallying point for women across many boundaries and has facilitated the creation of collaborative strategies for promoting and protecting the human rights of women.

While women have raised questions for a long time about why their rights are seen as ancillary to human rights, a coordinated effort to change this attitude using a human rights framework gained particular momentum in the early part of the 1990s. The opening of space for new debates afforded by the end of the Cold War facilitated the exchange of ideas and experiences among women around the world that led to strategizing about how to make women's human rights perspectives more visible. As women's activities developed globally during and following the United Nations' Decade for Women, more and more women raised the question of why "women's rights" and women's lives have been deemed secondary to the "human rights" and lives of men. Over the past decade, a movement around women's human rights has emerged to challenge limited notions of human rights, and it has focused particularly on violence against women as a prime example of the bias against women in human rights practice and theory.

The United Nations World Conference on Human Rights held in Vienna in 1993 was the first such meeting since 1968, and it became a natural vehicle to highlight the new visions of human rights thinking and practice being developed by women. Its initial call did not mention women nor did it recognize any gender-specific aspects of human rights in its proposed agenda. Since the conference represented an historic reassessment of the status of human rights, it became the unifying public focus of a worldwide Global Campaign for Women's Human Rights-a broad and loose international collaborative effort to advance women's human rights. The campaign launched a petition calling upon the World Conference "to comprehensively address women's human rights at every level of its proceedings" and to recognize "gender violence, a universal phenomenon which takes many forms across culture, race, and class... as a violation of human rights requiring immediate action."

The petition was eventually translated into 23 languages, and was used by over 1,000 sponsoring groups who gathered a half million signatures from 124 countries. The petition and its demands instigated discussions about why women's rights and gender-based violence in particular, were left out of human rights considerations, and served to mobilize women around the World Conference. Women acted to inject issues of women's human rights into the entire pre-conference preparatory process: Women from all regions demanded that women's human rights be discussed at the preparatory meetings held in Tunis, San Jose, and Bangkok, as well as at other non-governmental and national preparatory events. The idea of women's human rights was a framework for women to articulate and collaborate around broad and similar concerns about the status of women; it also provided women with a way to elaborate on the most pressing human rights issues specific to particular political, geographic, economic, and cultural contexts.

By the time the World Conference convened, the idea that "women's rights are human rights" had become the rallying call of thousands of people all over the world and one of the most discussed "new" human rights debates. The Vienna Declaration and Program of Action, which is the product of the conference and is meant to signal the agreement of the international community on the status of human rights, states unequivocally that:

> The human rights of women and of the girl-child are an inalienable, integral and indivisible part of universal human rights.

VIENNA DECLARATION

Women continued to lobby for and gain wider recognition of women's human rights at subsequent United Nations

Conferences. So, for example, at the International Conference on Population and Development in Cairo in 1994, women's reproductive rights were explicitly recognized as human rights. A particularly significant development was the way in which the Platform for Action at the IV World Conference on Women in Beijing in 1995 became virtually an agenda about the human rights of women. This signaled the successful mainstreaming of women's rights as human rights.

The agreements that are produced by such conferences are not legally binding; however, they do have ethical and political weight and can be used to pursue regional, national, or local objectives. Conference documents can also be used to reinforce and interpret international treaties such as the Covenant on Civil and Political Rights, or the Covenant of Social, Economic and Cultural Rights. These covenants, when signed by a country, do have the status of international law and have been used in courts by lawyers seeking redress for human rights violations. The most important international treaty specifically addressing women's human rights is the Convention on the Elimination of All Forms of Discrimination Against Women (CEDAW) which was initiated during the UN Decade for Women and has been ratified by over 130 countries. Further, local women's groups have integrated the women's human rights framework into their legal literacy programs and legal strategies.

Although the framework of women's human rights has been tremendously useful in efforts to lobby for legislative and policy changes at local, national and international levels, it has been an equally as important tool for grassroots organizing. Women's human rights not only teach women about the range of rights that their governments must honor; it also functions as a kind of gestalt by which to organize analyses of their experiences and plan action for change. The human rights framework creates a space in which the possibility for a different account of women's lives can be developed. What is so useful about this framework is that it provides women with principles by which to develop alternative visions of their lives without suggesting the substance of those visions.

The fundamental principles of human rights that accord to each and every person the entitlement to human dignity give women a vocabulary for describing both violations and impediments to the exercise of their human rights. The large body of international covenants, agreements and commitments about human rights gives women political leverage and a tenable point of reference. And finally, the idea of women's human rights enables women to define and articulate the specificity of the experiences in their lives at the same time that it provides a vocabulary for women to share the experiences of other women around the world and work collaboratively for change.

HUMAN RIGHTS ARE WOMEN'S RIGHTS

Women form half of the human beings inhabiting planet Earth. Since human rights are the rights of all human beings, male and female alike, human rights are women's rights. By the same token, a society in which men are not willing to extend human rights to their mothers, the women who bore and nurtured them; their daughters, products of their own loins; and their wives, the women who bear and raise their treasured sons, is a society in which men are unwilling to extend human rights to men of another family, tribe, language, religion, race, ethnic tradition, or nation. If a society does not hold justice and equality for all women in the highest regard, neither will it hold justice and equality for the many varieties of men in high regard. In a very real sense, women's rights are the basis of all human rights. Women's rights belong to women as members of the human family, and, as such, are not dependent either on a woman's marital status or on the number or sex of the children she has borne.

From time to time, it behooves us to examine human rights in the special context of women's rights. Some, but by no means all, of women's rights, which are part of the rights of all human beings, both male and female, are listed below. Since the primary responsibility of any society is to bear and raise future generations of male and female human beings, women's roles in reproduction must be held in the highest esteem and must not be permitted to become the basis for discrimination against women as women. Further, the responsibility for raising and nurturing future generations must fall upon men and women equally. Parents, male and female alike, have the right to guide the upbringing of their children according to the dictates of their consciences. A woman's important and, often, unpaid contribution to the family and the community must be considered in the event of a divorce, the death of the family's primary wage earner, and a woman's own death. Since a husband and wife are equal partners in creating and maintaining a family, upon her husband's death, one-half of the family's property is to be considered the property of the widow, property which she helped to create by her labour in the interests of the family unit.

Women, equal to men in the eyes of the law, shall be subjected to the same laws, no more and no less, as men. All laws that restricts women as women are null and void. Women have the right to the same access as men to food, clothing, shelter, medicine, an education, job training, and employment. Women, like men, have the right to rest and leisure, including a reasonable limitation on working hours, a living wage for a reasonable number of hours worked, and periodic holidays. Women have the right to equal pay for the same work as men. Just as woman has the right to enter the place of public execution, woman has the right to enter the place of public acclaim for her accomplishments. Women, like men, have the right to freely participate in the cultural life of the community, to enjoy the arts and to share in scientific, economic, and cultural advancement and their benefits.

Women, equal to men in the eyes of the law, shall be subjected to the same laws, no more and no less, as men. For the violation of any law, women shall be subject to the same punishment as men, no more and no less. Women have the same rights as men to life, liberty, property, security, and the pursuit of happiness and can be denied these things only by the due process of law. Consequently, "Crimes of honor" are, indeed, crimes, violations of human rights, and must be prosecuted to the fullest extent of the law. Women have the right to be free from all forms of domestic violence. Women have the same right to bodily autonomy as men, especially as regards their reproductive organs. Surgical alteration of a woman's sexual organs for any reason other than her health is a violation of her human rights.

Compelling women to bear unwanted children and forbidding women from bearing wanted children are violations of women's human rights. Any act of unwanted sex, including child molestation, forced prostitution, military sexual slavery, trafficking in women, forced participation in the creation of pornography, sex by extortion, marriage by rape, rape as an instrument of war, rape as a means of terror or torture, acquaintance rape, and marital rape, is a violation of girls' and women's human rights. Selective abortion based on the sex of the fetus, female infanticide, and sex selections of embryos are violations of women's and girls' human rights. The laws of both marriage and divorce apply equally to men and women. Marriage shall be entered into only with the free and full informed consent of the intending spouses. Children are not capable of providing informed consent to such an important undertaking.

Neither education nor any profession may be closed to any qualified woman. Women, like men, have the right to assemble peacefully, for whatever reason their conscience dictates including, but not limited to, teaching, learning, debating, discussing, worshipping, owning and operating businesses either as individuals or as groups, creating and maintaining local, state, national, and international non-governmental organizations, such as institutions to promote the arts, the humanities, and the sciences, professional societies, educational establishments, medical facilities, social services organizations, churches, synagogues, mosques, temples, and other religious organizations, sports clubs, legal and legal aide societies, self-help groups, co-operatives, and trade unions, and engaging in all group endeavors in both social and civic arenas of life.

Women have the same rights as men to equal access to service provided by her government, including, but not limited to, services in such areas as education, medicine, law, finance and banking, farm assistance, technical assistance, transportation, sanitation, electricity, communications, water, social support services, land redistribution, home building, and public sector employment. Women are entitled to engage in the same legal public and private activities as men, including the right to travel with only the same restrictions as imposed upon men. Women have the right to own and to control their own passports regardless of marital status. Women are entitled to a nationality, regardless of their martial status and regardless of the nationality or actions of their husbands, fathers, sons, or other family members.

The right to consent to the form of government under which one resides and to consent to the laws which govern one's actions are widely recognized as human rights, the rights of men and women alike. As such, a constitution is null and void if the majority of individuals comprising the nation or their representatives have not cooperated in drafting it. The equal voice of women must be present in the drafting of a nation's constitution. The right of suffrage, the right to vote by secret ballot, for the people to represent them in all levels of government including village, city, county, state, and national offices applies to women, as well as, men. All male and female citizens, equal in the eyes of the law, have the right to run for public office and to serve in those offices, if elected. As citizens, women have an obligation to the state to sit on juries to assist in determining the guilt or innocence of an accused man or woman. Women have the right to have other women sit on a jury to help determine their guilt or innocence when charged with a crime.

Women have a right to interpret the laws of the land as legal scholars, court officials, and magistrates. Women have a right to help to enforce the laws of the land both as police officers and as other civil officials responsible for uncovering suspected criminals and bringing them to a court of law. Women, as well as men, must be equally admitted to all honors, positions, and public employment according to their capacity and without other distinctions besides those of their virtues and talents. Women, as well as men, must participate in the formation and implementation of all public policies. Women, as well as men, have the right as public officials to represent their government agency to local, state, national, and international non-governmental organizations, to various levels of other government agencies of their own nation's political structure, to foreign governments, and to international political institutions. Women, like men, have the right to petition the government for a redress of their grievances.

No woman shall be held in slavery or involuntary servitude, except as punishment for a crime. Sexual slavery and trafficking in women are human rights violations. No man or woman shall be subjected to torture or to cruel, inhuman, or degrading treatment or punishment, including genital mutilation and rape. Men and women alike are entitled to the equal protection of the law. No one shall be subjected to detention, regardless of whether the place of detention is a public place like a prison or a jail, or a private place like a house, without due process of law. Women, like men, have the right to enter into contracts and to own and administer property.

The free communication of ideas and opinions, through the spoken, written, and printed word, is one of the most precious human rights for women, as well as, for men. As such, women have the right to Speak the name of the man who raped her, the name of the father of her illegitimate child, the name of a man who beats her, Learn to read and write,Teach the history of the women who came before her, Describe the myriad of ways in which government and social policies affect her, both positively and negatively, as a woman, Participate in all aspects of her religious faith and religious traditions both in public, as from the pulpit, and in private, as in personal prayer with her family and friend, and Contribute to the development of the arts, literature, humanities, religion, culture, and the sciences.

Sources of international law are the materials and processes out of which the rules and principles regulating the international community are developed. They have been influenced by a range of political and legal theories. During the 19th century, it was recognised by legal positivists that a sovereign could limit its authority to act by consenting to an agreement according to the principle pacta sunt servanda. This consensual view of international law was reflected in the 1920 Statute of the Permanent Court of International Justice, and preserved in Article 38(1) of the 1946 Statute of the International Court of Justice.

Article 38(1) is generally recognised as a definitive statement of the sources of international law. It requires the Court to apply, among other things, (a) international conventions "expressly recognized by the contesting states", and (b) "international custom, as evidence of a general practice accepted as law". To avoid the possibility of non liquet, sub-paragraph (c) added the requirement that the general principles applied by the Court were those that had been "the general principles of the law recognized by civilized nations". As it is states that by consent determine the content of international law, sub-paragraph (d) acknowledges that the Court is entitled to refer to "judicial decisions" and the most highly qualified juristic writings "as subsidiary means for the determination of rules of law".

On the question of preference between sources of international law, rules established by treaty will take preference if such an instrument exists. It is also argued however that international treaties and international custom are sources of international law of equal validity; this is that new custom may supersede older treaties and new treaties may override older custom. Certainly, judicial decisions and juristic writings are regarded as auxiliary sources of international, whereas it is unclear whether the general principles of law recognized by 'civilized nations' should be recognized as a principal or auxiliary source of international law. It may be argued that the practice of international organizations, most notably that of the United Nations, as it appears in the resolutions of the Security Council and the General Assembly, are an additional source of international law, even though it is not mentioned as such in Article 38(1) of the 1946 Statute of the International Court of Justice.

Article 38(1) is closely based on the corresponding provision of the 1920 Statute of the Permanent Court of International Justice, thus predating the role that international organizations have come to play in the international plane. That is, the provision of Article 38(1) may be regarded as *dated*, and this can most vividly be seen in the mention made to 'civilized nations', a mentioning that appears all the more quaint after the decolonization process that took place in the early 1960s and the participation of nearly all nations of the world in the United Nations. It is also possible, though less common, for a treaty to be modified by practices arising between the parties to that treaty. The other situation in which a rule would take precedence over a treaty provision would be where the rule has the special status of being part of the jus cogens.

INTERNATIONAL CUSTOM

"International custom" as a source of international law, specifically emphasizing the two requirements of state practice plus acceptance of the practice as obligatory or opinio juris sive necessitatis (usually abbreviated as opinio juris). Derived from the consistent practice of (originally) Western states accompanied by opinio juris (the conviction of States that the consistent practice is required by a legal obligation), customary international law is differentiated from acts of comity by the presence of opinio juris (although in some instances, acts of comity have developed into customary international law, i.e. diplomatic immunity).

Treaties have gradually displaced much customary international law. This development is similar to the replacement of customary or common law by codified law in municipal legal settings, but customary international law continues to play a significant role in international law.

STATE PRACTICE

When examining state practice to determine relevant rules of international law, it is necessary to take into account every activity of the organs and officials of states that relate to that purpose. There has been continuing debate over where a distinction should be drawn as to the weight that should be attributed to what states do, rather than what they say represents the law. In its most extreme form, this would involve rejecting what states say as practice and relegating it to the status of evidence of opinio juris. A more moderate version would evaluate what a state says by reference to the occasion on which the statement was made. It is only relatively powerful countries with extensive international contacts and interests that have regular opportunities of contributing by deed to the practice of international law.

The principal means of contribution to state practice for the majority of states will be at meetings of international organisations, particularly the UN General Assembly, by voting and otherwise expressing their view on matters under consideration. Moreover, there are circumstances in which what states say may be the only evidence of their view as to what conduct is required in a particular situation. The notion of practice establishing a customary rule implies that the practice is followed regularly, or that such state practice must be "common, consistent and concordant". Given the size of the international community, the practice does not have to encompass all states or be completely uniform. There has to be a sufficient degree of participation, especially on the part of states whose interests are likely be most affected, and an absence of substantial dissent.

There have been a number of occasions on which the ICJ has rejected claims that a customary rule existed because of a lack of consistency in the practice brought to its attention. Within the context of a specific dispute, however, it is not necessary to establish the generality of practice. A rule may apply if a state has accepted the rule as applicable to it individually, or because the two states belong to a group of states between which the rule applies. A dissenting state is entitled to deny the opposability of a rule in question if it can demonstrate its persistent objection to that rule, either as a member of a regional group or by virtue of its membership of the international community. It is not easy for a single state to maintain its dissent. Also, rules of the jus cogens have a universal character and apply to all states, irrespective of their wishes.

Demand for rules that are responsive to increasingly rapid changes has led to the suggestion that there can be, in appropriate circumstances, such a concept as "instant custom". Even within traditional doctrine, the ICJ has recognised that passage of a short period of time is not necessarily a bar to the formation of a new rule. Because of this, the question is sometimes raised as to whether the word "custom" is suitable to a process that could occur with great rapidity.

Opinio juris

A wealth of state practice will usually carry with it a presumption that opinio juris exists. It would then be for the state against which the rule is pleaded to rebut that presumption by demonstrating the absence of opinio juris in the activities being relied upon by the other party. In cases where practice (of which evidence is given) comprises abstentions from acting, consistency of conduct might not establish the existence of a rule of customary international law. The fact that no nuclear weapons have been used since 1945, for example, does not render their use illegal on the basis of a customary obligation because the necessary opinio juris was lacking.

Although the ICJ has frequently referred to opinio juris as being an equal footing with state practice, the role of the psychological element in the creation of customary law is uncertain.

Jus cogens

A peremptory norm or jus cogens (Latin for "compelling law" or "strong law") is a principle of international law considered so fundamental that it overrides all other sources of international law, including even the Charter of the United Nations. The principle of jus cogens is enshrined in Article 53 of the Vienna Convention on the Law of Treaties:

For the purposes of the present Convention, a peremptory norm of general international law is a norm accepted and recognised by the international community of States as a whole as a norm from which no derogation is permitted and which can be modified only by a subsequent norm of general international law having the same character.

Rules of jus cogens generally require or forbid the state to do particular acts or respect certain rights. However, some define criminal offences which the state must enforce against individuals. Generally included on lists of such norms are prohibitions of such crimes and internationally wrongful acts as waging aggressive war, war crimes, crimes against humanity, piracy, genocide, apartheid, slavery and torture.

The evidence supporting the emergence of a rule of jus cogens will be essentially similar to that required to establish the creation of a new rule of customary international law. Indeed, jus cogens could be thought of as a special principle of custom with a superadded opinio juris. The European Court of Human Rights has stressed the international public policy aspect of the jus cogens.

TREATIES AS LAW

Treaties can play the role of contracts between two or more parties, such as an extradition treaty or a defence pact. They can also be legislation to regulate a particular aspect of international relations, or form the constitutions of international organisations. Whether or not all treaties can be regarded as sources of law, they are sources of obligation for the parties to them. Article 38(1)(a), which uses the term "international conventions", concentrates upon treaties as a source of contractual obligation but also acknowledges the possibility of a state expressly accepting the obligations of a treaty to which it is not formally a party.

For a treaty-based rule to be a source of law, rather than simply a source of obligation, it must either be capable of affecting non-parties or have consequences for parties more extensive than those specifically imposed by the treaty itself.

TREATIES AS CUSTOM

Some treaties are the result of codifying existing customary law, such as laws governing the global commons, and jus ad bellum. While the purpose is to establish a code of general application, its effectiveness depends upon the number of states that ratify or accede to the particular convention. Relatively few such instruments have a sufficient number of parties to be regarded as international law in their own right. The most obvious examples are the 1949 Geneva Conventions for the Protection of War Victims.

Most multi-lateral treaties fall short of achieving such a near universal degree of formal acceptance, and are dependent upon their provisions being regarded as representing customary international law and, by this indirect route, as binding upon non-parties. This outcome is possible in a number of ways:

- When the treaty rule reproduces an existing rule of customary law, the rule will be clarified in terms of the treaty provision. A notable example is the Vienna Convention on the Law of Treaties 1969, which was considered by the ICJ to be law even before it had been brought into force.
- When a customary rule is in the process of development, its incorporation in a multilateral treaty may have the effect of consolidating or crystallising the law in the form of that rule. It is not always easy to identify when this occurs. Where the practice is less developed, the treaty provision may not be enough to crystallise the rule as part of customary international law.
- Even if the rule is new, the drafting of the treaty provision may be the impetus for its adoption in the practice of states, and it is the subsequent acceptance of the rule by states that renders it effective as part of customary law. If a broad definition is adopted of state practice, the making of a treaty would fall within the definition. Alternatively, it is possible to regard the treaty as the final act of state practice required to establish the rule in

question, or as the necessary articulation of the rule to give it the opinio juris of customary international law.

- Convention-based "instant custom" has been identified by the ICJ on several occasions as representing customary law without explanation of whether the provision in question was supported by state practice. This has happened with respect to a number of provisions of the Vienna Convention on the Law of Treaties 1969. If "instant custom" is valid as law, it could deny to third parties the normal consequences of non-accession to the treaty.

GENERAL PRINCIPLES OF LAW

The scope of general principles of law, to which Article 38(1) of the Statute of the ICJ refers, is unclear and controversial but may include such legal principles that are common to a large number of systems of municipal law. Given the limits of treaties or custom as sources of international law, Article 38(1) may be looked upon as a directive to the Court to fill any gap in the law and prevent a non liquet by reference to the general principles. In earlier stages of the development of international law, rules were frequently drawn from municipal law. In the 19th century, legal positivists rejected the idea that international law could come from any source that did not involve state will or consent, but were prepared to allow for the application of general principles of law, provided that they had in some way been accepted by states as part of the legal order. Thus Article 38(1)(c), for example, speaks of general principles "recognised" by states.

An area that demonstrates the adoption of municipal approaches is the law applied to the relationship between international officials and their employing organisations, although today the principles are regarded as established international law. The significance of general principles has undoubtedly been lessened by the increased intensity of treaty and institutional relations between states. Nevertheless, the concepts of estoppel and equity have been employed in the adjudication of international disputes. For example, a state that has, by its conduct, encouraged another state to believe in the existence of a certain legal or factual situation, and to rely upon that belief, may be estopped from asserting a contrary situation in its dealings.

The principle of good faith was said by the ICJ to be "[o]ne of the basic principles governing the creation and performance of legal obligations". Similarly, there have been frequent references to equity. It is generally agreed that equity cannot be employed to subvert legal rules (that is, operate contra legem). This "equity as law" perception is reinforced by references to equitable principles in the text of the United Nations Convention on the Law of the Sea 1982, though this may be little more than an admission as to the existence, and legitimation, of the discretion of the adjudicator. However, the principles of estoppel and equity in the international context do not retain all the connotations they do under common law.

The reference to the principles as "general" signify that, if rules were to be adapted from municipal law, they should be at a sufficient level of generality to encompass similar rules existing in many municipal systems. Principles of municipal law should be regarded as sources of inspiration rather than as sources of rules of direct application.

EQUITY (LAW)

Equity is the name given to the set of legal principles, in jurisdictions following the English common law tradition, which supplement strict rules of law where their application would operate harshly, so as to achieve what is sometimes referred to as "natural justice". It is often confusingly contrasted with "law", which in this context refers to "statutory law" (the laws enacted by a legislature, such as Parliament), and "common law" (the principles established by judges when they decide cases).

In modern practice, perhaps the most important distinction between law and equity is the set of remedies each offers. The most common civil remedy a court of law can award is monetary damages. Equity, however, enters injunctions or decrees directing someone either to act or to forbear from acting. Often this form of relief is in practical terms more valuable to a litigant; for example, a plaintiff whose neighbor will not return his only milk cow, which had wandered onto the neighbor's property, may want that particular cow back, and not just its monetary value.

However, in general, a litigant cannot obtain equitable relief unless there is "no adequate remedy at law"; that is, a court will not grant an injunction unless monetary damages are an insufficient remedy for the injury in question. Law courts also enter orders, called "writs" (such as a writ of habeas corpus), but they are less flexible and less easily obtained than an injunction. Another distinction is the unavailability of a jury in equity: the judge is the trier of fact. In the American legal system, the right of jury trial in civil cases tried in federal court is guaranteed by the Seventh Amendment, but only "[i]n Suits at common law," i.e., in cases that traditionally would have been handled by the law courts.

The question of whether a case should be determined by a jury depends largely on the type of relief the plaintiff requests. If a plaintiff requests damages in the form of money or certain other forms of relief, such as the return of a specific item of property, the remedy is considered legal, and a jury is available as the fact-finder. On the other hand, if the plaintiff requests an injunction, declaratory judgment, specific performance, or modification of contract, or some other non-monetary relief, the claim would usually be one in equity. A final important distinction between law and equity is the source of the rules governing the decisions. In law, decisions are made by reference either to legal doctrines or to statutes.

In contrast, equity, with its emphasis on fairness and flexibility, has only general guides known as the maxims of equity. As noted below, a historic criticism of equity as it developed was that it had no fixed rules of its own, with the Lord Chancellor from time to time judging in the main according to his own conscience. As time went on the rules of equity did lose much of their flexibility, and from the 17th century onwards equity was rapidly consolidated into a system of precedents much like its common-law cousin. Charles Dickens' Bleak House parodied the excessive time and expense associated with the Court of Chancery, the court that heard suits in equity in 19th-century England.

The distinction between "law" and "equity" is an accident of history. The "law courts" or "courts of law" were the courts in England that enforced the king's laws in medieval times. At the end of the 13th century the courts of law gradually froze the types of claims they would hear, and the procedure that governed the hearing of those claims. Because the range of legal claims at that time was quite narrow, legal procedures were painfully hypertechnical, with the result that many deserving plaintiffs were denied relief. However, remedies could also be obtained through filing a petition with the king, who held residual judicial power; these filings were usually phrased in terms of throwing oneself upon the king's mercy or conscience.

Eventually, the king began to regularly delegate the function of resolving such petitions to the Chancellor, an important member of the King's Council. At the time, the Chancellor was usually a clergyman and the King's confessor, so he was literally the keeper of the King's conscience. Soon the Chancery, the Crown's secretarial department, began to resemble a judicial body and became known as the "Court of Chancery". By the 15th century, the judicial power of the Chancery was recognised.

Equity, as a body of rules, varied from Chancellor to Chancellor, until the end of the 16th century. After the end of the 17th century, only lawyers were appointed to the office of Chancellor. One area in which the Court of Chancery assumed a vital role was the enforcement of uses, a role which the rigid framework of land law could not accommodate. This role gave rise to the basic distinction between legal and equitable interests.

THE NATURE AND DEVELOPMENT OF INTERNATIONAL LAW

According to Bentham's classic definition, international law is a collection of rules governing relations between states.

It is a mark of how far international law has evolved that this original definition omits individuals and international organizations—two of the most dynamic and vital elements of modern international law. Furthermore, it is no longer accurate to view international law as simply a collection of rules; rather, it is a rapidly developing complex of rules and influential—though not directly binding—principles, practices, and assertions coupled with increasingly sophisticated structures and processes. In its broadest sense, international law provides normative guidelines as well as methods, mechanisms, and a common conceptual language to international actors—i.e., primarily sovereign states but also increasingly international organizations and some individuals.

The range of subjects and actors directly concerned with international law has widened considerably, moving beyond the classical questions of war, peace, and diplomacy to include human rights, economic and trade issues, space law, and international organizations. Although international law is a legal order and not an ethical one, it has been influenced significantly by ethical principles and concerns, particularly in the sphere of human rights. International law is distinct from international comity, which comprises legally nonbinding practices adopted by states for reasons of courtesy (e.g., the saluting of the flags of foreign warships at sea). In addition, the study of international law, or public international law, is distinguished from the field of conflict of laws, or private international law, which is concerned with the rules of municipal law—as international lawyers term the domestic law of states—of different countries where foreign elements are involved.

International law is an independent system of law existing outside the legal orders of particular states. It differs from domestic legal systems in a number of respects. For example, although the United Nations (UN) General Assembly, which consists of representatives of some 190 countries, has the outward appearances of a legislature, it has no power to issue binding laws. Rather, its resolutions serve only as recommendations—except in specific cases and for certain purposes within the UN system, such as determining the UN budget, admitting new members of the UN, and, with the involvement of the Security Council, electing new judges to the International Court of Justice (ICJ). Also, there is no system of courts with comprehensive jurisdiction in international law. The ICJ's jurisdiction in contentious cases is founded upon the consent of the particular states involved.

There is no international police force or comprehensive system of law enforcement, and there also is no supreme executive authority. The UN Security Council may authorize the use of force to compel states to comply with its decisions, but only in specific and limited circumstances; essentially, there must be a prior act of aggression or the threat of such an act. Moreover, any such enforcement action can be vetoed by any of the council's five permanent members (China, France, Russia, the United Kingdom, and the United States). Because there is no standing UN military, the forces involved must be assembled from member states on an ad hoc basis.

International law is a distinctive part of the general structure of international relations. In contemplating responses to a particular international situation, states usually consider relevant international laws. Although considerable attention is invariably focused on violations of international law, states generally are careful to ensure that their actions conform to the rules and principles of international law, because acting otherwise would be regarded negatively by the international community.

The rules of international law are rarely enforced by military means or even by the use of economic sanctions. Instead, the system is sustained by reciprocity or a sense of enlightened self-interest. States that breach international rules suffer a decline in credibility that may prejudice them in future relations with other states. Thus, a violation of a treaty by one state to its advantage may induce other states to breach other treaties and thereby cause harm to the original violator. Furthermore, it is generally realized that consistent rule violations would jeopardize the value that the system brings to the community of states, international organizations, and other actors. This value consists in the certainty, predictability, and sense of common purpose in international affairs that derives from the existence of a set of rules accepted by all international actors. International law also provides a framework and a set of procedures for international interaction, as well as a common set of concepts for understanding it.

THE INTERNATIONAL SYSTEM

In the following, much will be said about the substance of international law, the method of its creation and the legal persons or 'subjects' who may be governed by it. The purpose of this first chapter is, however, to examine the very nature and quality of this subject called 'international law'. Historically, international law has been derided or disregarded by many of the world's foremost jurists and legal commentators. They have questioned, first, the existence of *any* set of rules governing inter-state relations; second, its entitlement to be called 'law'; and, third, its effectiveness in controlling states and other international actors in 'real life' situations. In the early years of the twenty-first century, this theoretical rejection of the prescriptive quality of international law seemed to be borne out in practice as a number of states, groups and individuals became engaged in internationally 'unlawful' action without even the remote possibility that their conduct could be checked by the international legal system.

Whatever the legal merits of the US-led invasion of Iraq or the Israeli invasion of Lebanon, or the detention of terrorist suspects without trial, or the unhindered resort to terrorism by groups based in existing states (with or without the support of another state's government), or the rejection by some of international minimum standards for the protection of the environment, the *perception* has been that international law is failing in one of its primary purposes – the maintenance of an ordered community where the weak are protected from arbitrary action by the strong. Some commentators have even suggested that we are witnessing the demise of this subject as a *legal discipline* and should now recognise it as having political and moral force, but not necessarily legal content.

There is, of course, some truth in these criticisms, but let us not pretend that we are arguing that international law is a perfect legal system. It is not, but neither is the national legal system of any state. Historically, there have been successes and failures for the international legal system. The invasion of Kuwait by Iraq in 1990 may have produced a significant response from the international community, both legally and militarily, but the United Nations failed in Bosnia, Somalia and Sudan and was impotent as Israel invaded Lebanon in July 2006. Likewise, the denial of procedural and substantive rights to those being held in detention by the USA at Guantanamo Bay may well constitute a violation of the international law of human rights worthy of much criticism, but it pales beside the activities of Pol Pot in Cambodia in the late 1970s or the Rwandan genocide of the 1990s. On the other hand, these episodes can be contrasted with the successful UN-led efforts to bring self-determination and then independence to East Timor in 2002, the groundbreaking establishment and operation of the International Criminal Court responsible for prosecuting individuals for violation of fundamental international human rights and the continuing impact of the International Court of Justice in regulating states' use of the world's oceans and their natural resources.

In other words, the story of international law and the international legal system, like so many other legal systems, is one with successes and failures. So, in much the same way that we would not suggest that the law of the UK is somehow 'not law' because it is currently proving impossible to control internet crime, it does not necessarily follow that international law should be dismissed as a system of law because there are international actors that seem determined to ignore it. The way in which the international system deals with these practical issues and the many others that occur on a daily basis whenever the members of the international community interact, goes to the heart of the debate about whether 'international law' exists as a *system of law*. However, to some extent, this debate about the nature of international law is unproductive and even irrelevant.

The most obvious and most frequently used test for judging the 'existence' or 'success' of international law is to compare it with national legal systems such as that operating in the UK or Japan or anywhere at all. National law and its institutions - courts, legislative assemblies and enforcement agencies - are held up as the definitive model of what 'the law' and 'a legal system' should be like. Then, because international law sometimes falls short of these 'standards', it is argued that it cannot be regarded as 'true' law. Yet, it is not at all clear why *any* form of national law should be regarded as the appropriate standard for judging international law, especially since the rationale of the former is fundamentally different from that of the latter. National law is concerned primarily with the legal rights and duties of legal persons (individuals) within a body politic - the state or similar entity.

This 'law' commonly is derived from a legal superior, recognised as competent by the society to whom the law is addressed (e.g. in a constitution), and having both the authority and practical competence to make and enforce that law. International law, at least as originally conceived, is different. It is concerned with the rights and duties of the states themselves. In their relations with each other it is neither likely nor desirable that a relationship of *legal* superiority exists. States are legal equals and the legal system which regulates their actions *inter se* must reflect this. Such a legal system must *facilitate* the interaction of these legal equals rather than control or compel them in imitation of the control and compulsion that national law exerts over its subjects. Of course, as international law develops and matures it may come to encompass the legal relations of non-state entities, such as 'peoples', territories, individuals or multi-national companies, and it must then develop institutions and procedures which imitate in part the functions of the institutions of national legal systems.

Indeed, the re-casting of international law as a system based less on state sovereignty and more on individual liberty is an aim of many contemporary international lawyers and there is no doubt that very great strides have been made in this direction in recent years. The establishment of the

International Criminal Court is perhaps the most powerful evidence of this trend. However, whatever we might hope for in the future for international law, it is crucial to remember that at the very heart of the system lies a set of rules designed to regulate states' conduct with each other, and it is this central fact that makes precise analogies with national law at present misleading and inappropriate.

THE ROLE OF INTERNATIONAL LAW

In simple terms, international law comprises a system of rules and principles that govern the international relations between sovereign states and other institutional subjects of international law such as the United Nations and the African Union (formerly the OAU). As we shall see, that is not to say that international law is unconcerned with the rights or obligations of the individual. Rather, it is that the rules of international law are created primarily by states, either for their own purposes or as a means of facilitating the functions of organisations of which they are members. Rules of international law cover almost every facet of inter-state activity. There are laws regulating the use of the sea, outer space and Antarctica. There are rules governing international telecommunications, postal services, the carriage of goods and passengers by air and the transfer of money. International law is a primary tool for the conduct of international trade. It is concerned with nationality, extradition, the use of armed force, human rights, protection of the environment and the security of nations.

In short, there is very little that is done in the international arena that is not regulated by international law and it can now govern some aspects of relations between distinct units *within* a sovereign state, such as the territories of federal Canada or the devolved regions of the UK. International law is the vital mechanism without which an increasingly interdependent world could not function. In this sense, international law facilitates the functioning of the international community. However, that is not all. Modern international law also seeks to control states by inhibiting or directing their conduct both in their relations with other states (e.g. the law prohibiting the use of armed force to settle disputes) and in relation to individuals, both individuals of other states (e.g. issues concerning the exercise of criminal jurisdiction) and its own nationals (e.g. the law of human rights). It is the evolution of international law from a system that was concerned primarily with facilitating international co-operation among its subjects (states), to a system that is now much more engaged in the control of its subjects that is the pre-eminent feature of the history of international law in the last sixty years.

It is also important to realise that the practice of international law is intrinsically bound up with diplomacy, politics and the conduct of foreign relations. It is a fallacy to regard international law as the only facilitator or controller of state conduct. It cannot be this and, more significantly, it is not designed to do it. International law does not operate in a sterile environment and international legal rules may be just one of the factors which a state or government will consider before deciding whether to embark on a particular course of action. In fact, in many cases, legal considerations will prevail, but it is perfectly possible that a state may decide to forfeit legality in favour of self-interest, expediency or 'humanity', as with the Iraqi invasion of Kuwait in 1990 and the US-led invasion of Iraq some thirteen years later.

There is nothing surprising in this and it is a feature of the behaviour of every legal person in every legal system, including that of the UK. If it were not so, there would be, for example, no theft and no murder. Indeed, in international society, where politics are so much a part of law, it may be that contextual and flexible rules, so evident in international law, are a strength rather than a weakness.

THE EXISTENCE OF INTERNATIONAL RULES AS A SYSTEM OF LAW

The most cogent argument for the existence of international law as a system of law is that members of the international community recognise that there exists a body of rules binding upon them as law. States believe international law exists. When Iraq invaded Kuwait in 1990, or earlier when Tanzania invaded Uganda in 1978/79, the great majority of states regarded the action as 'unlawful', not merely 'immoral' or 'unacceptable'. The same is true of the war crimes committed in Bosnia and Rwanda, and this is given concrete form when the United Nations Security Council imposes sanctions on a delinquent state, as with the embargoes on Libya (now lifted) following the Lockerbie bombing. The criticism of the US-led invasion of Iraq in March 2003 and of Israel's forceful intervention in Lebanon in July 2006 followed a similar pattern, both being cast by a majority of the international community as a violation of law, not merely as unethical, immoral or undesirable.

Similarly, those arguing in support of these uses of force do not dismiss international law as irrelevant or voluntary, but seek instead to justify the invasions as lawful under the legal rules concerning collective security and self-defence. In other words, even the international actors who engage in potentially unlawful activity do not deny the relevance of international law or its prescriptive quality. This acceptance of the reality of international law by the very persons to whom it is addressed exposes the weakness of those who argue that international law does not exist.

Of course, this does not answer questions about its effectiveness, nor does it settle whether it is 'law' in the same sense as that of the UK or of other states. Yet, it does reflect accurately the reality of international relations. How then do we know that states believe that there is a set of rules binding on them as law? What evidence is there of this 'law habit'?

a. International law is practised on a daily basis in the Foreign Offices, national courts and other governmental organs of states, as well as in international organizations such as the United Nations and the Organisation of American States. Foreign Offices have legal departments whose task is to advise on questions of international law and to assist in the drafting of international agreements and the like. National courts are frequently concerned with substantive questions of international law, as with the series of Pinochet cases in the UK concerning questions of immunity and human rights and the House of Lords judgment in R v Jones concerning the meaning of the international crime of aggression and its impact on domestic law. In reading the judgment of Lord Bingham in that case, no-one could doubt the legal validity of the system of international law. Similarly, international organisations, in all their forms, use lawyers, employing the language of the law, to conduct their everyday business. These organisations and their state-members accept that they are 'legally bound' to behave in a certain way and will pursue claims against each other alleging a 'breach' of international law.

b. It is a fact of the utmost significance that states - still the most important of the subjects of international law - do not claim that they are above the law or that international law does not bind them. When Iraq invaded Kuwait it did not claim that the law prohibiting armed force did not apply to it or was irrelevant. Rather,Iraq argued that international law 'justified' its action; in other words, that it was 'legal' by reference to some other rule of international law. Likewise, in the Case Concerning the Application of the Convention on the Prevention and Punishment of the Crime of Genocide ICJ 2007, Serbia did not deny the existence of rules of law concerning genocide, but contended rather that it was not internationally responsible for the violations of international law that had taken place. In fact there is no modern day example of a state claiming that it is not bound by general rules of international law, although there is often a great deal of debate as to the precise obligations imposed by that law (as in the Bosnia Serbia Genocide Case where there was argument over the precise obligations imposed by the Genocide Convention). This is powerful evidence that states follow rules of international law as a matter of obligation, not simply as a matter of choice or morality.

If this were not so, there would be no need for states to justify their action in legal terms when they departed from a legal norm.

c. The most convincing evidence of the existence of international law is that the overwhelming majority of international legal rules are consistently obeyed. Of course, there will be occasions when the law is ignored or flouted, just as there will be murder and theft in national law. Indeed, the apparent ineffectiveness of international law stems from the fact that it is the occasions of law-breaking that receive the most publicity. Some of the modern day and notorious failures of international law, such as the US invasion of Grenada in 1983, the genocide of the Kurds at the hands of the Iraqis and the invasions of Afghanistan, Iraq and Lebanon in pursuit of 'the war on terrorism' are not representative of the whole. Outside of the exceptional cases, the everyday operation of international law goes on in a smooth and uninterrupted fashion. The occasions when a state disregards its treaty or customary law obligations are but a small fraction of the occasions on which those obligations are observed. The same is true of the law of diplomatic immunities, state responsibility and the law of the sea. In short, the vast majority of the rules of international law are obeyed most of the time. Such observance is not headline news.

d. It is a function of all legal systems to resolve disputed questions of fact and law. International law has to do this and, because it has only a limited number of developed legal institutions, it sometimes fails. That, however, is no reason to doubt its validity as a system of law. Rather, it suggests that if international law is to be on a par with national law, it needs to develop better institutions responsible for law creation and enforcement. In comparison with national law, international law may be regarded as 'weak' law, not because of its binding quality, but because of its less organised approach to the problems of adjudication and enforcement. On the other hand, it has been suggested above that the existence of such institutions is a feature of national law that may be out of place in an international system, or at least not merited to the same degree. For example, given that international law regulates the conduct of legal equals, it might be unwise to have a formal and coercive process of law enforcement. All states are powerful in some measure and all have the practical ability to inflict harm on each other whether that be economic, political or military. With such a reality, it may be that the best way to regulate state conduct is to proceed on the basis of a system of law that is voluntarily accepted and voluntarily enforced. This does not mean that international law forfeits the right to be called law - because it still obliges states to do certain things.

It means, rather, that it is not the same kind of law as national law. Moreover, in those areas where international law does function in a similar manner to national law - as where individuals are given enforceable rights or are subject to personal obligations (e.g. war crimes) - international law has indeed developed institutional mechanisms similar to those existing in national legal systems. The well-established European Court of Human Rights, the War Crimes Tribunals for Bosnia, Rwanda and Somalia and the International Criminal Court are good examples.

THE ENFORCEMENT OF INTERNATIONAL LAW

Many jurists claim that the hallmark of a system of law is that its rules are capable of being enforced against malefactors. Consequently, one of the most frequent arguments used against international law is that it is not 'true' law because it is not generally enforceable. This raises two issues. First, as a matter of principle, does the existence of any system of law depend on the chances of effective enforcement? Secondly, is it true that international law is not enforceable or effective? In national legal systems it is assumed that the law will be enforced. If someone steals, provided they are caught, they will be punished. In international law this may not be the case. There was, for example, no formal enforcement action taken against the USA after its illegal invasion of Grenada and no formal condemnation of Israel for invading Lebanon in 2006. We might even suggest that on those occasions when the United Nations has acted (e.g. against Iraq after its invasion of Kuwait), it is more in the way of keeping or restoring the peace than of enforcing the law. Yet is it really true that the test of the binding quality of any 'law' is the presence or absence of assured enforcement of its rules? It may be that the assumed certainty of enforcement of national law masks its true basis and, in the same way, enforcement may be irrelevant to the binding quality of international law. For example, a better view of national law may be that it is 'law' not because it will be enforced, but because it is generally accepted as such by the community to whom it is addressed: the local population.

The national society recognises that there must be some rules governing its life and, so long as these come into existence in the manner accepted as authoritative (e.g. in the UK through Act of Parliament), they are binding. In other words, the validity of 'law' may depend on the way it is created, that being the method regarded as authoritative by the legal subjects to whom it is addressed. The fact of enforcement may be a reason why individuals obey the law (and that is not certain), but it is not the reason why it is actually law. In international law, then, the fact that rules come into being in the manner accepted and recognised by states as authoritative is enough to ensure that 'law' exists. Less effective enforcement procedures may encourage states to flout the law more frequently than the individual does in national legal systems (although this is arguable), but that is a question about motives for compliance with law, not about its quality as 'law'.

If international law is regarded as a system of 'law', it is axiomatic that all states are under a legal obligation to abide by its rules. Evidence of the existence of this obligation has been presented above. What, however, of the methods which international law does possess for enforcing these legal obligations? While international law has never been wholly dependent on a system of institutionalized enforcement, the absence of a 'police force' or compulsory court of general competence does not mean that international law is impotent. In fact there are enforcement procedures and these are considered below. Reference should also be made to section 1.4 on the reasons for compliance with international law.

THE EFFECTIVENESS OF INTERNATIONAL LAW

It has already been suggested that the great majority of the rules of international law are followed consistently every day as a matter of course. It is normal to obey international law. This is something that is overlooked by some critics of the system and it goes a long way to refute their claims that international law is nothing more than a haphazard collection of principles that can be ignored at will. In this section we will examine some of the reasons why international law does work.

The common good there is no doubt that a very important practical reason for the effectiveness of international law is that it is based on common self-interest and necessity. Today, international society is more interdependent than ever and the volume of interstate activity continues to grow. International law is needed in order to ensure a stable and orderly international society. It is in every state's interest to abide by the rules of international law, for they lay down orderly and predictable principles for the conduct of international relations and international commerce. For example, it is vital that the allocation of the scarce resources of the high seas and ocean floor is achieved smoothly and equitably and it is only through rules of international law - binding on all states - that this can be achieved. Likewise with the protection of the environment and the management of climate change. Thus, a major reason why international law works is that it provides a stable and authoritative regime for the conduct of international relations and the regulation of global issues in an increasingly interdependent world.

THE PRACTITIONERS OF INTERNATIONAL LAW

International law operates hand in glove with international politics and diplomacy. Its most potent field of operations is, in fact, in the Foreign Offices and legal departments of the world's governments and in international organisations. While it is tempting to think of international law as operating in the abstract and impersonal terms of 'governments', 'organisations' and 'states', in practice the application of international law is a matter for the considered judgment of some individual somewhere. This may be a judge of the ICJ or national court, a legal adviser at the UN or a government official. Along with the army of legal advisers available to nongovernmental organisations, these are the actual practitioners of international law. The crucial point is that the great majority of these officials will have been trained in the national law of their own countries and they are likely to approach international law in the same way as they would any other legal system. The practitioners of international law may have a 'habit of obedience' derived from their own training as national lawyers which serves to encourage respect for international law.

The flexible nature of international law

International law is not an 'adversarial' system of law. As we shall see when considering the sources of international law, many of its rules have evolved from the practice of states and often these do not stipulate rigid obligations or confer overriding legal rights. Indeed, in some circumstances, the substance of a rule may be unclear, as was the case with the law on the breadth of the territorial sea until the deliberations of the Third UN Conference on the Law of the Sea. It is a fact of the system that in many areas it may not be possible to achieve a clear and unambiguous statement of a state's legal position. This is the flexible nature of international law. This flexibility may be perceived as a weakness, for states need to know with some degree of certainty the precise scope of their legal obligations and the extent of their legal rights.

Uncertainty is the mother of instability. In international law, however, the flexible or open-ended nature of the rules means that disputes are less likely to be seen as 'right' versus 'wrong'. The absence of rigid and precise obligations leads to modest claims and, because there may be no objectively 'right' answer, there is a premium on compromise. Moreover, the flexible nature of international law means that a state may be able to choose from a range of policies, all of which will be legal. It will not be hamstrung or feel 'boxed in'. The fact that international law rarely leaves the state with only one course of action is a great advantage for a system so bound up with politics and diplomacy.

THE WEAKNESS OF INTERNATIONAL LAW

It would be a mistake to conclude that international law is a perfect system. There is much that could be reformed and enhanced. However, as a practical matter, the development of international law can be achieved only by states themselves. The United Nations, other international organisations and the International Law Commission may propose substantive changes in the law or changes in procedure, but the development of the system depends ultimately on the political will of sovereign states. If the system is believed to work satisfactorily for most of the time, as most states appear to believe, there will be no great movement to reform, especially if this involves a diminution of state power.

This is not to underestimate the role that non-governmental organisations play in pushing for reform, but in the final analysis it is only states that can enter into effective multilateral treaties concerning questions of global significance and only states whose practice can influence the speedy development of customary rules of international law. The creation of the International Criminal Court is a good example of when this succeeds, but we still wait for effective international rules on such matters as climate change and the protection of ethnic minorities in existing states.

THE JURIDICAL BASIS OF INTERNATIONAL LAW

If, then, we accept that international law is 'law', albeit a very different kind of law from that which we find in national legal systems, from where does it derive its legal validity? What is the juridical origin or source of international law? Why is it law? These are questions that have vexed jurists for many years and a number of theories have been developed. These are considered below.

The command theory

John Austin was one of the greatest legal philosophers of the nineteenth century. His view of 'law' was that it comprised a series of commands or orders, issued by a sovereign, and backed by the threat of sanctions (enforcement) if the commands were disobeyed. Consequently, unless the rules of a system amounted to a collection of orders backed by threats, emanating from a sovereign, they were not 'positive law'. This theory has had a profound and, perhaps, unwarranted impact on the search for the juridical origin of international law. According to Austin, 'international law' is not 'positive law' because it does not result from the commands of a sovereign.

Customary law, for example, develops through state practice and treaty law develops through consent. Thus, international law, because it is not made up of commands, is properly to be regarded as a species of 'positive morality' and is not within the province of jurisprudence. As a general description of what law is, this theory has now been largely discredited. The picture of law as a series of commands issued by a sovereign and backed by threats does not even describe national law accurately, let alone international law. Moreover, Austinian theory may be dismissed in so far as it suggests that international law is the same sort of animal as national law. The sovereignty theory misinterprets the function of international law because its primary purpose is not to coerce or command states, but to enable them to interact freely by laying down orderly, predictable and binding principles. Austinian theory cannot explain why states themselves regard international law as binding even when there is no 'sovereign'.

THE CONSENSUAL THEORY

The basic tenet of the consensual theory is that the binding quality of international law – its existence as 'law' – flows from the consent of states. It is said to be a 'positivistic' system of law based on the actual practice of states. In its pure form, this consensual or positivist theory stipulates that no international law can be created without the consent of the state which is to be bound. Thus, 'new' states would not be bound by pre-existing rules because consent is the source of all legal obligations. International law is said to flow from the will of the state. It is formed from the realities of international life rather than its desirabilities. It is created by what actually goes on (consent), rather than according to some higher moral principles.

This theory recognises that a state's consent may be given in a variety of ways - express in treaties or implied in custom - but essentially the system of international law is based on voluntary self-restriction. In this regard, the consensual theory has certain attractions, for it appears to reflect accurately what goes on in international society. The rule that states are bound by their treaty obligations (pacta sunt servanda - treaties must be observed) seems to be based on consent because, as we shall see, treaties are generally binding on a state only if it deliberately and positively accepts the terms. Similarly, it is not inconceivable to regard customary law as being consensual, for consistent state practice may be tantamount to agreeing to be bound by the rule that then develops.

However, there are certain difficulties with the consensual approach to international law, both theoretical and practical. First, as a matter of legal theory, it is not at all clear why states can be bound *only* by self-imposed obligations. There seems to be no necessary reason why this should be so, especially since many rules are not really referable to consent. Indeed, if there exists a rule that says 'states can create law only by consent', where did that rule come from? Where is the legal authority for the pacta sunt servanda/consent rule? If we say that states have always behaved as if consent was fundamental to the creation of legal norms, we can ask further why it is that customary practice should have the authority to validate legal rules?

In fact, the search for the legal source of the consent rule can go on ad infinitum, for we can always ask one more question and take one more step up the 'ladder of authority'. Second, on a practical level, consent does not explain the existence of all legal obligations. The last 25 years have witnessed the birth of many 'new' states, including former dependencies of colonial powers and former members of defunct federations (Yugoslavia, USSR). If consent is the basis of international law, how is it that these new states are bound by pre-existing rules of customary law? There is no doubt that they are bound by the general obligations of international law, yet they have not had the opportunity to accept or reject them. It has been suggested that consent for new states is implied, either specifically by their 'first act' of state practice under an existing rule, or generally by acceptance of membership of the international community.

This is, however, no more than a fiction, since it would allow states to 'opt out' of certain rules if the intention not to be bound was made known. This simply does not happen. To talk of consent in such circumstances is unrealistic and ignores the pre-existing validity of international law for new states. Similarly, a change in circumstances may expose an existing state to rules of customary law with which previously it was unconcerned, yet it is still bound without its prior consent.

For example, Panama and Liberia did not have the chance of objecting to customary maritime law before they became influential maritime states. In fact, even the binding quality of the ultimate consensual instrument - the treaty - cannot be explained fully by use of the consent theory. There is, for example, a limited class of treaties, known as dispositive treaties, which are mainly concerned with territorial issues and which bind all states.

After the UK ceded to China by treaty in 1997 that part of the Hong Kong colony which was sovereign UK territory, no other state claimed (or could claim) that the UK was still the sovereign by alleging that they were not a party to the UK/China bilateral treaty. Other states have not consented to this transfer of jurisdiction but they are bound by it. More importantly, there are certain fundamental rules of customary law (rules of jus cogens) which cannot be altered by the express agreement of states, even if in treaty form. If consent was the basis of international law, nothing would be unalterable by treaty. In general, then, the consensual theory is attractive but it does not describe accurately the reality of international law. When we consider the sources of international law, it will become apparent that consent is a method for creating binding rules of law, rather than the reason why they are binding.

NATURAL LAW

In almost complete contrast to the consensual approach is the theory of international law based on natural law doctrines or 'the law of nature'. This presupposes an ideal system of law, founded on the nature of man as a reasonable being. Thus, rules of law are derived from the dictates of nature as a matter of human reason. International law is said to derive its binding force from the application of 'the law of nature' to the methods of law creation used by states.

Natural law can be contrasted with positive (consensual) law, the latter being based on the actual practice of states while the former is based on objectively correct moral principles. Empirically, natural law theory finds little support in international law. Given that the method of law creation in international law is so heavily dependent on consent or practice, it is difficult to maintain that there is some guiding body of principles to which states defer when creating law. In general, concrete rules of international law are derived from what states actually do, rather than what 'the law of nature' supposes they should do.

However, 'natural law' may be a good descriptive label for such concepts as equity, justice and reasonableness which have been incorporated in substantive rules of law, such as those dealing with the continental shelf, human rights, war crimes and rules of jus cogens. In this sense, natural law may be part of the sources of international law under the category 'general principles recognised by civilised nations'. Natural law does not, however, explain why international law is binding, especially if we remember that the states of the world are so diverse that it is impossible to find any universal moral or ideological thread tying them together.

THE FUTURE OF INTERNATIONAL LAW

The 'decade of international law' (GA Res 45/90) has come and gone and the international community has entered the 21st century. At the start of the 1990s, the end of the 'cold war' brought uncertainty but actually heralded a new era of cooperation among the five permanent members of the Security Council and a consequential increase in the influence of the United Nations. The present decade is unlikely to witness such a fundamental realignment, but the challenges facing international law are no less pressing. The next few years will see the wider exercise of jurisdiction by the International Criminal Court and, no doubt, a widening of the scope of international law to embrace in even more detail non-state entities such as individuals, organizations and corporations. This is nothing new, but perhaps the pace of this development will gather speed. Likewise, to give but a few examples, there will be significant advances in international environmental law, in the law of international communications and more treaty codification of customary law.

In the United Nations itself, calls for the abolition of the 'veto' and/or an increase in the number of permanent members of the Security Council are becoming louder and more persistent. In contrast, many international lawyers believe that 'regionalisation' will replace 'universality' as the most effective template for managing the international community. So, perhaps, there will be different rules of international law for Europe, and Africa or North America. Certainly, regional organisations seem more prepared to take on the task of regulating the conduct of its members rather than submit to 'outside' regulation. There is uncertainty, but the world is changing and international law must change with it. All this will have an impact on a system of law that was conceived originally as a set of rules to govern sovereign states in their international relations.

Of course, it remains true that the majority of concrete rules of international law are created by states for states and that conceptions of 'sovereignty' and independence are deeply rooted in the fabric of international society. Nevertheless, it seems that the institutions of international law are changing, and will have to change further, to accommodate the slow but steady move to rules aimed at controlling states (even in their dealings with their own nationals inside their own territory) instead of rules which simply facilitate their interaction. Much will depend on how international law copes with the issue of effective enforcement. A set of rules that facilitates interaction between states without over-prescribing a particular course of action can survive with little or weak enforcement machinery. A set of rules that seeks to control states in their actions needs a stronger enforcement mechanism if it is to achieve its goals. Is this likely, or will the attempt fail and bring the whole edifice of international law into disrepute?

RELATIONSHIP BETWEEN INTERNATIONAL LAW AND MUNICIPAL

International Law is the law which governs the Relations of sovereign independent States inter se Municipal law or State law or national law is the law of a State or a country and in that respect is opposed to International Law which consists of rules which civilized States consider as binding upon them in their mutual relations. Kelsen observes that national law regulates the behaviour of individuals' International law the behaviour of States or as it is put whereas national law is concerned with the international relations the so called domestic affairs of the State. International Law is concerned with the external relations of the State its foreign affairs.

There is a divergence of opinion on the question as to whether International Law and Municipal Law on the various national laws can be said to form a unity being manifestations of a single conception of law or whether International Law constitutes an independent system of law essentially different from the Municipal Law. The former theory is called monistic and the latter dualistic. Monistic Theory: It maintains that the subject of the two systems of law namely, International Law and Municipal Law are essentially one in as much as the former regulates the conduct of States, while the latter of individuals.

According to this view law is essentially a command binding upon the subjects of the law independent of their will which is one case is the States and in the other individuals. According to it International Law and Municipal Law are two phases of one and the same thing. The former although directly addressed to the States as corporate bodies is as well applicable to individuals for States are only groups of individuals. Dualistic theory: According to the dualist view the systems of International Law and Municipal Law are separate and self contained to the extent to which rules of the one are not expressly or tacitly received into the other system. In the first place they differ as regards their sources.

The sources of Municipal Law are customs grown up within the boundaries of the State concerned and statutes enacted therein while the sources of International Law are customs grown up within the Family of Nations and law making treaties concluded by its members. In the second place Municipal Laws regulates relations between the individuals under the sway of a State or between the individuals and the State while International Law regulates relations between the member States of the Family of Nations. Lastly there is a difference with regard to the substance of the law in as much as Municipal Law is a law of the sovereign over individuals while International Law is a law between sovereign State which is arrived at an agreement among them. The latter is therefore a weak law.

Transformation Theory: According to this theory it is the transformation of the treaty into national legislation which alone validates the extension to individuals of the rules set out in international agreements. The transformation is not merely a formal but a substantial requirement. International Law according to this theory cannot find place in the national or Municipal Law unless the latter allows its machinery to be used for that purpose. This theory is fallacious in several respects. In the first place its premise that International Law and Municipal Law are two distinct systems is incorrect. In the second place the second premise that International Law binds States only whereas municipal law applies to individuals is also incorrect for International Law is the sum of the rules which have been accepted by civilized states as determining their conduct towards each other and towards each others subjects. In the third place the theory regards the transformation of treaties into national law for their enforcement.

This is not true in all cases for the practice of transforming treaties into national legislation is not uniform in all the countries. And this is certainly not true in the case of law making treaties. Delegation Theory: According to this theory there is the delegation of a right to every State to decide for itself when the provisions of a treaty or convention are to come into effect and in what manner they are to be incorporated in the law of the land or municipal law. There is no need of transformation of a treaty into national law but the act is merely an extension of one single act. The delegation theory is incomplete for it does not satisfactorily meet the main argument of the transformation theory. It assumes the primacy of international legal order but fails to explain the relations existing between municipal and international laws. It is settled by the leading English and American decisions that International Law forms part of the municipal law of those countries.

The United States has unambiguously applied the doctrine that International Law is part of the law of the land. All international conventions ratified by the USA and such customary International Law as has received the assent of the United States are binding upon American Courts even if they may be contrary to the statutory provisions. There is a presumption in cases of conflict that the United States Congress did not intend to overrule International Law. International law has the relationships between states as its primary focus, while municipal law is concerned with the domestic aspects of governance, with issues between individuals and issues between the individual and the administrative setup. There are various theories that govern the relationships of international and municipal law, ranging from monism, dualism, transformation, delegation and harmonization.

International law supersedes municipal law in the sense that non compliance to an international obligation cannot be brushed off by a state claiming that the action was in pursuit of its own municipal laws. The state can not use any provision within its internal legal structure to evade an international obligation. Treaties, executive certificates, and other principles of customary law provide a means for application of international law. Different countries however follow different methods in the approach and application of international law to municipal jurisdiction.

This study has analysed the norms of international law that are related to the right to adequate food in emergency situations. In so doing, it has focused on two main issues: the obligations of States and non-State entities to respect, protect and fulfil the right to adequate food in emergencies; and the principles and standards applicable to food and food-related aid programmes implemented by international humanitarian agencies. Under international human rights law, every human being has the right to have physical and economic access at all times to adequate food or to the means for its procurement. In order to progressively realize this right, each State has a legal obligation to take steps to the maximum of its available resources, both individually and through international assistance and cooperation.

As a fundamental human right, the right to adequate food applies in emergency situations, including both natural disasters and armed conflicts. The recognition of the right to adequate food embodied in human rights law is supplemented by norms contained in other branches of international law (refugee law, economic law, environmental law). Moreover, in armed conflicts, international humanitarian law is applicable. International human rights law and international humanitarian law (where applicable) are complementary. Human rights law, which is applicable (albeit to different degrees) in both peace and war, recognizes the right of individuals to have access at all times to safe and nutritious food or to the means for its procurement. Humanitarian law, on the other hand, applies only in armed conflicts (and in other related situations, like occupation) and is instrumental to protecting certain basic human rights, including the right to food, in these situations. Many of its provisions are aimed at ensuring that persons or groups not taking or no longer taking part in the hostilities are not denied food or access to food, by prescribing certain conduct and prohibiting certain behaviour.

Thus, international humanitarian law contains numerous provisions aimed at facilitating humanitarian assistance to persons in need, which impose obligations both upon the parties to the hostilities and upon States not taking part in the conflict. Parties to the conflict must allow humanitarian assistance whenever the basic needs of the civilian population, including food, are not fulfilled and an impartial humanitarian organization offers such assistance. Indeed, while humanitarian assistance is under international law subject to the consent of the affected State, the discretion of the latter in refusing consent is limited by several norms and principles of international (humanitarian and human rights) law: aid offers cannot be considered unfriendly acts; refusals must be justified by valid reasons; refusals could constitute violations of human rights law provisions on the right to food and the right to life; refusals could amount to deliberate starvation of civilians, war crime, genocide or crime against humanity, punishable under international law.

Under international humanitarian law, parties to the conflict must also protect relief consignments and facilitate their rapid distribution, and must refrain from delaying or diverting them. In addition, international humanitarian law limits the right of the parties to international and non-international armed conflicts to choose methods and means of warfare, and prohibits the use of starvation of civilians. A party to the conflict cannot attack, destroy, remove or render useless objects indispensable to the survival of the civilian population, such as foodstuff, crops, drinking water installations, or make these objects the target of reprisals. In specified circumstances, particularly serious violations of international law, including some forms of violation of the right to adequate food (e.g. the use of starvation of civilians as a method of warfare), constitute crimes punishable under international law, namely genocide, war crimes and crimes against humanity. Adjudication over these crimes rests with domestic courts and/or with international tribunals.

International economic law contains norms regulating the provision of food aid, which are binding for the States parties to the relevant treaties. Norms are embodied both within WTO instruments (Agreement on Agriculture; Decision on Least-Developed and Net Food-Importing Developing Countries) and within international commodity agreements (Food Aid Convention 1999, which is part of the International Grains Agreement). The Food Aid Convention provides for the supply of specified quantities of food aid by identified donor States, and for principles and criteria guiding such supply. WTO norms include criteria for domestic food aid (exempting it from reduction commitments concerning domestic support to agriculture) and for international food aid (particularly regulating the relationship between food aid and commercial transactions). International standards on food safety, animal and plant health are applicable in emergency situations.

Finally, principles and standards contained in internationally recognized codes of conduct adopted by humanitarian agencies and NGOs, which are not binding and outside the scope of international law, may provide insights on the interpretation and operationalization of some aspects of the right to adequate food in emergencies. As for the identification of principles and standards for food and food-related aid, several principles and standards have been identified, namely: impartiality and non-discrimination; special protection and assistance for vulnerable groups; gender approach; consideration for longer-term rehabilitation and development; participation; environment protection; and adequacy standards.

Impartiality and non-discrimination entail that aid must be distributed according to need only. Special protection and assistance must be provided to categories of particularly vulnerable groups, determined in international instruments or identified in each humanitarian programme. A gender approach is to be integrated in aid programmes, by avoiding discrimination against women and by taking women's special nutritional needs into account (especially with regard to expectant and nursing mothers). Although food and food-related aid aims at satisfying urgent and immediate needs, it must take into account longer-term rehabilitation and development concerns. Ways in which participation may be integrated within aid programmes are to be devised. While not required to carry out an environmental impact assessment before undertaking their relief programmes, humanitarian agencies should take into account environmental concerns in the design and implementation of their programmes, and respect plant and animal protection standards.

Finally, food and food-related aid must meet certain minimum requirements, especially in terms of food safety for human consumption. Due regard must be given to cultural acceptability.

U.S. foreign relations depend on legal order, operate within a legal framework, and require legal principles and concepts that influence policy and limit choices. To be sure, the United States derives benefits from international legal rules and agreements with other states. Legal rules keep international society functional, contribute to economic order and political stability, and provide a basis for common ventures and mutual intercourse. Given that international law serves to limit the actions of all governments, it therefore enhances the security and independence of the United States in its dealings with other states. International legal rules establish common standards where they are deemed by states to be desirable and make more predictable what behaviour to expect from states in their relations with each other. That is no less true for the United States in this age of globalization and increasing interdependence.

But international law also limits the freedom of the United States to act in its foreign affairs. The United States is obligated to certain restraints, irrespective of what its government might like to do when the time comes to act. Political arrangements legitimized by formal agreements are more difficult to unravel or modify. The predictability of state behaviour established by international law means that the United States is not free to be disorderly or promote changes on its own whim. To foster the security and independence of its own territory and limit the conduct of other governments, the United States must accept corresponding limitations on its own behaviour. To secure the confidence accrued from law, the United States must consent to being restricted in its ability to frustrate the expectations of other states. U.S. foreign policy therefore evolves in tandem with how international legal rules are regarded.

Each successive administration builds its foreign policy on the legal framework constructed by its predecessors. Since World War II, U.S. foreign policy has moved slowly but perceptibly away from pragmatic, nationalist principles toward a more legalist, international doctrine. With the end of the Cold War, this tendency has accelerated. In the early twenty-first century, U.S. foreign policy was moving toward more universal values, bound by increasing legal commitments in formal multilateral agreements. For American foreign policy, international law is most effective in regulating the rapidly expanding range of functional relations between the United States and other international actors. Such functional interstate relations are considered to be "low politics" (trade, communications, rules of diplomacy) and are motivated by a combination of idealism, moralism, and pragmatism.

National security issues, however, retain their critical importance as pragmatic considerations, though increasingly the tendency has been to negotiate arms control agreements whenever possible, as opposed to seeking a straightforward balance of power amongst military adversaries. For the United States the restraint of legal rules appears least effective when applied to "high politics," meaning its national security relations between sovereign states. Under these circumstances, realism and pragmatism are prone to fostering American unilateralism in foreign dealings. Yet the wide range of arms control agreements, environmental regulations, and rules for war negotiated through U.S. leadership suggests that recourse to international legal solutions to deal with "high politics" issues retains great sway for U.S. foreign policy as well.

The American experience demonstrates that international law best serves those who make it work over the long term. As the body of rules for the international relations game, international law provides the formal ways and means for communicating to U.S. policymakers the perceived international consensus on policy questions and legal issues. Thus, the United States employs international law in its foreign policy and contributes to its creation. This explains why, with few exceptions, the United States formally recognizes and agrees to respect fundamental rules and principles intended to guide its foreign policy behaviour. For the preeminent actor in international relations at the dawn of the twenty-first century, it cannot be otherwise.

Despite the appearance that women are gaining more options and the significant improvement in status, there are still countless unarticulated violations to the rights of Chinese women in the People's Republic of China today. The improvement of women's rights often comes with economic and social development and in man parts of rural China today, there are still alarmingly high incidences of abuse of women or the violation of their rights. It is only through modernization, a gradual change in the psyche of society about the equally significant role of women, and very importantly, educational opportunities that women in China can finally break free from these bonds. Affirmative action should be taken to make up for the past discrimination and to allow qualified women a level playing field, in all aspects of life, from family to education to employment. Women in modern China need to be empowered by being informed of their rights through education and exposure and must shift away from the traditionally weaker and more submissive sex to that of a more assertive role.

Much has been accomplished, yet a lot still remains to be done. The remaining injustices should be articulated, examined and tackled by society at large. Women have not been the passive recipients of miraculous changes in laws and human nature. Many generations of women have come together to affect these changes, through many more meetings, petition drives, lobbying, public speaking and non-violent resistance. But women have not gained full, or at least equitable freedom, even though they had taken equally tremendous risks throughout the society. Judging from the results of our project, women's rights have undeniably been violated. Yet, this is just part of the long and arduous journey just as how gender equality still generates passionate arguments. However there is a saying that goes "A journey of a thousand miles starts with the first step." At the preliminary stage of the championing of women's rights, we can conclude that with adequate attention and measures as well as an allowance of time, the feet long bound may once again see the light of day.

Bibliography

Afkhami, Mahnaz, ed. (1995) *Faith and Freedom: Women's Human Rights in the Muslim World.* Syracuse: Syracuse University Press.

Americas Watch (1991) *Criminal Injustice: Violence Against Women in Brazil.* New York: Human Rights Watch.

Amnesty International (1995) *Human Rights Are Women's Right.* New York, New York: Amnesty International.

Askin, Kelly D. And Doreen M. Koenig, eds. (1999) *Women and International Human Rights Law.* Ardsley, New York: Transnational.

Bunch, Charlotte (1990) Women's Rights as Human Rights: Toward a Re-Vision of Human Rights. *Human Rights Quarterly* 12(4):486-498.

Charlton, Sue Ellen M. (1984) *Women in Third World Development.* Boulder, Colorado: Westview Press.

Cook, Rebecca J. (1994) *Women's Health and Human Rights: The Promotion and Protection of Women's Health Through International Human Rights Law.* Geneva: World Health Organization.

Cook, Rebecca J., ed. (1994) *Human Rights of Women: National and International Perspectives.* Philadelphia, Pennsylvania: University of Pennsylvania Press.

Fraser, Arvonne S. (1999) Becoming Human: The Origins and Development of Women's Human Rights. *Human Rights Quarterly* 21:853-906.

Henever, N. (1983) *International Law and the Status of Women*. Boulder and London: Westview Press.

Human Rights Watch (1995) *The Human Rights Watch Global Report on Women's Human Rights*. New York and Washington: Human Rights Watch.

Maraskin, Roslyn (1999) *Women and Justice: Development of an International Policy*. Amsterdam: Gordon and Breach.

Moser, Caroline O.N. (1993) *Gender Planning and Development: Theory, Practice and Training*. London: Routledge.

O'Hare, Ursala A. (1999) Realizing Human Rights for Women. *Human Rights Quarterly* 21(2):364-402.

Overseas Development Institute (1995) *Making Aid Work For Women*. London. ODI.

Peters, Julie and Andrea Wolper, eds. (1995) *Women's Rights, Human Rights: International Feminist Perspectives*. New York: Routledge.

Peterson, V. Spike and Anne Sisson Runyan (1993) *Global Gender Issues*. Boulder, Colorado: Westview Press.

Sadasivam, Bharati (1997) The Impact of Structural Adjustment on Women: A Governance and Human Rights Agenda. *Human Rights Quarterly* 19(3):630-665.

Stiglmayer, Alexandra, ed. (1994) *Mass Rape: The War Against Women in Bosnia-Herzegovina*. Lincoln: University of Nebraska Press.

Tomasevski, Katarina (1993) *Women and Human Rights*. London: Zed Books.

United Nations High Commissioner for Refugees (1995) *Sexual Violence Against Refugees: Guidelines on Prevention and Response*. Geneva: UNHCR.

Vickers, Jeanne (1993) *Women and War*. London: Zed Books.

Vinding, Diana, ed. (1998) *Indigenous Women: The Right to*

a Voice. Copenhagen, Denmark: International Work Group for Indigenous Affairs.

Wetzel, Janice Wood (1993) *The World of Women: In Pursuit of Human Rights*. New York: New York University Press.

Index

I

J

L

N

O

P

R

S

T

V

W